‘The relevance of Machiavelli to current FE leadership is made horribly clear in this ingenious, fresh and challenging collection of essays. Political theory is used to devastating but useful [illegible] space in which it is possible to think about power and the principal differently.’

Stephen J. Ball , Distinguished Service Professor of Sociology of Education, UCL Institute of Education

‘Just when I was wondering what more damage politicians could possibly do to the vital FE sector, this book arrives with disturbing comparative studies, unsettling, critical research and deliciously subversive irony. Together these 25 authors offer the sector the democratic practices needed for a journey of hope.’

Frank Coffield, Emeritus Professor, UCL Institute of Education

‘This book shines light on the dark arts of political street fighting in colleges. Machiavelli is the prism through which you will learn about how power between governments and colleges, and management and teachers, is exercised, resisted, exercised and resisted again. While the book shows just how brutal the exercise of power can be in the college sector, it also tells of resistance, courage, and hope. This is a book for all students of education. It is gripping reading.’

Leesa Wheelahan, William G. Davis Chair in Community College Leadership, University of Toronto

‘A direct and provocative challenge to every principal and senior leader in FE. It raises difficult but pertinent ethical, strategic, professional and pragmatic questions concerning the whole system as well as policy, students, practitioners, motivation, action and self justification alongside the potential, or actual, use and abuse of power. The thread of irony running throughout the book is used to clever effect and may, at times, require an open, inquiring, reflective, honest and tolerant mind from any reader currently in a leadership position.
This is a deeply refreshing and important contribution to the leadership literature of FE, written from the perspective of voices seldom heard. If read widely and taken seriously this book could revolutionise FE leadership discourse, professionalism and p

Dr Lynne Sedgmore CBE, former FE college
Chief Executive of the 157 Group (2008–15)
Centre for Excellence in Leadership (200

'The need for a dynamic further education system is greater than it has ever been, but too often the sector has been hampered by weak governance and limited ambition. This volume confronts those limitations head on and sets out an alternative prospectus for the sector that is both imaginative and audacious. Much more than an argument for "second chance" education, the contributors open up the possibility of genuine transformatory change. This book could not be more timely.'

Professor Howard Stevenson, Director of Research, School of Education, University of Nottingham

The Principal

In polities like Rome and Athens, the people are princes.

Niccolò Machiavelli, *Discourses*

This book is dedicated to principled FE colleagues committed to ethical, collegiate leadership; and to the indomitable democratic professionals who hold the sector's powerful to account.

The Principal:

Power and professionalism in FE

Edited by Maire Daley, Kevin Orr and Joel Petrie

is an imprint of

First published in 2017 by the UCL Institute of Education Press, University College London, 20 Bedford Way, London WC1H 0AL

www.ucl-ioe-press.com

British Library Cataloguing in Publication Data:
A catalogue record for this publication is available from the British Library

ISBNs
978-1-85856-844-7 (paperback)
978-1-85856-845-4 (PDF eBook)
978-1-85856-846-1 (ePub eBook)
978-1-85856-847-8 (Kindle eBook)

Typeset by Quadrant Infotech (India) Pvt Ltd
Printed by CPI Group (UK) Ltd, Croydon, CR0 4YY

Cover image: Portrait of Niccolò Machiavelli by Santi di Tito, in the Palazzo Vecchio, Florence. Reproduced by kind permission of Musei Civici Fiorentini.

Contents

Part 4 Introduction: FE Utopia: Towards a New Republic

Kevin Orr

List of figures

List of abbreviations

AE	adult education
AoC	Association of Colleges
ARPCE	Association for Research in Post-Compulsory Education
ASA	Advertising Standards Authority
BERA	British Educational Research Association
CBHE	college-based higher education
CIF	common inspection framework
COOCs	Community Open Online Courses
CoVE	Centre of Vocational Excellence
CPD	continuing professional development
DBS	Disclosure and Barring Service
DCSF	Department for Children, Schools and Families
DfE	Department for Education
DIUS	Department for Innovation, Universities and Skills
DYW	Commission for Developing Scotland's Young Workforce
EFA	Education Funding Agency
ESOL	English for speakers of other languages
ESRC	Economic and Social Research Council
EU	European Union
EWC	Education Workforce Council (Wales)
FAS	An Foras Áiseanna Saothair (Training and Employment Authority)
FE	further education
FEC	further education college
FET	further education and training
FETL	Further Education Trust for Leadership
FOFO	'Fuck off and find out'
GTCW	General Teaching Council Wales
HE	higher education
HEFCE	Higher Education Funding Council for England
HMI	Her Majesty's Inspectorate
IfL	Institute for Learning
ISP	inspection service providers
ITE	initial teacher education
LA	local authority
LEP	local enterprise partnership

LSRN	Learning and Skills Research Network
MOOC	massive open online courses
NATECLA	National Association for Teaching English and Community Languages to Adults
NATFHE	National Association of Teachers in Further and Higher Education
NIACE	National Institute for Adult Continuing Education
NPISH	non-profit institutions serving households
NPM	new public management
NUS	National Union of Students
NVQ	National Vocational Qualification
OECD	Organisation for Economic Co-operation and Development
Ofsted	Office for Standards in Education, Children's Services and Skills
OTL	observation of teaching and learning
QIA	Quality Improvement Agency
RaPAL	Research and Practice in Adult Literacy
SFA	Skills Funding Agency
SLT	senior leadership team
SNP	Scottish National Party
SOLAS	An tSeirbhís Oideachais Leanúnaigh agus Scileanna (Further Education and Training Authority)
SWCETT	South West Centre for Excellence in Teacher Training
TAFE	technical and further education
TELL	Teacher Education in Lifelong Learning
TES	*Times Educational Supplement*
TLA	teaching, learning and assessment
TUC	Trades Union Congress
UCU	University and College Union
UCU Cymru	University and College Union Wales

About the contributors

Dr Mike Aiello worked in FE for approximately fifteen years in the areas of learning and teaching and management and leadership development. He pursued these interests in HE for a similar period of time, and continues to explore leadership development through critical learning in his current role as Associate Dean Leadership at Liverpool Business School.

Daniel Altés is originally from Barcelona and currently works as an FE Graphic Design lecturer in Liverpool. He is a practitioner in graphic design, illustration and printmaking.

James Avis left school at the age of 16. He is currently Professor of Post-Compulsory Education and Training at the University of Huddersfield. He taught in FE for a number of years during which time he studied for a PhD at the Centre for Contemporary Cultural Studies at the University of Birmingham.

Eric Bari is studying on the Extended Diploma in Art and Design at the University for the Creative Arts, Rochester, and would like to travel the world and pursue many careers.

Ann-Marie Bathmaker is Professor of Vocational and Higher Education at the University of Birmingham. She has a particular interest in the role of further education colleges and their international equivalents in the provision of education and training. Her research focuses on questions of equity and inequality in vocational, post-compulsory and higher education. She was the specialist adviser to the House of Lords Select Committee on Social Mobility School to Work (2015–16).

Geoff Brown has been active as a trade unionist and socialist for many years, working most of the time as a union tutor. He is currently writing a history-from-below of the Manchester area in the long 1970s.

Steve Brown is Curriculum and Quality Leader of the Languages Department at West College Scotland.

Siobhan Carmichael is an FE lecturer in visual arts, a multi-disciplinary artist, an exhibition curator and a community artist.

Lexie Cave is studying on the Extended Diploma in Art and Design at the University for the Creative Arts, Rochester; and hopes to have a future in 3-dimensional design, visual art and concept art.

Gabi Clarke is course coordinator of both the Extended Diploma in Creative Media Production and Technology and the Extended Diploma in Art and Design at the University for the Creative Arts, Rochester.

Dr Jim Crawley is a senior lecturer in Education Studies and a teaching fellow at Bath Spa University, where he led post-compulsory teacher education for twelve years. He chaired the Post-16 Committee of the Universities' Council for the Education of Teachers (UCET) between 2012 and 2015, and convenes the Teacher Education in Lifelong Learning (TELL) research network.

Maire Daley taught in FE for more than thirty years, latterly as a teacher educator, before her retirement. An active trade unionist, she was a member of the National Executive Committee in NATFHE and UCU, chair of UCU's Education Committee, and a member of the Women's, LGBT and International committees. As a feminist and socialist her research interests focus on education for liberation and the democratization of education.

Callum Davis is studying on the Extended Diploma in Art and Design at the University for the Creative Arts, Rochester; and would love to create more illustration work with pen and watercolour and inspire people with his images.

Dr Carol Azumah Dennis is a programme director for Postgraduate Taught Programmes (MA) at the University of Hull. She spent several years as a teacher and manager in FE before working in HE.

Dr Vicky Duckworth, a former FE student and teacher, is a Reader in Education at Edge Hill University. She is committed to challenging inequality through emancipatory approaches to education, widening participation, inclusion, community action, and research with a social justice agenda. She is leading a UCU-funded research project (with Dr Rob Smith) which aims to evidence how FE transforms lives and communities.

Alex Dunedin is the Director of the Ragged University project and a long-term beneficiary of learning through informal relationships with diverse people and communities. He researches widely in order to develop ideas to open up opportunities for those outside formal education; this forms part of his practice of active citizenship and social justice.

Geoffrey Elliott has taught in comprehensives and in further, adult and higher education, is an FE college governor, and serves on the board of the Office of the Independent Adjudicator for Higher Education. He edits the journal *Research in Post-Compulsory Education*, and is Professor of Post-Compulsory Education at the University of Worcester.

Paige Elliott is studying on the Extended Diploma in Art and Design at the University for the Creative Arts, Rochester; she plans to use the ideas and experience from UCA to influence and mould her future direction.

John Field began teaching in FE at the Northern College, Barnsley, which he left after seven years to join the University of Warwick. He has published widely on adult learning and skills, and is an active blogger and policy advocate for adult learning. He is Professor Emeritus in Education at the University of Stirling.

Fergal Finnegan is Lecturer in Adult and Community Education at the Department of Adult and Community Education, National University of Ireland, Maynooth, Ireland.

Eryn Hadrill is studying for the Extended Diploma in Art and Design at the University for the Creative Arts, Rochester, and is aiming to go on to a degree course in Asia Pacific Studies, while still enjoying art as a hobby.

Rania Hafez has 25 years as a lecturer in FE and HE, and is currently programme leader for the MA in Education at the University of Greenwich. She was a non-executive director of the IfL, is co-chair of the Learning and Skills Research Network (London and South-East), and has published on professionalism, teacher education and faith in education.

Aylin Hall is studying on the Extended Diploma in Art and Design at the University for the Creative Arts, Rochester; and hopes to have a career in fashion after university.

Dr Craig Hammond was recently appointed as a Senior Lecturer in Education at Liverpool John Moores University. He worked for eighteen years across all aspects of FE provision at Blackburn College, and has published *Hope, Utopia, and Creativity in Higher Education: Pedagogical Tactics for Alternative Futures* (Bloomsbury, 2017).

Dr Gary Husband is a lecturer in Professional Education and Leadership in the Faculty of Social Science at the University of Stirling. Following a career as a lecturer and curriculum manager in FE, he now has teaching and research interests in the learning of professionals in all sectors of education.

Peter Jones has been an active trade unionist for over fifty years and as an FE teacher was a member of the National Executive Committee of NATFHE. He was chair of UCU Cymru and active in its opposition to the imposition of the Education Workforce Council. He now writes short stories and poetry.

Rajiv Khosla has worked in the post-compulsory education sector for almost twenty years as an assessor, lecturer, manager and additional inspector. His current research is focused on examining alternative systems of classroom observations.

Bronek Kram mainly teaches in FE, sometimes exhibits in art, rarely performs in music, and no longer talks in poetry.

Shakira Martin is the mother of two beautiful girls, and recently graduated with a Diploma in Education and Training. She was the NUS vice-president for FE in 2015–17, launching the #FEunplugged campaign and securing apprentice representation within the Institute for Apprenticeships. She was elected President of the National Union of Students (NUS) in 2017, and aspires to be a college principal.

Gavin Moodie is adjunct professor in the University of Toronto's Ontario Institute for Studies in Education. He was an administrator at two of Australia's 'dual-sector' universities, which conduct research, offer PhDs and have over twenty per cent of their teaching in each of FE and HE.

Mia Moore is studying on the Extended Diploma in Art and Design at the University for the Creative Arts, Rochester, after which she wishes to pursue a career in children's illustration.

Lou Mycroft has been a social purpose teacher educator since 2003 and is a qualified Thinking Environment coach. She defines herself as a philosopher of praxis and is a pioneer of distributed, rhizomatic working, blending digital and face-to-face experiences of learning and leadership. She is studying for a doctorate and is committed to world-changing educational approaches.

Tony O'Connell teaches in FE. He is leftist, punk, rude-boy, queer and Buddhist, and dedicated to subverting hierarchical imagery.

Kevin Orr is Professor of Work and Learning at the University of Huddersfield, where he has worked since 2006. Before that he was an FE teacher in colleges in and around Manchester, mainly on ESOL and teacher education courses. He has been a branch officer for NATFHE and UCU throughout his career.

Damien Page began his teaching career in a large inner-city FE college in London as a lecturer in English Language and Literature. He is currently Professor of Education and Dean of the Carnegie School of Education at Leeds Beckett University.

Joel Petrie has worked in post-compulsory education for over two decades as a lecturer, teacher educator, manager and trade union activist. He is currently undertaking an educational doctorate focusing on leadership in FE at the University of Huddersfield.

Rob Peutrell has worked in FE for over 25 years as an ESOL and learning support tutor. He is active in UCU and the National Association for Teaching English and Community Languages to Adults.

Dr David Powell started his FE career at Stafford College in 1986. He moved from a senior management role, via staff development, into initial teacher education (ITE), and is director of the Education and Training Consortium, a partnership between twenty FE colleges and the University of Huddersfield.

Dr Simon Reddy has been a plumber for over thirty years, and teaches and researches in the English FE sector.

James Richards is studying on the Extended Diploma in Art and Design at the University for the Creative Arts, Rochester, after which he hopes to become a storyboard artist for television and major movie productions.

Rob Roach teaches on the Extended Diploma in Creative Media Production and Technology at the University for the Creative Arts, Rochester, in a range of disciplines. He has taught in some capacity from the age of 16. His polymathic approach to teaching is heavily based on the practical facilitation of studio work for students, where inclusive pedagogies and equality are central to his practice.

Peter Shukie teaches in FE and HE courses in FE, and is an educator whose interests straddle formal education as a critical pedagogy, technology, and free community spaces of learning, on community open online courses (COOCs).

Dr Rob Smith is a Reader in Education at Birmingham City University. His work explores marketization and education. Recent research with Vicky Duckworth focuses on FE as a space for transformative learning.

Becy Spendley is studying on the Extended Diploma in Art and Design at the University for the Creative Arts, Rochester, and would like to become a skin illustrator and help people feel more confident and happy with themselves.

Linda Stephens works as a visual arts facilitator in FE. She is passionate about textile techniques, print making and keeping art and design accessible to all.

Curtis Tappenden is a senior lecturer in FE at the University for the Creative Arts, Rochester, and teaches on the Extended Diploma in Art and Design. He has worked as an illustrator and painter for the past 28 years, is an editorial artist for a national newspaper in London, has written 23 books on art and design practice, and is a performing poet. His most recent collaborations involve visually recording aspects of international circus life, and he is currently completing a PhD in education, exploring maverick educators in HE.

Mason Thew is studying on the Extended Diploma in Art and Design at the University for the Creative Arts, Rochester. He wants to see how far he will go in art, study for his master's degree in art and design, and have his own shop or teach classes when he is older.

Jane Weatherby has worked in adult and further education for more than 25 years, and has benefited from its transformative power as both a student and a teacher. She firmly believes in sustaining FE's capacity to be bold, creative and disruptive.

Bethany Williams is studying on the Extended Diploma in Art and Design at the University for the Creative Arts, Rochester, and would like to do something within fine art in her own way, or become an art therapist and work with children.

Jake Wood is studying on the Extended Diploma in Art and Design at the University for the Creative Arts, Rochester, and would like to have a career as a fine art photographer or an art historian.

Acknowledgements

Azumah Dennis wishes to acknowledge that the research informing her chapter was made possible by a grant from the Further Education Trust for Leadership (FETL) from 2014–16.

Alex Dunedin would like to thank all the supporters, participants and contributors who make the Ragged University, and all those in academia who carry their love of knowledge and teaching beyond the gates, as well as bringing the learning and thinking outside formal education in.

Maire Daley, Kevin Orr and Joel Petrie extend their warm thanks to Dr Daniel O'Neill for sharing his expertise on early educational texts during our initial discussions about this book. This collection would not have been possible without the commitment of often time-poor colleagues to produce their chapters and illustrations, and we are very grateful for their input.

We also wish to recognize the ongoing, invaluable guidance and consistent good humour of Gillian Klein, our publisher at Trentham, and of the support of the wider publishing team at the UCL IOE Press: Nicky Platt, Jonathan Dore, Sally Sigmund and Margie Coughlin, who have been a pleasure to work with.

Finally, we are grateful to Claudia Bardelloni of Museo di Palazzo Vecchio in Florence for her assistance in providing Santi di Tito's portrait of Machiavelli, and it has been our privilege to work with Curtis Tappenden as the book's art director. Special thanks are due to Curtis's student illustrators from the University for the Creative Arts, Rochester, whose sophisticated images so enrich this book: Eric Bari, Lexie Cave, Callum Davis, Paige Elliott, Eryn Hadrill, Aylin Hall, Mia Moore, James Richards, Becy Spendley, Mason Thew, Bethany Williams and Jake Wood.

Figure 0.1: The student illustrators

Preface

Geoffrey Elliott

> [T]here is nothing more difficult to take in hand, more perilous to conduct, or more uncertain in its success, than to take the lead in the introduction of a new order of things.
>
> (Niccolò Machiavelli, *The Prince*)

Nearly a quarter of a century has passed since the incorporation of the further education (FE) sector, a policy shift that signalled the most radical transformation of post-school education since the consolidation of technical education towards the end of the nineteenth century. During this period of change at the end of the last century, the theoretical literature on the FE sector was replete with terms such as fragmentation, confusion, complexity and competition, to describe a policy landscape in which FE colleges were removed from local authority control and awarded the autonomy, freedoms and authority that supposedly came with independence, much to the approval of many college principals at the time and since. Perilous times, these, in which the crosswinds of the education market so created have brought about the dissolution of many colleges, a good number of mergers and a resulting dramatic reduction in the number of FE colleges across the UK.

Education has at its core a moral purpose – to make a difference, to bring about improvements, to be transformational – therefore effective leadership practice in education is of necessity rooted in values. To remove moral choices and judgements from the domain of educational leadership carries with it the danger of managerialism, in which executive decision making is reduced to a means–ends calculation, and the consequences of actions for teaching and learning are secondary to compliance, meeting targets and personal gain. Importantly, ethical decision making is a whole-institution matter. It is to do with culture, norms, expectations and an explicit set of values that are highly visible internally and externally and which provide the overarching framework for organizational aims, objectives and outcomes.

The new order of things raises many important questions, not least for those educational leaders and managers in the sector who put students first and see themselves as leaders of learning who must try to get to grips with whether and how post-compulsory education organizations can be effectively led, changed and improved through an uncertain, not to say hostile, environment.

How can research help to answer these questions? A vital connection exists between openness to research, especially a qualitative kind that empowers participants, and capacity to break out of the assumptive world of managerialist educational language and action. However, *a posteriori*, many of those who lead and manage colleges discharge their responsibilities with little exposure to or understanding of educational research and how it might inform their practice. I have written at various points over the last twenty years concerning the absence of a research tradition in FE. A number of factors have contributed to this gap, one of which is the combined effects of a cumulative tradition of differentiation within post-compulsory education. The education policy of successive governments, following the White Paper 'A plan for polytechnics and other colleges' in 1966 (Department of Education and Science), was to withdraw higher-education work from FE colleges, which served to distance research activity from the sector, with most post-A-level work concentrated within regional and area colleges. Despite the significant increase of directly and indirectly funded HE taught in FE colleges, the many and varied pressures on the time of teaching and professional support staff leaves little room or energy for research, and it is rarely recognized as a legitimate and resourced part of an FE teacher's contract. Added to this, at the time of writing the Independent Review of Professionalism in Further Education, chaired by Lord Lingfield (2012), has led to the requirement for teachers in FE to have a teaching qualification – and thus some exposure to educational research – being quietly abandoned by government. Accompanying the paucity of research done in FE is a paucity of research *on* FE: historically the sector has been significantly under-represented as a focus of educational research. A significant reason for this is that many researchers have little or no experience of the FE sector themselves, having followed traditional school and university pathways. There is little funding to support research on the sector, while the ESRC-funded project Transforming Learning Cultures in Further Education is a notable exception that proves the rule.

The generation and maintenance of a research culture in an FE college appears problematic. The Ofsted surveillance mechanisms in place to deliver performance management and accountability, and the gaming strategies in which all are players in effecting compliance, leave little or no space for systematic critical enquiry. For principals who must ensure that achievement rates line up with Ofsted expectations, there is nothing more difficult to take in hand than inconvenient noise from research that might skew the orbit of the assumptive world in which they are complicit. Failure to challenge carries a high price. A research culture might encourage ethical, responsive and adaptive management styles, better suited to the policy maelstrom that surrounds FE colleges. Options for partnerships and alliances could be identified by sensitive research strategies, and an institutional response formulated. Trends could be mapped where they can be identified, and policies on learning and teaching and on staff and curriculum development adjusted continually within a flexible planning model. Only research that is prepared to challenge the status quo can approach this level of sophistication and relevance to action; it contrasts dramatically with the 'fix it quick' reactive approach familiar to many who work in the FE sector. Unfortunately, the latter approach is more convenient and less bother. Deeper controversial enquiry is unlikely to be initiated or supported by those who presently determine and implement policy for the FE sector. The reasons for this may well be rooted in their reluctance to support an activity that has the potential to be dangerous; the threat of heresy that rides on the back of intellectual innovation is one that stifles opposition and fuels performativity.

There are, however, three solid platforms on which to build a research culture in FE. Some well-established international peer-reviewed academic journals regularly feature research in and on FE, including *Research in Post-Compulsory Education* (which will have a special issue on 'Re-imagining FE' in 2018), the *Journal of Further and Higher Education* and the *Journal of Vocational Education and Training*. Research and development organizations serving the FE sector have come and gone with some regularity over the last thirty years; however, a few have endured, and they consistently attract a core membership from FE practitioners as well as from academic researchers, including the Association for Research in Post-Compulsory Education (ARPCE), the Post-Compulsory Education Special Interest Group of the British Educational Research Association (BERA), Teacher Education in Lifelong Learning (TELL), and the Learning and Skills Research Network (LSRN), which was highlighted in Yvonne Hillier's conclusion to this volume's prequel, *Further Education and the Twelve Dancing Princesses* (Daley *et al.*, 2015). In addition, the Association of Colleges (AoC) has become more active in commissioning and supporting research and scholarship in FE. The third platform that has contributed particularly to FE research is the FE monograph written and contributed to by FE practitioners, representing a growing tradition of scholarly books that give a thoughtful and critical lens to change and opportunity in FE. The current volume, with its predecessor, is an outstanding example of this tradition. In it, contributors systematically apply detailed analysis and critique to the FE landscape and their lived experience of it. What gives this volume its power is the force of its foray into the secret garden of FE, the corporate world inhabited by principals and the extent to which this space is or is not shaped by educational values. The contributors have stood up to be counted; they inhabit a subversive land that questions orthodoxy, challenges the narrow empiricist logic of the neoliberal market, and posits alternative futures that draw their inspiration from a UNESCO-informed vision of lifelong learning as the conceptual framework and organizing principle for education in the twenty-first century. These research foundations in post-compulsory education are part of a wider movement of academics and teachers across all sectors to reclaim education's higher moral purpose and to resist narrow instrumental formulations of education systems and institutions.

The current volume draws upon much original research that challenges the status quo, a quality that is critical to the enduring legacy of Machiavelli, and offers a fresh and different vision, as good research should do. It is a call to arms to abandon reductionist education policies and to work collaboratively and tirelessly towards a conception of FE in particular that values lifelong learning, learning for its own sake, teaching as a values-driven moral art, and students as skilful and valued participants in their own and others' learning (showing and sharing what Alex Dunedin in his contribution to this volume calls 'valuable knowledge' and 'working knowledge'). On such a foundation, economic wealth, social prosperity, institutional health, professional status and individual fulfilment can all be achieved. It is research that has uncovered the truths to be found herein, and it is around research that all who value FE and desire it to flourish must gather to conspire and to plot a different future.

References

Daley, M., Orr, K., and Petrie, J. (eds) (2015) *Further Education and the Twelve Dancing Princesses*. Stoke-on-Trent: Trentham Books.

Department of Education and Science (1966) 'A plan for polytechnics and other colleges: Higher education in the further education system'. White Paper. London: HMSO.

Lingfield, R. (chair) (2012) 'Professionalism in further education: Final report of the independent review panel'. BIS/12/1198. London: Department of Business, Innovation and Skills. Online. www.gov.uk/government/uploads/system/uploads/attachment_data/file/422247/bis-12-1198-professionalism-in-further-education-review-final-report.pdf (accessed 24 June 2017).

Introduction: FE's Machiavellian moment and its Promethean promise

Joel Petrie

> And at his mother's home, Hermes …
> Slipped sideways through the keyhole,
> Like fog on an autumn breeze.
> (Anon. (trans. Lewis Hyde), *Homeric Hymn to Hermes*)

From princesses to princes

Further Education and the Twelve Dancing Princesses (Daley *et al.*, 2015) challenged Cinderella as the dominant deficit metaphor for English further education (FE). It instead celebrated collective professional spaces that could still be exploited, albeit behind a locked door guarded by the King. To what extent this aspiration succeeded is for others to judge. We were, though, pleased that the *Times Educational Supplement* (*TES*) subsequently decreed that the C-word was beyond the pale (Exley, 2016), while being disappointed that Ofsted's new Chief Inspector undermined her celebration of FE's importance with a reference to the lacklustre and gendered fairy-tale cliché (Spielman, 2017). In this sequel the focus shifts from princesses to princes, and we slip through the keyhole to directly interrogate how formal power is exercised in FE (whether ethically or problematically). We cover teacher resistance and professionalism, the agency of students and communities, and leadership practice in its broadest sense as the appropriate prerogative of individuals at all organizational and sectoral levels. What explicitly links the two books is an intention to be playful but deadly serious in considering power, agency and professionalism in FE through a metaphorical lens: in the current project the lens is *The Prince,* Machiavelli's celebrated and contested treatise on the exercise of power.

The Machiavellian trichotomy

In recent political discourse Machiavelli is having something of a renaissance: in the aftermath of the UK's Brexit vote and the Conservative Party leadership election it engendered, the former Secretary of State for

Education Michael Gove was described as a Machiavellian psychopath by supporters of his rival Boris Johnson (Ross and Hope, 2016); similarly in the American presidential election Ignatius (2016) suggested Donald Trump embodies the leadership traits of dishonesty and bullying Machiavelli lauded in Italian potentates. In reviewing Machiavelli one encounters 'one expression of moral outrage after another' (Breckman, 2015: 239), including some from the Jesuits, for whom he was in league with Satan; for Thayer only 'Judas Iscariot has been more detested than Machiavelli' (1892: 476), and Berlin attributes to Bertrand Russell the view that *The Prince* is 'a handbook for gangsters' (2013: 44).

Machiavelli can equally be interpreted as a utopian, and in *Discourses on Livy* he 'expresses his preference for republics and his sympathies for the plebeians' (Breckman, 2015: 241). Pocock posits the notion of a Machiavellian moment: the historical point at which Machiavelli wrote *The Prince*, but also one of two inseparable moments at which the 'foundation of a "republic" appears possible or ... at which its formation is seen to be precarious and entails a crisis' (Pocock, 1975: 554). Benner (2017) argues that Machiavelli was fundamentally democratic in his sensibilities. Similarly, Kahn highlights Gentili's *De legationibus libri tres* (1585) description of the Florentine as a '"laudator democratiae" (eulogist of democracy)' (1994: 128). For Salman Rushdie, who featured a fictional Machiavelli in *The Enchantress of Florence*, he is a profoundly humanist philosopher of republicanism (Tonkin, 2008). Breckman points out that key commentators of the Left such as Marx admired Machiavelli, and that 'Gramsci described *The Prince* as a manifesto that is both "revolutionary" *and* "utopian"' (2015: 240).

A third reading of Machiavelli, particularly in relation to *The Prince*, positions him as an ironist or a trickster. According to Hyde, trickster archetypes such as Hermes and Prometheus are the 'mythical embodiment of ambiguity and ambivalence, doubleness and duplicity, contradiction and paradox' (Hyde, 2008: 7). This interpretation is evident in a letter from Machiavelli to a close acquaintance, in which he describes them both as serious men who are additionally 'petty, fickle, lascivious, and ... directed towards chimerical matters' (Atkinson and Sices, 1996: 312).

Sedgmore (2015) highlights FE's noble tradition of humorous dissent, appealing to sector leaders to laugh along and thus learn something. There is unquestionably a leitmotif of wit running through this volume, along with various perspectives sympathetic to the trichotomy of interpretations of Machiavelli and, indeed, of power. The book's chapters are organized thematically into parts, each of which begins with a contextualizing introduction, and each chapter is associated with an image by an FE student or lecturer that illustrates a quotation about power. The chapters in the first part of the book deal with issues of power in FE, including governmental, sectoral and senior managerial authority. In the second part five authors explore aspects of Scottish, Welsh, Irish, English and Australian power dynamics in post-compulsory education. The chapters in the third part analyse citizenship, community and professionalism in FE. The final part makes explicit the book's underlying aspirational, radical and democratic vision for FE, which is in sympathy with Machiavelli's less prominently celebrated republicanism and utopianism.

FE's Promethean promise

Breckman argues that to recover the 'theoretical legacy of the Florentine thinker seems a fitting task in what might be our own Machiavellian moment' of contested relationships between 'citizens and states, plebeians and elites' (2015: 253, 252). Hodgson and Spours suggest that the era of FE incorporation has reached a crossroads, and that top-down managerialism and marketization should be replaced by more collegiate, democratic accountability: 'a new era with more altruistic and collaborative institutions' (2015: 215). This view chimes with that of FETL (the Further Education Trust for Leadership), which argues that FE requires leadership that looks 'beyond the current crisis that engulfs it ... [and] a new narrative to secure its place in the future. To do this requires an environment where the leadership of thinking is second nature' (Kahn, 2015). In *Further Education and the Twelve Dancing Princesses* we suggested that after a generation of neglect the sector's cinders should be reignited, but we didn't fully anticipate the policy conflagration to come. Like Prometheus the arch-trickster, the sector must steal back its fire from any authority that limits its agency to transform. A Promethean as much as a Machiavellian moment is increasingly urgent: the principled democratic leadership of powerful FE professionals is the critical spark the sector requires.

References

Atkinson, J.B. and Sices, D. (eds) (1996) *Machiavelli and His Friends: Their personal correspondence*. DeKalb: Northern Illinois University Press.

Benner, E. (2017) *Be Like the Fox: Machiavelli's lifelong quest for freedom*. London: Allen Lane.

Berlin, I. (2013) 'The originality of Machiavelli'. In Hardy, H. (ed.) *Against the Current: Essays in the history of ideas*. Princeton: Princeton University Press, 33–100.

Breckman, W. (2015) 'The power and the void: Radical democracy, post-Marxism, and the Machiavellian moment'. In Smulewicz-Zucker, G. and Thompson, M.J. (eds) *Radical Intellectuals and the Subversion of Progressive Politics: The betrayal of politics*. New York: Palgrave Macmillan, 237–54.

Daley, M., Orr, K., and Petrie, J. (2015) *Further Education and the Twelve Dancing Princesses*. Stoke-on-Trent: Trentham Books.

Exley, S. (2016) 'Why we ban the C-word'. *TES*, 23 December. Online. www.tes.com/news/further-education/breaking-views/why-we-ban-c-word (accessed 21 February 2017).

Hodgson, A. and Spours, K. (2015) 'The future for FE colleges in England: The case for a new post-incorporation model'. In Hodgson, A. (ed.) *The Coming of Age for FE? Reflections on the past and future role of further education colleges in England*. London: Institute of Education Press, 199–219.

Hyde, L. (2008) *Trickster Makes This World: How disruptive imagination creates culture*. Edinburgh: Canongate.

Ignatius, D. (2016) 'Donald Trump is the American Machiavelli'. *Washington Post*, 10 November. Online. www.washingtonpost.com/opinions/donald-trump-is-the-american-machiavelli/2016/11/10/8ebfae16-a794-11e6-ba59-a7d93165c6d4_story.html?utm_term=.49d0d2742611 (accessed 21 February 2017).

Kahn, V. (1994) *Machiavellian Rhetoric: From the Counter-Reformation to Milton*. Princeton: Princeton University Press.

Khan, A. (2015) 'Thinking up a future for FE and skills'. *FE Week*, 13 November. Online. http://feweek.co.uk/2015/11/13/thinking-up-a-future-for-fe-and-skills/ (accessed 4 April 2017).

Pocock, J.G.A. (1975) *The Machiavellian Moment: Florentine political thought and the Atlantic republican tradition*. Princeton: Princeton University Press.

Ross, T. and Hope, C. (2016) 'Boris Johnson allies accuse Michael Gove of being a "Machiavellian psychopath" who plotted to win leadership "from the beginning"'. *The Telegraph*, 3 July. Online. www.telegraph.co.uk/news/2016/07/03/boris-johnson-allies-accuse-michael-gove-of-being-a-machiavellia/ (accessed 21 February 2017).

Sedgmore, L. (2015) 'If we attempt to stifle satire, the joke's on us'. *TES*, 6 February. Online. www.tes.com/news/tes-archive/tes-publication/if-we-attempt-stifle-satire-jokes-us (accessed 4 April 2017).

Spielman, A. (2017) 'Amanda Spielman's speech at the Association of Colleges Ofsted conference: "A new direction"'. Online. www.gov.uk/government/speeches/amanda-spielmans-speech-at-the-association-of-colleges-ofsted-conference-a-new-direction (accessed 3 April 2017).

Thayer, W.R. (1892) 'Machiavelli's Prince'. *International Journal of Ethics*, 2 (4), 476–92.

Tonkin, B. (2008) 'Salman Rushdie: "Fiction saved my life"'. *The Independent*, 10 April. Online. www.independent.co.uk/arts-entertainment/books/features/salman-rushdie-fiction-saved-my-life-807501.html (accessed 4 April 2017).

Part One

1

Introduction: Power and Principals

Mike Aiello

The title and focus of the book and the contributions in this part prompted me to revisit and reflect on not only where we have travelled since incorporation (1992) but also, in the style of Machiavelli, on a number of complex questions. The analysis of power is one such question. The scrutiny of power in FE, as the sector struggles to survive and develop within the context of marketization and austerity, presents us with a potentially bewildering array of strategies, policies and practices. This publication is thus well timed and important.

Contributions in this part highlight the increasingly uncertain future of FE and suggest that issues we have engaged with since incorporation are still live and significant a quarter of a century later. The prognosis for FE appears bleak. However, it is publications such as this, and the ongoing work of activists across the sector, that provide evidence of an ongoing and healthy struggle to ensure professionalism and care across all aspects of FE. The value of activism, scholarship and criticality is evident throughout this part, and for making sense of what appears to be an uncertain, inconsistent and fluctuating approach to power and the principal in FE the decision to revisit Machiavelli proves inspired. It has clearly provided a prompt and a framework for all the contributors in this part.

Revisiting the source and the many commentaries on Machiavelli, I enjoyed reeling in the years and re-examining the extensive Machiavelli opus. It ranges from what we in management development would call simple normative approaches – that is, Machiavelli provides a blueprint for successful practice through universal examples of good practice – to more insightful and nuanced work on Machiavelli and insights on appearance and virtue, or to what I think is most significant for this part, the work on Machiavelli as ironist. *The Prince* is resplendent with ambiguity. Ambiguity provides the basis for irony. Irony is a significantly powerful tool for political criticism and insight into power. Contributors in this part dazzle in their use of irony, and this reflects the trickster qualities of Machiavelli explored in Joel Petrie's introduction.

This part consists of contributions which in different but significant ways seek to use Machiavelli's *The Prince* as a trigger to raise key questions about power and the principal in FE. In one sense this is a diverse mixture of contributions. Some adopt the style and tone of the original to offer leadership and career advice for current and aspiring principals, while other contributors take aspects of Machiavelli and use them to critique current policy and practice.

Rob Smith starts the part with an exploration of the impact of area reviews and the end of incorporation: a Machiavellian moment. The chapter provides a contemporary account of the state of FE with a potentially tragic outcome. If the quest for a new leadership model is unsuccessful FE may be in ruins. Chapter 2 is in stark contrast. In '*Il Principe*, a handbook for career-makers in further education', Geoff Brown provides sage, good advice for the aspiring careerist. Machiavelli would appreciate the insights, experience and tone of this ironist. The chapter provides salutary warnings as well as advice for rampant careerists and the victims of their success. A similar engagement with the original is then provided by Carol Azumah Dennis. Adopting a Machiavellian letter-from-exile approach she provides a series of insights into leadership, what kind of leaders there are and how leadership is gained and kept. There are significant universal insights and lessons: it is a letter for all of FE and not merely the recipient, the 'esteemed principal and chief executive'. The part finishes with a Machiavellian justification of the principal. In '"For one will always find malcontents": In defence of the principal', Damien Page highlights a host of questions for activists and malcontents to consider and answer.

This part should enthuse and energize readers to revisit Machiavellianism, and prompted me to revisit my extensive professional practice working with managers, principals and other colleagues in post-compulsory provision. FE is a complex and dynamic environment. I have worked in, or with colleagues in, FE in the north-west of England since 1980, and my experience confirms that there are no easy solutions or approaches to power and the principal. However, this does not mean there are no answers.

During the 1997–2010 FE expansionist era of Blair and Brown several principals in the North West of England demonstrated their commitment to growth as set out by Machiavelli, and created FE institutions as a significant resource for their community. In more straitened and politically hostile times, such as now, collegial approaches to leadership and development may provide an appropriate and enduring model of practice. I co-delivered a very successful partner-based MA programme between 2002 and 2006 with a principal – Kevin – whose perspective on college leadership was to remain focused on what made him become a teacher in the first place, namely an abiding interest in teaching and learning and the belief that the best prospect of developing a questioning, reflective and self-motivated student body lies in the nurturing of a questioning, motivated and self-motivated staff (Aiello and Watson, 2007). He has since maintained and developed his collegial-learning-based philosophy of leadership in a number of appointments in London. The approach has led to his current college being recognized as a beacon of excellence, as an Investors in People champion, and more importantly as the best of all London colleges for academic and vocational achievement. Kevin as principal evidences the effectiveness of an explicitly collegial approach to leadership in FE. This may be the model required not only in expansionist or straitened times, but at all times.

Reference

Aiello, M. and Watson, K. (2007) 'An alternative approach to CPD: An evaluation of the impact on individual and institutional development of an action learning programme run in partnership by an HE institution (HEI) and a sixth form college (SFC)'. In Townsend, T. and Bates, R. (eds) *Handbook of Teacher Education: Globalization, standards and professionalism in times of change*. Dordrecht: Springer, 457–64.

Becy Spendley

[P]art of the whole technique of disempowering people is to make sure that the real agents of change fall out of history, and are never recognized in the culture for what they are. So it's necessary to distort history and make it look as if Great Men did everything – that's part of how you teach people they can't do anything, they're helpless.

Noam Chomsky

Chapter 1

Area reviews and the end of incorporation: A Machiavellian moment

Rob Smith

At first glance, FE is over-populated by would-be princes. That is primarily because the sector has been profoundly influenced by neoliberal structures of governance and cultures of performance management that assert colleges' autonomy. This supposed autonomy confers and promotes a type of leadership that is individual, entrepreneurial and competitive. We might therefore imagine that every town has its own FE principality and each principal is busy planning how, ruthlessly, to expand her or his empire. However, the deep cuts to FE budgets experienced since 2009 and the national programme of area reviews launched in September 2015, which are reorganizing FE provision, have made principals' princely robes look decidedly threadbare. Drawing on findings from a recent research project, this chapter will explore the implications for FE leadership of these recent sectoral developments.

Beginning in 1993, the era of incorporation required a particular kind of leadership that positioned FE principals at the intersection between the college and the wider policy environment. Managerialist cultures dominated, and financial responsibility, managing local competition and delivering educational outcomes were key aspects of coordinating a local FE service. At the same time, links with local authorities were severed and replaced with a relationship with centralized governance. Above all, incorporation required college leaders to develop an expertise in funding and the management of performance data to satisfy funding bodies and policy-makers.

The model of leadership that underpinned incorporation fits snugly with *The Prince*. By coming out from local authority control, each principal was granted a mini-fiefdom and told to compete. Elsewhere I've written about the perception that, after 1993, many principals considered themselves 'masters of their universe' (Smith, 2015: 26). But it's important to view the clamour about the increased 'freedom' colleges were enjoying with great scepticism, because the gravitational pull of state involvement in FE appears to have strengthened as policy initiatives have come thick and fast (e.g., the 16–19 Diploma 2008, Functional Skills 2008, Train to Gain 2009, the Technical Baccalaureate 2013, Study Programmes 2013, Apprenticeships 2013). While previous local authority (LA) involvement may have been sometimes prescriptive or negligent, it has been replaced by a gradual ratcheting up of 'arm's-length' state control (Public Administration Select Committee, 2014: 5).

FE's annualized funding model, always integrating a success or achievement factor, provides a better purchase for the kind of governmentality (Burchell *et al.*, 1991) that characterizes neoliberal models of governance. Here I am taking neoliberalism to mean a 'hegemonic ideological fix' (Peck, 2010: 32) that has at its heart an emphasis on market fundamentalism originating in the Chicago school of economics (Davies, W., 2014). Foucault's definition of governmentality sees it as:

> The ensemble formed by the institutions, procedures, analyses and reflections, the calculations and tactics that allow the exercise of this very specific albeit complex form of power, which has as its target population, as its principal form of knowledge political economy and as its essential technical means apparatuses of security.
>
> (Burchell *et al.*, 1991: 102)

FE's annualized funding model, integrating as it always has a success or achievement factor, tied to the performance of students in the qualifications they undertake, provides a key to understanding the difference between FE and other sectors (including the model currently emerging in HE). The so-called success rate (retention × achievement) provides a supposedly absolute measure of the quality of the provision. Unlike with schools or universities, the Success Rate allows for the imposition of a funding penalty if colleges fail to achieve national benchmarks. This means that college teachers are under pressure to ensure that all the students they recruit to their courses pass. Unlike in schools, recruitment is identified as their responsibility, as is the pass rate. What sounds innocuous leads in actuality to a range of optimization behaviour, gaming and unforeseen consequences (see Goldstein, 2013; Wolf, 2011; Smith, forthcoming). In this way, teachers are forced to produce positive performance data as part of the institutional simulationist projects all colleges engage in. The centrality of data production operates on teachers as internalized surveillance or panopticism, almost as though the state were sitting in the corner of every classroom.

Funding arrangements, complemented by governance and accountability structures that carried the whiff of a feudal system of annual tribute, dramatically shaped models of FE leadership in the years following incorporation. The structural imperative underpinning incorporation was that principals had to demonstrate competence in their newly acquired positions of power in order to continue to receive the same funding. However, in 2015, there were strong signals that these models of leadership were coming to an end. The series of area reviews commenced at that time provided a clear indication that the existing model of stratified governmentality was breaking down.

Triggers

Calls for austerity measures in the wake of the banking crisis of 2008/9 tolled like the chimes of midnight for FE. After FE had enjoyed unprecedented levels of investment during the first years of the new millennium, not least due to New Labour's Skills for Life programme, the Comprehensive Spending Reviews that sought to implement austerity across the public sector appeared to target FE budgets. Unlike schools, FE was not granted ring-fenced funding protection (hollow though that promise has turned out to be), and between 2009 and 2014 funding cuts hit FE particularly hard. Some sources estimated that cuts in adult courses amounted to between 24 and 35 per cent (UCU, 2015). As the cuts to FE mounted year on year, a growing number of colleges posted an annual deficit. The policy response to this was the appointment of the FE Commissioner (or Czar), Dr David Collins.

Collins was one of a series of czars – public figures appointed variously to tackle endemic poor quality in particular areas of the public sector. The appointment of these designated experts as a way of responding to perceived crises originates in US politics but has recently manifested itself in British political life. This policy invention (we have had an Enterprise Czar, a Drugs Czar and, in education, a Behaviour Czar) signals crisis while at the same time legitimizing and operationalizing governmental intervention. Czars are symbolic figures, apparently equipped with relevant insider knowledge, and capable of tackling problems impervious to the blunt instrument of government bureaucracy. They have, we can surmise, objective and universal insights that transcend specific contexts. Thus, their experience and acuity raise them above the contextual pressures of affiliation and emotion within colleges and give their insights a detached and dispassionate objectivity that enables them to make depoliticized decisions based on technical judgements alone. As an invented policy identity, in

Foucault's terms the Czar represents a tool of continuity, the personalized manifestation and affirmation of a centralized agenda. In the case of the area reviews, this means a realignment of corporate FE finances that attempts to secure, for the time being, the creaking system of FE governance.

Before the announcement of area reviews, Collins was appointed as Commissioner to turn around poor provision. In a letter of 13 June 2014, he explained his progress:

> In each of the FE Colleges recently under review the intervention process has been triggered by financial health and/or control concerns. ... In most of the colleges I have visited to date, it would be true to say there hasn't been the level of challenge and scrutiny by the governing body that might be expected in an organisation that is dealing with financial concerns. This is often because some governing bodies do not have sufficient financial expertise within their membership to oversee complex multi-million pound organisations.
>
> (BIS, 2014: [1], [2])

This is one of a series of letters that focuses on the governance and leadership within FE colleges. Collins was more explicit in a letter of October 2015 in which he spoke of 'tighter government funding' and acknowledged that 'for the first time since incorporation the sector as a whole has posted an annual deficit' (BIS, 2015a: [1]). In an earlier letter he had listed a number of features that might be identified as possible indicators that any given college could be in trouble and heading for a poor inspection. Among them were:

- Average student attendance rates are below 85%–90%
- Success rates (Retention x Achievement) are 5% below benchmark and not improving
- Teacher observation grades of good or better, independently verified, are below 80%
- Student surveys/focus groups show levels of satisfaction below 90%
- Quality Improvement plans ... do not state clearly for each issue the college's starting position, the targeted outcome [and] actions that will be taken to achieve that outcome ... .

(BIS 2015b, [2])

The language of targets and the use of numerical performance metrics are familiar to FE staff. Poor provision and failing colleges are part of a hegemonic lexicon that also includes financial health, Key Performance Indicators and efficiency. Since incorporation, efficiency has been a totem in the political economy of FE, a thoroughly ingrained concept. But it is only possible to operationalize it once the success rate has been established and linked, through national benchmarks, to funding. Once the link between a target and a benchmark is set and a notional cost attached, then efficiency, the achievement of the same outcomes for less money, can be contemplated, and required, by funders.

Despite the Czar's busy schedule, by 2015 estimates of the number of colleges in deficit ranged from 50 to 110 (Cooney, 2015; Gaunt, 2015; NAO, 2015). The growing number of insolvent colleges and the seeming inability of the Czar to remedy the situation triggered the area review programme. In the context of seemingly intractable financial problems at the local college level, the aim of the reviews was to 'move towards fewer, larger, more resilient and efficient providers, and more effective collaboration across institution types' (BIS and DfE, 2016). As well as offering a solution to the funding crisis in up to a quarter of colleges, in the opinion of the FE Commissioner the reviews would address the fact that there were 'still major efficiencies to be made in existing institutions' (BIS, 2015a: [1]). In this respect, the merging and even closure of colleges was foreseen. According to Nick Boles, the then skills minister:

> A merger can mean that you save on a whole lot of administrative and management costs, so that you can actually put more money into paying for teachers doing the job we all want them to do.
>
> (Offord, 2015)

The reviews, which were to proceed region by region, were presented through the ideological trope of endless efficiency to provide 'better quality through the reduction/elimination of poor provision' (BIS, 2015a: [2]). After nearly a quarter of a century of incorporated FE, the need for area reviews suggests a cross-sectoral failure of governance that begs the question *What went wrong?* While we ponder that question, we might also consider area reviews as presenting us with the opportunity to look again at what leadership in FE colleges has been like and what it could and should look like.

This chapter draws on research data on the views of FE leaders gathered through semi-structured interviews between 2014 and 2016. Interviews were carried out face to face and by telephone with eleven individuals who had all held senior positions in FE settings. The sample included serving principals and vice-principals, ex-principals, policy advisers and leaders of national organizations connected to FE. The research project began before the announcement of area reviews, and to start with it focused on the key research questions:

1. What are FE leaders' views on the efficacy and appropriateness of the current model of funding and governance?
2. How are FE leaders negotiating the tensions between external market cultures and local cultures of teaching and learning within their colleges?
3. What are the key challenges for FE leadership currently?

The interviews were transcribed, and emerging themes were highlighted after transcription. For the purposes of this chapter, I will draw on the views of four participants out of the eleven. These were participants who were interviewed later in the project when the area reviews had begun or had been announced.

Themes from the data

Chapter 5 of *The Prince* begins:

> Whenever those states which have been acquired as stated have been accustomed to live under their own laws and in freedom, there are three courses for those who wish to hold them: the first is to ruin them, the next is to reside there in person, the third is to permit them to live under their own laws, drawing a tribute, and establishing within it an oligarchy which will keep it friendly to you. Because such a government, being created by the prince, knows that it cannot stand without his friendship and interest, and does its utmost to support him … .
>
> (Machiavelli, 1908: 20)

This passage illustrates how tribute was used in Machiavelli's time in the domination and domestication of occupied states as a tool of governance. We have already touched on how panopticism carries the state into teachers' classrooms, but the notion of tribute is also a useful one to explain how quality, accountability and funding currently combine in the governance of FE. A regime of tribute is legitimized through the conferring of conditional autonomy. Colleges were granted the freedom to compete within the newly marketized sector, but this freedom was dependent on colleges' ability to demonstrate compliance with policy demands around three interlinked areas: quality/standards, curriculum and, pre-eminently, efficiency.

Leaders in the sample flagged up the problematic nature of colleges' freedom. One talked about LA 'shackles' and decried the idea of going back under LA control; however, others complained of the centralized control of funding, claiming it significantly constrained colleges' development, hindering autonomy in investment and planning and severely restricting other activities. There was a strong consensus amongst the participants that the combination of funding cuts and the actual challenges faced by colleges made the job of leading 'inherently unmanageable' and 'unfeasible'.

> When you look at the list of challenges, I mean only fantasists could willingly take on the challenge.
>
> (Greg, ex-principal and ex-LA officer)

The normalization of the link between funding and success rates is a key aspect of this unmanageability. The hegemonic bonding of the two means that demands for increased efficiency are potentially limitless. Terri, an active leader and national figure in the sector, commented:

> We are expected to get a hundred per cent success rates. They don't know what they're talking about. These are human beings. There are exam systems where you will never get a hundred per cent pass rates anyway [but] ... falling short of that a hundred per cent is seen as a failure in the system.
>
> (Terri)

A primary theme to emerge from the research relates to the regimes of simulation that have been established and sustained through funding and accountability arrangements in the sector. Closure and merger have always been integral features of the FE market. At the time of writing, the number of colleges has reduced from 427 in 1993 to 325 (AoC, n.d.). This difference is accounted for by mergers and closures, which illustrates the pressure facing colleges and also explains how gaming and the manipulation of performance metrics are incentivized, something one participant commented on:

> If you were designing a corrupting system you'd pretty much put in place the sort of things we have now.
>
> (Terri)

Looked at through the lens of tribute, college leaders have to demonstrate loyalty to central government by annually offering up performance data as tokens of compliance; in exchange for this, they receive the state's backing in the form of funding. However, this compliance comes at a cost. The systems approach to management can be perceived as exerting a powerful negative influence on teachers' practice, but the all-pervasive language and culture of performativity also serves to widen a discursive hiatus that neoliberalism opens up between performance accountability to the state and the nurturing process of teaching and learning. Principals and other leaders act as coordinators of this disjunction. This was described by one participant in the following terms:

> My job as a chief exec is to fit the values of teaching into a presentational form that satisfies those who ultimately fund us, because the language of teaching and learning does not resonate down at the DfE. That is not language that is going to achieve funding for you. I now have to present our business to a set of funders, whether it's EFA, SFA or HEFCE or whoever, in a language and with impact measures that they buy into.
>
> (Maria, principal)

Not only was Maria aware of the importance of the discourse of fealty that college leadership requires mastery of, but she was also aware of the potential it has to undermine the values of the teaching and learning it is supposed to oversee. Talking about the need of leaders to encourage 'expansive' cultures (Fuller and Unwin, 2004) to support teaching and learning, she stated:

> How do I encourage and enable that, while the wiring that sits behind it belongs to a completely different set of values and uses a different language in order to sustain the operation?
>
> (Maria, principal)

The question is not an easy one to answer. However, across the sector the precariousness of college finances means gaming is all-pervasive as an effect of structure (see Smith, forthcoming). This requires a different definition of gaming that applies not to the teachers who change and adapt their practices and record-keeping in order to produce positive data outcomes, but to the leaders of FE colleges who suspend critical engagement with the real context of teaching and learning practices in the institutions they lead. Knowingly, they collate and consolidate performance data from different courses into an institutional package to present as tribute to funding agencies. This systemic simulation feeds into a self-perpetuating cycle that locks all colleges into the regime of fealty.

Participants found it particularly difficult to understand the justification for the extent of the cuts imposed as a result of the austerity measures after the 2008 international financial crisis. Several viewed this as sectoral victimization:

> It's almost as if the entire brunt of cuts and expenditure is being borne by FE ... Basically, it's the tenth year of cuts in budgets.
>
> (Adam, ex-principal)

Other participants, too, were convinced that the sector had been singled out, one seeing this as due to 'prejudice'. According to another, policy-makers and politicians simply do not understand FE:

> None of them have the vaguest understanding or idea of what it is like to work in an FE college, they have no understanding of what an FE college does, and no understanding of the kind of service that it provides for some 3.5 million people nationally.
>
> (Adam, ex-principal)

But one aspect of this ignorance is that it might be a designed-in feature of arm's-length governance. Incorporation was seen as a way of dividing FE from its community, having the effect of eroding its (locally defined and realized) purposes:

> In a way, incorporation was FE's downfall in policy terms. … At local authority level there was no question that FE colleges were needed and existed and at local level there is always support and interest in the colleges because they are part of the community and part of the fabric. But … nationally they are just like pins on a map. … They can be moved this way, that way.
>
> (Terri)

In this turbulent funding context, the area reviews were seen by one participant, Greg, as a symptom of system failure. Too many colleges had built up serious financial debts that, aggravated by the cuts imposed because of austerity, rather like those imposed on NHS hospitals (Triggle, 2016), had precipitated a 'tipping point' that would see colleges closing unless drastic action was taken:

> History may judge the area reviews as being a great big smokescreen for getting the bailout funds from the Treasury.
>
> (Greg)

Greg put the system failure down to the level of skills and knowledge needed by principals and governing bodies in a highly regulated and straitened funding environment. He believed that the demands and complexity of college leadership, given the current funding and accountability system, were beyond some college leaders:

> You have to ask yourself, with this incorporated and autonomous model, why do we keep having a significant slug of colleges who

can't run their own affairs? Very weak governors don't make the best appointments, not willing to take the action necessary.

(Greg)

Greg's view suggests that nationally there isn't the capacity to have a corporation in every college. In addition, Greg saw incorporation as having effectively stripped out a developmental layer of local supra-college leadership. Despite this perception of system breakdown, there are few signs that the centralized policy culture of 'deliverology' (Ball *et al.*, 2012) and its imposed spreadsheet regime of tribute are losing their dominance. Instead, the area reviews constitute a realignment of governmentality; leadership is more remote, its vision is intensified, and it is more tightly wedded to centrally determined discourses of fealty and simulation.

So, who is the Prince in FE in the era of area reviews? Do these new principals of the merged and ever-larger colleges qualify? Or is it perhaps the so-called Czar, the FE Commissioner? The real Prince is none of these, and the area reviews illustrate this. While the discourse of performance data and accountability continues to be countenanced, believed and acted on by sectoral leaders, then, the true Prince is the marketized system of incorporated simulation itself. Our problem is that this royal simulation depends for its legitimation on the fealty of FE leaders and their willingness to continue to participate. If we return to Chapter 5 of *The Prince* and look again at the Prince's alternatives, we can see how the options for FE governmentality are narrowing. The second option, 'to reside there in person', achieved through panopticism, and the third, the tribute option, appear close to being exhausted.

That leaves option one: to ruin FE. In the absence of any loyalty on the part of policy-makers to FE as a sector, ruin may indeed be in prospect. The market proponents' notion of allowing disfavoured public sector organizations to wither on the vine is well established (see for example Davies, N., 1999). The key variables that will determine FE's ultimate destination are the state of public finances and the fealty of college leaders to the current regime of simulation. That being the case, what is called for now is a new kind of leadership.

References

AoC (Association of Colleges) (n.d.) 'College mergers'. Online. www.aoc.co.uk/about-colleges/college-mergers (accessed 12 September 2016).

— (2015) *College Key Facts 2015/16*. London: Association of Colleges. Online. www.aoc.co.uk/sites/default/files/AoC%20College%20Key%20Facts%202015-16%20WEB.pdf (accessed 12 September 2016).

Ball, S., Maguire, M., Braun, A., Perryman, J., and Hoskins, K. (2012) 'Assessment technologies in schools: "Deliverology" and the "play of dominations"'. *Research Papers in Education*, 27 (5), 513–33.

BIS (Department for Business, Innovation and Skills) (2014) 'Financial challenges with rigour and responsiveness in skills: FE Commissioner letter'. Letter from Further Education (FE) Commissioner, Dr David Collins CBE, to chairs and principals, 13 June. Department of Business, Innovation & Skills. Online. www.gov.uk/government/uploads/system/uploads/attachment_data/file/319424/further-education-commissioner-letter-june_2014.pdf (accessed 4 June 2017).

BIS (Department for Business, Innovation and Skills) (2015a) 'Area reviews and the reshaping of the college sector'. Letter from Further Education (FE) Commissioner, Dr David Collins CBE, to chairs and principals, 30 October. Online. www.gov.uk/government/uploads/system/uploads/attachment_data/file/473452/area-reviews-and-reshaping-college-sector-FE-commissioner-letter.pdf (accessed 13 May 2017).

BIS (Department for Business, Innovation and Skills) (2015b) 'Organisational improvement with rigour and responsiveness in skills'. Letter from Further Education (FE) Commissioner, Dr David Collins CBE, to chairs and principals, 27 March. Online. www.gov.uk/government/uploads/system/uploads/attachment_data/file/418315/Organisational_improvement_with_rigour_and_responsiveness_in_skills_-_FE_Commissioner_letter.pdf (accessed 4 June 2017).

BIS (Department for Business, Innovation and Skills) and DfE (Department for Education) (2016) 'Reviewing post-16 education and training institutions: Area reviews'. Online. www.gov.uk/government/publications/reviewing-post-16-education-and-training-institutions-list-of-area-reviews (accessed 13 May 2017).

Burchell, G., Gordon, C., and Miller, P. (eds) (1991) *The Foucault Effect: Studies in governmentality*. Chicago: University of Chicago Press.

Cooney, R. (2015) 'Financial difficulties at "50 colleges"'. *FE Week*, 9 February. Online. http://feweek.co.uk/2015/02/09/financial-difficulties-at-50-colleges/ (accessed 8 September 2016).

Davies, N. (1999) 'Schools in crisis: Political coup bred educational disaster'. *The Guardian*, 16 September. Online. www.theguardian.com/uk/1999/sep/16/nickdavies (accessed 16 September 2016).

Davies, W. (2014) *The Limits of Neoliberalism: Authority, sovereignty and the logic of competition*. London: SAGE Publications.

Fuller, A. and Unwin, L. (2004) 'Expansive learning environments: Integrating organizational and personal development'. In Rainbird, H., Fuller, A., and Munro, A. (eds) *Workplace Learning in Context*. London: Routledge, 126–44.

Gaunt, C. (2015) 'More than a quarter of FE colleges face financial meltdown'. *Nursery World*, 16 December. Online. www.nurseryworld.co.uk/nursery-world/news/1155233/more-than-a-quarter-of-fe-colleges-face-financial-meltdown (accessed 7 September 2016).

Goldstein, H. (2013) 'Evaluating educational changes: A statistical perspective'. *Ensaio: Avaliação e Políticas Públicas em Educação,* 21 (78), 101–14.

Machiavelli, N. (1908) *The Prince*. Trans. Marriott, W.K. Originally 1515. Online. www.constitution.org/mac/prince.pdf (accessed 13 April 2017).

NAO (National Audit Office) (2015) *Overseeing Financial Sustainability in the Further Education Sector*. London: National Audit Office. Online. www.nao.org.uk/wp-content/uploads/2015/07/Overseeing-financial-sustainability-in-the-further-education-sector.pdf (accessed 8 September 2016).

Offord, P. (2015) 'Skills Minister Nick Boles issues "nothing to fear from college mergers" assurance'. *FE Week*, 26 October. Online. http://feweek.co.uk/2015/10/26/skills-minister-nick-boles-issues-nothing-to-fear-from-college-mergers-assurance/ (accessed 23 August 2016).

Peck, J. (2010) *Constructions of Neoliberal Reason*. Oxford: Oxford University Press.

Public Administration Select Committee (2014) *Who's Accountable? Relationships between government and arm's-length bodies: First report of session 2014–15*. London: The Stationery Office. Online. www.publications.parliament.uk/pa/cm201415/cmselect/cmpubadm/110/110.pdf (accessed 12 September 2016).

Smith, R. (2015) 'College re-culturing, marketisation and knowledge: The meaning of incorporation'. *Journal of Educational Administration and History*, 47 (1), 18–39.

Smith, R. (forthcoming) 'Democratic governance and the teachers' real: Performance data in further education in England'. *British Journal of the Sociology of Education*.

Triggle, N. (2016) 'Virtually all hospitals now in deficit'. *BBC News*, 19 February. Online. www.bbc.co.uk/news/health-35608992 (accessed 11 September 2016).

UCU (University and College Union) (2015) 'UCU briefing on 24% cuts to adult further education budget in England'. Online. www.ucu.org.uk/media/7108/FE-England-budget-cuts-2015-16---a-UCU-briefing/pdf/ucu_fecutsbriefing_feb15.pdf (accessed 9 September 2016).

Wolf, A. (2011) *Review of Vocational Education: The Wolf report*. London: The Stationery Office. Online. www.gov.uk/government/uploads/system/uploads/attachment_data/file/180504/DFE-00031-2011.pdf (accessed 17 November, 2015).

Paige Elliott

The man of power is ruined by power, the man of money by money, the submissive man by subservience, the pleasure seeker by pleasure.

Hermann Hesse (*Steppenwolf*)

Chapter 2

Il Principe, a handbook for career-makers in FE

Geoff Brown

To start, a note of encouragement: do not think that those who climb to the top need any special talents. With a sharp political nose and the courage to seize the moment you need only the good fortune to be in the right place at the right time.

From the very beginning, be sure to take your reputation seriously. However, if it fits the time, as it did in the late 1960s and early 1970s, do not let this put you off being a wild young thing. It does no harm to spend your early years as a union activist and thereafter dropping occasional hints of having been one, as this will assist your reputation as feisty. We should remember the leading polytechnic director who boasted of his youthful prowess as a street fighter. This did not weaken his credibility in the corridors of Whitehall. Indeed, time spent as a member of the hard left may provide some useful political education. Not least, such a record may act as a smokescreen during later career moves, confusing colleagues as to your motives and objectives. However these early years are spent, be sure to make yourself popular, with a reputation for good humour and a general concern for others, but take care not to be overfamiliar or fast. Intimacy can lead to nasty rumours. Be sure to understand that the time and effort given to such schmoozing is a valuable, and indeed necessary, investment in your future.

Have no scruples in how you learn the ropes and establish your network. For example, there should be no hesitation in operating as the principal's secret informant in the staffroom. In return for the help rendered, you are entitled to expect that conversations with the principal will yield valuable advance notice of new posts and other changes as well as lesser titbits that can be used to establish yourself as someone in the know.

It should go without saying that keeping your eye out for the main chance must never slip your mind. Whatever your status as a union activist, promotion opportunities must be seized without scruple. Neither betrayal of colleagues nor breach of union policy should be ruled out, and likewise the elimination of potential rivals for promotion by whatever means needed for you to advance. Do not forget, though, that such perfidy has a price. There will be those who bear a grudge and spread their version of the truth at every opportunity. So, careful judgement is needed to assess when to sacrifice scruple and take the opportunity.

All politics is local; therefore establishing a local base is a *sine qua non*. Much of the time this requires is no more than an extension of what is already being done in the college. The network must be established, respecting the existing powers that be with uncounted hours spent as the one always willing to get stuck in, swallow the sexist jokes, be ready to buy a round and support the local interest. As you are beginning now to mix seriously with others on the political career path, it will become clear to you there are no particular qualifications required to get to the top apart from those already mentioned.

Campaigning for a good cause, such as the defence of a local NHS facility, can now be the key to candidacy for high public office, for example when an opportunity arises as the current Member of Parliament nears retirement. The success or otherwise of the campaign is a secondary matter, but, again, do not underestimate the labours involved. There will need to be many a tedious conversation while consuming alcohol round tables in local pubs and clubs. But only through such efforts can nomination for office be made credible.

You must understand that high politics is a dangerous affair, with great prizes for the winners and often a heavy price paid by the losers. A strong local base will not suffice as protection when national figures take part. They may pick and choose what local figures they will. At the same time, they also are bound by the laws of political calculation. Every decision has a cost that must be paid. Thus, losing out in contesting a nomination does not mean all investment is wasted. Rather, ensuring your own interests are at the heart of any such agreement, you may agree to withdraw peacefully and so put yourself in a more favourable light in any future applications for promotion.

Such deals with political superiors must take into account the powers and objectives of those now sometimes referred to in the popular media as the movers and shakers or even the local mafia. Politics is no longer dominated by a municipal pride but by that business philosophy known as entrepreneurialism (Harvey, 1989). Cities now compete. Big is beautiful in the provision of palaces of culture, airports, universities and colleges. To this door property development is the golden key. Forget the foolishness of Investors in People, think rather of Investors in Property. As cities are reshaped with fancy flats, shops and grand office blocks for prestigious tenants, so should the city leaders require what is in effect your property; the only question is 'How much?' Be sure, though, as the bulldozers move into your valuable city centre site, that you are ready to proclaim that the shift of college resources is being directed to meet the needs of those whose need is greatest. It should be added that property, or rather the use of it, can be dispensed as a gift to worthy organizations in the locality, an excellent means to build the local base that conveniently escapes the prying eyes of the auditors. It is barely worth mentioning that all principals worthy of the name require a tame chair of governors, one who is, for whatever reason, afraid of you and will accept your plans without serious question.

As the market becomes god and government hastens to castrate the local state, so college incorporation or amalgamation seems inevitable, transforming the power of the principal within the local elite: no longer employee but player. As always, size matters and understanding the new political environment, the possibilities, nay the necessity of expansion – eat or be eaten – means cultivating political contacts. When the moment arrives to merge the city's colleges, your political preparation will be decisive. Any weakness and you will be lost. There are in practice no college mergers, only takeovers. Ask yourself, 'Will you eat or be eaten?'

Do not spend too much time schmoozing in Whitehall and Westminster. The key contacts are in the City Hall and surrounding pubs and hotels. Still, the advantages gained by a 'heads-up' about a new funding stream from some ministerial flunkey are real. Seizing them quickly brings the greatest benefit, recognizing that as others follow so qualifying criteria will tighten. Be careful though. As the creativity involved in interpreting these criteria begins to backfire, so the lifespan of these monies is often curtailed. And there may be determined journalists digging into the detail, on occasion assisted by whistle-blowers trying to revenge themselves for perceived injustices. All the more reason to move with speed.

Be ready for the gift from heaven, that is, being in the right place at the right time, and when it comes, use it to the full. If a huge circus comes to town, and it's just for a fortnight, money is being spent like there is no tomorrow. Remember that colleges have resources that can be turned to many uses and rented out at a most lucrative price, no matter if it be in the form of goods that have a long-term value rather than cash.

Be sure to keep your subordinates in their proper place. Not just respect but fear is the appropriate attitude for them to hold towards you. This by no means excludes the use of favours, such as the chance to travel briefly on college business, petty promotions and the like. Be sure to dispense these trifles not only to sustain motivation but also to keep your underlings under control, factionalizing against each other rather than against you. Our motto remains '*Divide et impera*'.

Always be ready to use the talents of others, even those – such as people with a record of union activism – who on the face of it may appear unreliable. Experience shows that once they have taken the management shilling the opposite is generally the case. There is always the danger of managers fleeing the pressures involved. This can be simply dealt with by giving them a salary above any they can obtain elsewhere. Take care with the overachievers who, in seeking to emulate your success by being as ruthlessness as you are, may lack the skills and resources, so their bullying may become known. Such publicity can only reflect badly on you and delay the moment when you get a proper gong that marks you as having arrived among the great and the good.

Always bear in mind that heading up the greasy pole is less a matter of not forgetting where you came from than of recognizing that being seen as 'one of us', a local princess or prince, remains as important as ever. To achieve this, it does no harm to let drop that you are continuing to refuse invitations to take up a national role. Coupled with this, it is of the greatest importance that, as the empire grows, you present yourself as accountable, indeed squeaky-clean, on all matters concerning money. Failure to do so will be taken by your enemies as an invitation to label you as corrupt. A target-driven culture helps you to keep your hands clean: your subordinates may well be forced to bend or even break the rules to achieve the figures demanded of them, but can easily be disowned if the auditors should spot their creativity. Be careful too with your powers of appointment when it comes to your power base in the locality. Nothing points more quickly to corruption than cronies with jobs in the college. Some below you in the chain of command may well see themselves as secret oppositionists. Do not let this perturb you overmuch. They may successfully resist the tendency to bully and nevertheless achieve the goals set them. In which case, so what if they are secretly disloyal? So long as the money comes in.

Remember that Deep Throat had it right. The key advice to understanding the world and successfully using that knowledge is 'Follow the money' (Pakula *et al.*, 1976). When cost cutting is of the essence and staffing is your main cost, then the prize comes to that principal who most successfully introduces new, cheaper contracts. If you can, present this as a step forwards with phrasing such as 'bringing the training to those that need it, where they need it'. Then, while confusing the opposition below, you will doubly strengthen your position with those above you. Encourage your managers to be similarly inventive. For example, when funds flow to those with high pass rates, they must shift the curriculum to easier courses where everyone will pass.

Ruthlessness does not mean being an assassin with the dagger in your hand. That is for others to do on your behalf. It makes sense to have deputies assigned this task (well rewarded to ensure they do not stray from their role), leaving your image untainted when things go wrong and someone has to appear in an employment tribunal. Do not underestimate the difficulties involved. There will be times when those with a different political agenda to yours will challenge you, however bluff your manner. Under no circumstances lose control of yourself. Do not say, or yet more seriously write, what might discredit your image.

In a world without age limits, you can go on and on but only so long as the politics will allow. When Whitehall falls to hostile forces, the political will from above that wants a big college to be a success disappears. Never say die, but this may be the time to abdicate.

References

Harvey, D. (1989) 'From managerialism to entrepreneurialism: The transformation in urban governance in late capitalism'. *Geografiska Annaler: Series B, Human Geography*, 71 (1), 3–17.

Pakula, A.J., Goldman, W., Bernstein, C., and Woodward, B. (1976) *All the President's Men*. Film. Burbank, CA: Warner Bros. Online. www.imdb.com/title/tt0074119/quotes (accessed 11 January 2017).

Daniel Altés

Nearly all men can stand adversity, but if you want to test a man's character give him power.

Abraham Lincoln

Chapter 3

A letter from Niccolò: Machiavellian indulgences and strategic myths

Carol Azumah Dennis

20th July 1516

Esteemed Principal and Chief Executive,

May I take this opportunity to make myself known to you? Indeed, given that I have for many years been well established as a diplomat, a strategist, a poet, an academic and a political thinker, you may already be familiar with my work. I have, for example, presented at numerous international conferences, enjoyed the sponsorship of wealthy donors and established partnerships with community governors. I am confident that my reputation (largely due to my associations) precedes me.

I suspect that much of what you have heard about me is misplaced. It is true that after some years in the most prestigious positions in further education (FE) colleges, some of which enjoy a national reputation for excellence, I write this letter to you from a place of exile. It is in this state of exile that I seem to have acquired an unsavoury reputation. It is true that my experience in the archaeology of policy may not seem the ideal vantage point from which to comment on leadership and the contemporary FE college. And yet, I ask for a moment of pause before you conclude that my advice – offered to you here as a gift, yours to keep or dispose of howsoever you choose – is of little relevance. You will see that my years spent listening to those who lead FE colleges, your colleagues, counterparts and competitors, have not been wasted. It is at the expense of these esteemed others that I have gained insight. No inducement would entice me to share my perceptions with agitators, activists or trade unionists who would find in my words provocation to weaken your principalship; my only obligation is to you, to secure your flourishing.

My advice is based on an extended period of structured conversation and observation. I have worked with a team of researchers over a period of fifteen months, speaking to principals, vice-principals and college leadership teams, observing management meetings at the highest level, and generating answers to a series of formal written questions, which have resulted in a huge data set. I have noted everything in these conversations, and that has profited me. My considered analysis – undertaken with the help of specialist software and codes – owes much to the guidance of Strauss and Corbin (1990). My labour has been systematic and robust. Framed within the idea of ethics, I have given myself over to my subject. I have thought deeply and debated extensively on these questions: What is FE leadership? What kinds of leaders are there? How is leadership gained, and how is it kept?

What is FE leadership?

Your recent shift from college principal to chief executive indicates to me that you have been engaged in a similar deliberation. As chief executive, you have become firmly entrenched in my world. That so many of you have made such a shift emboldens me. I need no longer remain figuratively in the shadows of leadership discourse. I claim only what I justly deserve: to be accorded a place in the leadership canon (Jackson and Grace, 2013). What I distinctly offer leaders is a practical methodology. I speak across contexts – from warring Italian cities to the usually more peaceable FE college. I speak also across time scales, gliding between and across centuries. What I have learnt about ruling a state is germane to the problems of leading an organization. And college life – like corporate life, and not unlike military life – is about power – sovereign, disciplinary and bio (Lilja and Vinthagen, 2014). That is, when I advise that for the college leader it is better to be feared than to be loved – and if not better certainly safer – I offer an effective truth – a truth that accepts how the world is, not how it ought to be. I have yet to meet a chief executive who was not first a pragmatist, and a visionary only as afterthought. To be an effective chief executive of a college, you will need to gain, hold and expend political power. When the staff who work in your college love you, they love you at their pleasure. They may love and they may unlove you as the circumstances require. When they fear you, they fear you at your pleasure.

The advice that I offer has had a mixed reception. By some I am hailed for my political acumen. By others I am maligned as an amoral (my detractors have gone so far as to suggest malevolent) influence. This is of course a perfect echo of the equivocality of your own situation. Does it surprise you that I call your position equivocal? You may feel that your work is premised on an entirely transparent undertaking. You are there, after all, to meet the needs of your community, to provide education and training, to build local competitiveness and individual prosperity. Could anything be clearer? Yet, in this undertaking, in calling yourself a chief executive, you claim the status of a business person operating within a market. As every business person knows – even ones who market their niche as an ethical enterprise – what matters is the bottom line.

The dilemma your profession faces in an age of austerity is this: how to maintain a convincing balance between ethical and financial exigencies. Several of my informants make this clear to me. *Do the right thing* is a useful refrain here. It sounds like an ethical obligation. But it is a qualified ethical commitment that ensures values are subservient to finance.

What kinds of leaders are there?

As chief executive it is your task to ensure the future viability of the college. To do this successfully you need to live in the real world. The three principles of advice I offer, then, are addressed to the real of college life, the actual. I have stripped the advice of idealism, as this is a luxury you cannot afford. At a time when many chief executives are enjoying salaries that may be counted as a fraction of one million pounds – I mean here, a quarter of a million – £250,000 – or a third of a million – £330,000 (Robertson, 2016) – it may seem somewhat misplaced to suggest there is any luxury that a college leader might not be able to afford. But the point I make stands. Your wealth, whether earned through hard work or merely through good fortune, should not cause you to rest. Your promotion has been rapid, a mark of your sheer charisma and utter brilliance.

The responsibility invested in you is enormous. You are the steward of an organization upon which so many rely. The students (I should, of course, say 'customers'), the local business community, the national economy – yes, indeed, the national economy and its capacity to compete in an increasingly international and interconnected global system of capital flows – rely on you to provide literate, numerate workers endowed with dispositions that enable them to fit into their allotted place in a shrinking labour market (Bowles and Gintis, 1976). They must be willing to endure moments of unemployment, flexible destitution and precarity.

The country needs you to produce a labour force that accepts without question the sweetly framed deceptions of their elected representatives. You must, if you can, encourage in them a post-colonial melancholic yearning (Gilroy, 2005) for the days when Britain was a proud independent nation. (That such a moment has never existed does not matter.) Let them believe that they have no need for Europe when they have a formerly colonized Empire longing to be reconquered. If you are indeed the leader of a pedagogic enterprise, as you claim, your task is to ensure they are willing to accept want, disease, ignorance, squalor and idleness as acts of a secular god. You are not alone in this endeavour. Others will aid and abet. What matters is that your students learn that collectivism – be it institutional, European, or global – is dangerous and undesirable. Your FE college is essential for the survival of capital, and capital needs a skilled, and a subsidiary, labour force. But there is another, closer and deeper, aspect to survival – one that impacts upon your person.

Does it help to rehearse the multiple ways in which this climate has changed the quotidian life of the college? A weighty catalogue of additional burdens has been placed on those working in FE – reductions in staffing, increases in teaching hours, intensified workloads, top-heavy management structures – all accompanied by the insatiable demands of neoliberalism (Mather and Seifert, 2004), accountability, inspection, the sheer terror of performativity (Ball 2003). All of these things exact their toll (Kinman and Wray, 2014). Sleepless nights, the physicality of stress, the lingering discomfort of guilt and the awkward intellectual contortions necessary to justify the unjustifiable, are all reminders that survival is personal. Its intensity is felt in your body (Morley, 2005). As a contemporary college chief executive, you need a survival strategy – one that allows you to resist changes that risk the ongoing existence of the college (where, after all, do persistent funding cuts lead, if not to the obliteration of the sector?) while maintaining your capacity to acquiesce to policy demands.

I must say again, that I have met and conversed at some length with several college chief executives, and I am yet to meet one who was not a pragmatist. Admittedly, their pragmatism might be principled or contingent (Moore *et al.*, 2002). But, in every case, it is a pragmatism driven by a desire to survive. I have frequently wondered about this Darwinian theme of survival. What is the entity that survives contingency, equivocation and compromise? To borrow from Ball and Olmedo (2013), I might accept that it is the mortal soul that survives; in more secular terms, the self. And yet, to make reference to Darwin is to make reference to the survival of the fittest. It is to make reference to a theme that requires us to move from the personal back to the institutional. Only lean organizations survive austerity. Only those organizations willing to assume the mantle of impoverishment survive; and when we examine as closely as we dare the impecunious post-austerity college, we have to consider not only precisely what it is that survives, but at what (and at whose) cost.

How is leadership gained?

There is a difference between calling yourself a principal and calling yourself a chief executive. The distinction I notice here is connected, but not restricted, to biography. If you are an accountant who has become a college leader after a successful career as a merchant banker, you may well wish to be known as a chief executive. After all, when you attend the local chamber of commerce meetings, 'chief executive' is a title that your counterparts know, recognize and respect. Given the changes that have taken place in FE colleges over the past few years, it is unsurprising that 'chief executive' has become the preferred title. The 1990s managerial myth – that the management of public sector organizations is energized by professional self-interest – has created opportunities for a new type of college leader, one unencumbered by the luxuries of ethics. Being thus unencumbered has its advantages. Indeed, the situation that colleges now find themselves in might even demand it. In the absence of actual ethics, one thing that every college leader, principal or chief executive has recourse to is an ethical mantra, a mantra that resonates powerfully across the sector with sufficient ambiguity to justify anything.

I would suggest that you develop, and regularly use, a mantra that has all the appearance of an ethical principle, but little of its content. It is wise to link this mantra to some distant educational radical – Freire and Dewey are good examples, but several others will do. Once the association is made, you may use, reuse and misuse this notion in as many ways as the situation requires. The mantra *Do the right thing* coupled with an ethics of survival will convince your staff, through love or fear, to descend with you to the depths of hell. They will do anything.

It is hard to argue that cuts to provision are in the interest of students. Once their evening course has gone they may never improve their life chances or attend a literacy class; they may have no other social contact; indeed, they may never leave the house. Yet, you must frame the choice thus: either accept a 60 per cent cut to provision this year, or risk provision altogether next year. For the long-term future of the college, for your own reputation as a chief executive who stands up in the face of hard decisions, for the sake of a six-figure salary (Robertson, 2016), to implement a 60 per cent cut is to *do the right thing*.

Another cohort impacted by cuts is those lecturers and managers who remain in post. It may be to the detriment of staff to have their terms and conditions dramatically changed overnight. There are now instances of staff who, in the name of flexibility, have no upper limits on their contractual teaching hours per year (Dennis, 2014). This is to their personal detriment. But is it the right thing to do? Yes. Your college survey makes it clear: high levels of staff stress correlate with high levels of student satisfaction. This is unambiguous. And the distress is worth it. We are here to meet the needs of our customers. The student is always right.

Any protest against these conditions of service must be silenced. And this is the third and final beneficial use of the ethical mantra. It allows you to appear ethical, while remaining silent on the damage policy does to your students, your staff, your college and the communities you serve. You are earnest in your belief that you always *do the right thing*. There is no need to confuse the issue with caveats. *Do the right thing* might be more accurately phrased as *do the best we can under the circumstances*. It might be the best course of action when confronted with a series of unwholesome alternatives (even if those alternatives are never explicitly articulated). It is more often the best compromise we can make, in a certain situation. It has the surface appearance of an ethical ideal. But it is better to ignore any suggestion that a compromise we are prepared to live with, and can persuade others to live with, might not be the right thing.

How is leadership kept?

Finding a compromise you can live with is not quite the same as doing the right thing. It entails a complex series of choices. Your confident assertion that you always *do the right thing* is something you tell yourself, and others tell themselves, to avoid an unpalatable truth. I cannot stress enough just how much, and how frequently, this phrase is repeated to me in conversations. However, it would be simplistic, and naïve, to accept that it means precisely what it says. What this commitment to *do the right thing* suggests is that college leaders are indeed concerned with the ethics of their behaviour and the organizations they lead. Ethics matter. A lot of work goes into considering what the right thing to do actually is, and every college strategy statement contains some kind of ethical commitment. I then have to explain why it is that these statements must be treated as a Machiavellian indulgence, a strategic myth.

If you are to maintain your position as Chief Executive, it is important that you hide your wickedity. I should of course say the wickedity of college life. The subterfuge this hints at is suggested for reasons other than those you might imagine. Let me explain. Your college is a complex adaptive system (Plsek and Greenhalgh, 2001). That is, it is a collection of individual agents who behave in unpredictable ways. Please refer to Dejours and Deranty (2010): the 'real' work of organizations. In a complex adaptive system all actions are interconnected. The actions of one individual change the context within which others act. This situation is characterized by paradox, creativity, surprise and emergence. The inherent wickedity of College Leadership is sketched against this background. I am indebted here to Rittel and Weber (1973). A wicked problem has no formulaic identifiers. It is not entirely and immediately clear precisely what the problem is, and any solution is impossible to definitively grasp. Any number of approaches might well be possible, plausible and even desirable. In most instances there are unanticipated outcomes. The preferred solution, therefore, is not an all-times all-places response. It is a preferred response to a unique situation. 'Every solution counts' (Wright, 2011: 350). There is no means to test whether a preferred solution is right or wrong. There are but perpetual retrospective arguments about whether it is better or worse. Wicked problems cannot be resolved by simple, linear, reductionist techniques.

The invocation to *do the right thing* is the ultimate in a linear, reductionist, one-size-fits-all solution. It purports to act as an ethical satellite navigational device, while providing a deceptive rhetorical ruse that submerges the inherent wickedity of the challenges you face. It merely offers a placebo, that reassures, but does nothing to address the real work within which you are embroiled. But it is a good device. It garners support for any action you wish to take. The brilliance of this strategy is to your credit. My contribution is merely to notice and elaborate upon its effectiveness and advise how this may be entrenched more fully in your leadership.

I end in the hope that you will accept the gift of my advice in the spirit in which I offer it. I implore you to read diligently and consider carefully what I have noted, and in these words recognize the purity of my desire that you attain the eminence you deserve. I want only to contribute towards your success. Should you, from your elevated position, feel the need to learn more of my conversations with your colleagues, counterparts and competitors, I would be most pleased to meet with you at your convenience. In my reduced circumstances, I am compelled to endure the 'keen and unremitting malignity of fortune' (Machiavelli, 1910: 7). But the indignity of my circumstances will not stop me from reaching out. I would see your esteemed self grasp not only national success, but international triumph. To this end, I place my insight at your disposal.

(Niccolò Machiavelli)

References

Ball, S.J. (2003) 'The teacher's soul and the terrors of performativity'. *Journal of Education Policy*, 18 (2), 215–28.

Ball, S.J. and Olmedo, A. (2013) 'Care of the self, resistance and subjectivity under neoliberal governmentalities'. *Critical Studies in Education*, 54 (1), 85–96.

Bowles, S. and Gintis, H. (1976) *Schooling in Capitalist America: Educational reform and the contradictions of economic life*. New York: Basic Books.

Dejours, C. and Deranty, J.-P. (2010) 'The centrality of work'. *Critical Horizons*, 11 (2), 167–80.

Dennis, C.A. (2014) 'Positioning further education and community colleges: Text, teachers and students as global discourse'. *Studies in the Education of Adults*, 46 (1), 91–107.

Gilroy, P. (2005) *Postcolonial Melancholia*. New York: Columbia University Press.

Jackson, M. and Grace, D. (2013) 'Machiavelli's echo in management'. *Management and Organizational History*, 8 (4), 400–14.

Kinman, G. and Wray, S. (2014) 'Taking its toll: Rising stress levels in further education (UCU stress survey 2014). London: University and College Union. Online. www.ucu.org.uk/media/pdf/q/b/ucu_festressreport14.pdf (accessed 21 April 2017).

Lilja, M. and Vinthagen, S. (2014) 'Sovereign power, disciplinary power and biopower: Resisting what power with what resistance?' *Journal of Political Power*, 7 (1), 107–26.

Machiavelli, N. (1910) *The Prince*. Trans. Thomson, N.H. New York: (Harvard Classics, 36, 1). New York: P.F. Collier & Son. New York: Bartleby.com, 2001. Online. www.bartleby.com/36/1/.

Mather, K. and Seifert, R. (2004) 'An examination of changes to the labour process of further education lecturers' (Working Paper WP008/04). University of Wolverhampton Business School. Online. http://citeseerx.ist.psu.edu/viewdoc/download?doi=10.1.1.564.5586&rep=rep1&type=pdf (accessed 21 April 2017).

Moore, A., Edwards, G., Halpin, D., and George, R. (2002) 'Compliance, resistance and pragmatism: The (re)construction of schoolteacher identities in a period of intensive educational reform'. *British Educational Research Journal*, 28 (4), 551–65.

Morley, L. (2005) 'The micropolitics of quality'. *Critical Quarterly*, 47 (1–2), 83–95.

Plsek, P.E. and Greenhalgh, T. (2001) 'Complexity science: The challenge of complexity in health care'. *British Medical Journal*, 323, 625–8.

Rittel, H.W.J. and Webber, M.M. (1973) 'Dilemmas in a general theory of planning'. *Policy Sciences*, 4 (2),155–69.

Robertson, A. (2016) 'Exclusive: Principal's salary doubles to over £330k'. *FE Week*, 12 March. Online. http://feweek.co.uk/2016/03/12/principals-salary-exceeds-300k-in-201415-according-to-sfa-data/ (accessed 12 March 2016).

Strauss, A. and Corbin, J. (1990) *Basics of Qualitative Research: Grounded theory procedures and techniques*. Newbury Park, CA: SAGE Publications.

Wright, N. (2011) 'Between "bastard" and "wicked" leadership? School leadership and the emerging policies of the UK Coalition Government'. *Journal of Educational Administration and History*, 43 (4), 345–62.

Curtis Tappenden

Contact with men who wield power and authority still leaves an intangible sense of repulsion. It's very like being in close proximity to fecal matter, the fecal embodiment of something unmentionable, and you wonder what it is made of and when it acquired its historically sacred character.

Jean Baudrillard

Chapter 4

'For one will always find malcontents': In defence of the principal

Damien Page

Introduction

It is easy to criticize the model of leadership espoused by Machiavelli in *The Prince*. It is easy to chide the suggestion that princes ought to inspire fear in their subjects or tut-tut the idea that we may learn from rulers who slaughtered their own people. Certainly the strategies espoused by Machiavelli conflict with our modern notions of ethical and authentic leadership, leadership that values and cherishes followers, wrapping them in a collaborative and collegial embrace. But then Machiavelli also departed from the prevailing leadership theories of his contemporaries, who praised virtue and faith in abstract principalities that 'have never been known or seen' (Machiavelli, 1908: 71). Machiavelli's intention was to get to the reality of leadership, forsaking the fantasy of ruling for the dark, violent realities. The world of *The Prince* was not a fairy tale, it was a place of political manoeuvring, plots, intrigues and usurpers, where nobles were greedy and ambitious and the people easily swayed to rebellion. One will always find malcontents, we are reminded. Is the world of FE any different? While the endless theories of educational leadership prize ethics and collaboration above all, few point back to the realities of leading a college. Few foreground the scheming union reps or the greedy senior leadership teams (SLTs) eager to depose the principal. Few acknowledge the treacherous throes of external fortune and the threat of invasions and undermining foreign forces. Instead, we deride our principals, we position them as managerialist tyrants who plunder the treasures of professionalism and autonomy from the people. This chapter, then, is a defence of the principal.

The problem of principalship

The interested reader does not need to look hard to find criticism of college principals: the academic literature is littered with it; the trade press is awash with it; social media thrives on it; the corridors and staffrooms of colleges consist of it. Principals are greedy, overpaid, uncaring, narcissistic, ignorant of pedagogy, deleterious to autonomy, the nemesis of professional practice. In short, principals embody the worst excesses of neoliberalism. Yet what is forgotten is the difficulty of being a principal. The environment is unstable, perpetually in turmoil, tossed on the winds of fortune that never quite know what to do with the FE sector. Colleges are large, complex organizations containing myriad tensions, financial, human and technological. While the temptation is to deify lecturers, every college has its fair share of malcontents. As Machiavelli states, 'the wish to acquire is in truth very natural and common, and men always do so when they can' (ibid.: 13): FE is no different, with union reps demanding fewer teaching hours and greater wage increases and SLTs demanding promotions and greater wage increases. Then there are technical staff demanding better IT facilities and catering staff demanding new cookers, students demanding better classrooms and better teaching, government demanding better results, better British Values, better use of less and less money, better skills, better progression and just being better. Principals and princes therefore 'ought to have two fears, one from within, on account of his subjects, the other from without, on account of external powers' (ibid.: 88). And this dual fear, the pressures from within and without, are the basis of the problems of principalship; the solution, from Machiavelli's perspective, is clear: the principal needs to become both fox and lion: 'a fox to discover the snares and a lion to terrify the wolves' (ibid.: 84).

Fortune and fortification

What is often forgotten when people engage in disparaging commentary about principals is the indomitable power of the external environment. The criticism often positions principals within a leadership vacuum where they are master of their own fiefdom, governing capriciously, for personal gain. Yes, principals may make swingeing cuts to their staffing and, yes, they may impose new contracts that increase contact hours or make more use of zero-hours contracts; and, yes, they may create environments where teachers are continually surveilled and evaluated. But let us remember that these are not the voluntary acts of managerialist despotism that they may at first appear: 'Fortune is the arbiter of one-half of our actions', Machiavelli states (ibid.: 120); the 'winds and variations of fortune' (ibid.: 85) force the actions of the principal, who acts not in a context of governmental concern for the FE sector but in a context where FE is an afterthought, an easy target of austerity funding cuts that creates little public outcry. Colleges are not isolated outposts in control of their destiny, they can be merged as a result of area reviews, they can have whole sections of a curriculum removed through financial strangulation, they can have GCSE retakes foisted upon them to the detriment of vocational education. The principal's sole responsibility is the survival of their college and the education of their students, so if that is threatened it is incumbent upon them to take whatever action is necessary, and pacifism in the face of an invading force is rarely successful. In dangerous times, the principal/prince 'cannot observe all those things for which men are esteemed, being often forced, in order to maintain the state, to act contrary to faith, friendship, humanity' (ibid.: 85). Principals must engage fortune on its own terms: neoliberal responses for neoliberal times, autocracy for an autocratic government. The lamentations of academics' insightful criticism of policy in peer-reviewed journals have not halted the march of funding cuts to colleges; the wailing of the left-wing press at the redundancies resulting from forced mergers has not stalled the march of devastation. No, principals are the ones keeping the neoliberal wolf from the door and ensuring students continue to be educated. The question is how. Machiavelli had a clear answer to this question:

> I believe also that he will be successful who directs his actions according to the spirit of the times, and that he whose actions do not accord with the times will not be successful.
>
> (ibid.: 121)

What is required from leaders is that they choose a strategy that is congruent with the context. Machiavelli himself was a product of his times and *The Prince* was written in a dangerous context of intrigue, political manoeuvring, torture and assassinations. It was no time to recommend virtue, fairness and pacifism; it was a time to choose behaviours and strategies that could adequately combat the dangers of political life. War was the only rational choice: a prince 'ought never, therefore, to have out of his thoughts this subject of war' (ibid.: 68), of aggression to ensure the survival of the kingdom. Principals, then, similarly need to select their actions according to the context, adopting a bullish neoliberalism to combat the invading horde of neoliberal governmental aggression. If colleges are forced to operate within a marketized topography, principals would be foolish if they didn't in turn ground their strategy within the most marketized strategy of marketization possible; when they are faced with performativity, the prudent strategy is to fashion the most performative institution they can create. In a context where colleges are vulnerable and facing the full onslaught of austerity and competition, the principal who survives, whose college survives, is the one who becomes a paragon of neoliberalism, a lion to terrify the wolves.

Within the walls

Yet to defend a kingdom, a prince must know it intimately, and, once again, Machiavelli provides guidance:

> As regards action, he ought above all things to keep his men well organized and drilled, to follow incessantly the chase, by which he accustoms his body to hardships, and learns something of the nature of localities, and gets to find out how the mountains rise, how the valleys open out, how the plains lie, and to understand the nature of rivers and marshes, and in all this to take the greatest care. ... [H]e learns to know his country, and is better able to undertake its defence.
>
> (ibid.: 68)

In order to ensure the survival of the college, the principal must know what is happening at all times and so – true to the need for a performative defence against performativity – the virtues of teacher surveillance come to the fore: internal inspections, learning walks, open-plan learning spaces, open-plan staffrooms, glass walls, the continuous collection of data, student voice activities, CCTV, all means to make the practices of education within a college perpetually visible, collectable and open to evaluation. The more intense the surveillance, the more the principal is able to plan, to strategize, to predict the outcomes of Ofsted's inspections, exam results and league tables, to sift out the bad apples and the malcontents before they risk the college defences, to fortify the areas of weakness and place the strongest troops in the vanguard. Only with such measures can the principal truly prepare against attack. Yet all they receive in return is opprobrium from the academic community, accusations of autocracy and invasive management, censure for a perceived lack of trust, admonition for managerialist incursions and perpetuating the performativity of the contemporary education system that strips what is good, what is real in teaching and learning. Staff in colleges would no doubt prefer to be left alone to their practice, resplendent within antiquated notions of professionalism, autonomy, academic judgement. They would no doubt prefer principals to have faith in their practice, to trust that they will operate in the best interests of the students and the college. But there be monsters: without a detailed knowledge of strength and weakness within the turrets, without intimacy of surveillance and judgement, who knows what an Ofsted inspector might find? Who could tell what exam results might ensue? How could such walls as these provide the steely embrace to keep out the wolves? To ensure the survival of the college, better performativity than trust:

> if everything is considered carefully, it will be found that something which looks like virtue, if followed, would be his ruin; whilst something else, which looks like vice, yet followed brings him security and prosperity.
>
> (ibid.: 72–3)

The threats within

While the prince must know the kingdom intimately in order to best defend it, they must also know their followers and the threats that they present. First, there are the ravenously ambitious nobles, the SLT in our FE context:

> The worst that a prince may expect from a hostile people is to be abandoned by them; but from hostile nobles he has not only to fear abandonment, but also that they will rise against him; for they, being in these affairs more far-seeing and astute, always come forward in time to save themselves, and to obtain favours from him whom they expect to prevail.
>
> (ibid.: 44)

The performatively armoured principal must select their SLT carefully: a prince is judged by the people around him, Machiavelli observes. To face the dangers of a neoliberal topography, one must assemble an appropriate force: yes, experts in pedagogy and the student experience may be able to contribute to the leadership of a college, but an accountant would be better; yes, someone with a background in education might have the odd good idea, but someone with a background in commercial banking would improve the bottom line. Principals need to understand that only a marketized nobility can combat a marketized environment, only the private sector can adequately defend against the privatization of education. And, where there is no choice but to employ a senior leader with a teaching background, the preferred candidate should be one who can morph into a corporate noble, tempering pedagogical concerns with the necessities of the market. The only problem with the SLT is the treachery, the dual fear of abandonment for promotion or being undermined and usurped. The former problem is inevitable and a result of princely success: the outstanding principal rarely leaves and so the ambitious members of the team have no choice but to seek promotion elsewhere to satisfy their careerism, leaving a vacuum that needs to be filled, a new noble to mould in the principal's own image. The latter problem is far more insidious. Colleges are grapevines and treachery spreads. An SLT that lacks sufficient fear or faith may conspire to undermine the principal, signalling ambivalence or – worse – outright rebellion. With external forces continually at the walls, anything less than total support presents a weakness in the security of the college.

And then there are the teachers. The problem for the contemporary principal is that teachers within colleges are too enmeshed within a historical setting, still harking back to an era of the terms and conditions within the old Silver Book as well as the long summer holidays, using these 'ancient privileges as a rallying point, which neither time nor benefits will ever cause [them] to forget' (ibid.: 21). Hence the continual calls of 'deprofessionalization' when they are asked to work a bit harder as a result of budget cuts and poor student outcomes, the union remonstrations when the performative environment forces principals to surveil ever more intently, and the alliance with university academics flinging Bourdieu and Foucault into peer-reviewed discourses that are resonant only in abstract principalities that 'have never been known or seen' (ibid.: 71). Here lie the snares the fox must discover, the bad apples waiting to topple an Ofsted inspection and bring down the retention statistics. Here are the ones who resist every new piece of technology, who go to the union whenever poor performance is challenged, who go on strike when colleges are merged for excellent reasons such as savings in back office costs, forcing the good ones to abandon the kingdom – and that is the real problem for the principal: the great teachers get tired of seeing their malcontent colleagues shirking work, employing sick leave as additional vacation, employing the old FOFO ('Fuck off and find out', a traditional pedagogical technique frequently employed by shirkers) as a continual substitute for actual teaching. Teacher retention, therefore, is not a matter of addressing workload or excessive administration. Teacher retention is solved by strength of leadership, a prince to terrify the internal as well as the external wolves, a prince who will savage the incompetent with the full force of arms; the alternative is unthinkable and causes the good followers to flee: 'a prince who does not understand the art of war ... cannot be respected by his soldiers, nor can he rely on them' (ibid.: 68). Only by being feared can the principal truly defend the college – and that is an uncomfortable truth.

Conclusion

In *Discourses* Machiavelli argues, 'when the deed accuses him, the result should excuse him' (1940: 20), and this should be the motif of the contemporary principal. While they may be criticized, lampooned, abused and vilified for their actions, all they are trying to do is ensure the survival of their colleges and educate students; that is the end that justifies their means. If student success is to be accomplished through strategies open to accusations of autocracy or managerialism, so be it. If the price of producing a viable vocational workforce to drive the economy forward is structural realignments and mergers, that is surely a price worth paying. What place equity, fairness, respect and trust when the very fabric of FE is being ripped apart? This is the central tenet of this defence: the principals we have are the principals we need and deserve. In times characterized by ferocity of competition, where colleges have become players within the commodified education marketplace, where the government imposes throttling systems of performativity, where the sector continues to be stripped of resources, there is no place for lambs; there is only a place for foxes and lions.

References and suggested reading

Bourdieu, P. (1992) *The Logic of Practice*. Trans. Nice, R. Cambridge: Polity Press.

Foucault, M. (1991) *Discipline and Punish: The birth of the prison*. Trans. Sheridan, A. London: Penguin.

Machiavelli, N. (1908) *The Prince*. Trans. Marriott, W.K. Originally 1515. Online. www.constitution.org/mac/prince.pdf (accessed 13 April 2017).

— (1940) *Discourses on the First Ten Books of Titus Livius*. Trans. Detmold, C.E. New York: The Modern Library. Originally 1517. Online. www.constitution.org/mac/disclivy.pdf (accessed 13 April 2017).

Watson, C. (2015) 'A sociologist walks into a bar (and other academic challenges): Towards a methodology of humour'. *Sociology*, 49 (3), 407–21.

Part Two

Introduction: Princes and Principalities

John Field

Analysing and comparing post-compulsory education systems can be challenging but rewarding. It is challenging because, unlike schools and universities, the institutions concerned differ widely in structure and mission, as do the types of students involved, and different countries' systems emerged from very different histories. Yet comparison is also a way of helping us understand not only why things are as they are, but also how they might be different. Machiavelli compared 'How many kinds of principalities there are, and by what means they are acquired', in order to help explain the different challenges they posed to the prince of each state.

This part explores aspects of power dynamics in post-compulsory education in Australia, England, the Republic of Ireland, Scotland and Wales. Unsurprisingly, given the shared histories of these nations, the chapters display important areas of similarity. However, by showing that each system has evolved and diverged from the others, they lead us to question the permanence and indeed the legitimacy of existing arrangements of power.

Wales, Scotland and England illustrate some of the contradictions and tensions of power in a relatively recently devolved system. While there have always been some distinctive national structures in education within the United Kingdom, devolution legislation created new national legislative assemblies for Wales, Northern Ireland and Scotland (but not England) that have created new power dynamics in – and indeed between - the education systems of the four nations.

Peter Jones's background in the trade union movement infuses his account of power and FE in Wales. As in a number of other countries, the General Teaching Council in Wales has extended its remit to cover the college sector, a process endorsed and underpinned by the Welsh Assembly Government. The result, Jones argues, is a significant loss of goodwill towards the sector's leaders and a loss of trust in the professional governance structures.

Post-compulsory education in Scotland is inspired by broad emancipatory goals. In ESOL, this means encouraging students to develop language skills in ways that help them shape their communities' aspirations and destinies. At the same time, the Government has pushed colleges to focus on full-time work-related provision for young adults, while also seeking significant cost savings by merging institutions. Steve Brown's chapter shows how damaging this process has been, and how it has taken place at the expense of some of the country's most vulnerable students.

Ireland has long had its own separate educational structures, pre-dating the creation of the independent state. It is fair to say, though, that

FE was far from the priorities of nation-building. A sharper policy focus came about in the late twentieth century that was due largely to external pressures from the European Union and the Organisation for Economic Co-operation and Development. Fergal Finnegan shows how the system came under pressure following the 2008 financial crisis and subsequent recession, leading to the downgrading of community education and the reorganization of FE to promote active labour market policies while securing greater managerial efficiency and organizational coherence. For Finnegan, these tendencies threaten to stifle the innovation and enterprise that might characterize a sector responsive to students.

Typically, policy-makers in England have oscillated between complete lack of interest in FE and an almost manic desire to re-create the supply of skills (Germany often being posed as the model). In neither case have they shown much interest in, or capacity for, intervention in the demand for skilled labour. Taking the case of the reformed apprenticeship system, Simon Reddy argues that artificially generated concerns over skills shortages are helping produce an over-supply of youngsters – as well as some adult returners – in occupations that are characterized by increasing precarity and low wages as a result.

The part is completed by Gavin Moodie's case study of Australian technical and further education. As in Britain, policy reform in the state of Victoria was justified in terms of greater commercial accountability; however, Victoria went further in opening up FE to private, for-profit providers, producing a highly predictable set of scandals that the government then had to intervene in, while simultaneously reducing funding levels and increasing its control over governing bodies. For Moodie, this provides a cautionary Shakespearean tragedy with a message.

Machiavelli's concern with the different kinds of principalities led him to distinguish those that are inherited, whose subjects are accustomed to live under a prince, and new principalities that were annexed by one means or another, whose authorities were accustomed to live in freedom, and where princes were as a result far more likely to make enemies. I suppose the equivalent in contemporary FE would be the contrast between systems that are relatively settled, and indeed regulated, as in Germany and Scandinavia, in which familiar routines allow incremental innovation, and those subject to permanent revolution from above, in which managers and staff are constantly required to adapt to the latest regime change, and are often seeking positional advantage within it. This begs the question, of course, of whether a completely different world of FE is possible – one in which the messy lives of students rather than the imposed changes of power are the main source of energy and innovation, and which sets out to transform the possibilities for its workforce as well as its students. As Machiavelli might have put it, we need to liberate FE from the barbarians.

Eric Bari

Washing one's hands of the conflict between the powerful and the powerless means to side with the powerful, not to be neutral.

Paulo Freire

Chapter 5

Mixed messages (or how to undermine your own policy): ESOL provision in the Scottish FE sector

Steve Brown

> One prince of the present time, whom it is not well to name, never preaches anything else but peace and good faith, and to both he is most hostile.
>
> (Machiavelli, *The Prince*)

Introduction

It's been a good millennium so far for the Scottish National Party (SNP). Having won a third term of office in the Scottish parliamentary election in 2016, the SNP is by far the largest political party in Scotland. The party's goal of achieving independence from the UK was very nearly achieved in 2014, and the following year it won 56 seats out of 59 Scottish constituencies in the UK general election. With Ed Miliband's Labour supporting the Conservatives' austerity agenda and the renewal of Trident, it was easy enough for the SNP to position itself as the only credible left-wing alternative in Scotland, championing social justice and an agenda that promoted equality. Since then, the referendum result that saw 62 per cent of Scots voting to remain in the European Union, while 52 per cent of the UK population as a whole voted to leave, has further highlighted political differences between Scotland and the rest of the UK, strengthening the SNP's case for independence.

In education, the SNP has taken the concept of Curriculum for Excellence that emerged out of a consultation exercise (Scottish Executive, 2002) and developed an approach that seeks to develop young people's capacities to become 'successful learners, confident individuals, responsible citizens [and] effective contributors' (Education Scotland, 2016). A similarly socially conscious ideology appears to exist in my own field, the teaching of English to speakers of other languages (ESOL). The National Adult ESOL Strategy (Scottish Executive, 2007) was refreshed in 2015 to reflect the needs of immigrant communities and support their involvement in the development of Scottish society. But to what extent does this socially conscious narrative pan out in practice? In terms of educational policy, the Scottish government has received criticism from various quarters over its implementation of Curriculum for Excellence (e.g. Holligan and Humes, 2009), and recent upheaval in the FE sector suggests that the needs of vulnerable members of society may be less of a priority than the SNP would have us believe. It is perhaps pertinent, then, to look more carefully at the Scottish government's approach to FE and establish the direction in which they are leading the sector.

The intention behind this chapter, therefore, is to identify conflicting ideological principles underlying the ESOL strategy and wider policies driving Scottish FE, which present considerable challenges for educational leaders. Problematizing the SNP's FE strategy raises questions about what the Scottish government actually expects from ESOL providers within the FE sector, as well as casting doubt over the party's social conscience, and the 'peace and good faith' (Machiavelli, 1908: 86) that the SNP ostensibly promotes.

ESOL policy and its underlying agenda

Like the rest of the UK, Scotland experienced a significant increase in net migration at the start of the millennium. This has predominantly been a consequence of globalization, which requires the development of 'a flexible workforce to be deployed at the discretion of global capital' (Guo, 2010: 144). EU expansion in 2004 facilitated freedom of movement, prompting a rise in immigration from accession states such as Poland. The dispersal of asylum seekers to the west of Scotland following the Immigration and Asylum Act (UK Government, 1999) also increased the number and diversity of immigrants to Scotland over the same period. Immigrants to Scotland whose first language is not English face considerable challenges in terms of their ability to integrate successfully, to fulfil their potential and to avoid marginalization or disenfranchisement. The provision of ESOL programmes to develop English language skills is therefore important for avoiding ghettoization and promoting social inclusion, as documented for other parts of the UK (e.g. Ward, 2007; Cooke, 2006).

To this end, a national ESOL strategy for Scotland was devised in 2007, with the following vision:

> That all Scottish residents for whom English is not a first language have the opportunity to access high quality English language provision so that they can acquire the language skills to enable them to participate in Scottish life: in the workplace, through further study, within the family, the local community, Scottish society and the economy.
>
> (Scottish Executive, 2007: 4)

Additional funding to support this strategy was used across Scotland to increase the quantity and enhance the quality of provision for ESOL students. In my own college, for example, we set up community-based partnerships with local authorities and voluntary organizations to provide courses for those who were unable to access college-based programmes, specifically those with childcare needs and health issues. Lesson content focused heavily on language and skills that allowed students to function effectively in an English-speaking environment, and the students themselves had considerable input into programme design.

Since gaining power in 2007, the SNP Government has continued to support the Adult ESOL Strategy and developed the policy further with a refreshed version for 2015–20 (Education Scotland, 2015) to reflect the changing profiles of ESOL students – asylum seekers becoming refugees with indefinite leave to remain in the country, migrant workers from EU states choosing to settle in Scotland – and the resulting need to integrate as permanent, rather than transient, residents in Scotland.

The revised strategy retains the vision statement of the original policy, but also includes five strategic objectives, related to access, relevance, impact on society, impact on policy and support. The language used in the vision statement demonstrates a clear intent to use ESOL provision as a means of empowering immigrant communities. But the newly added objectives appear to go further, facilitating immigrants' capacities not only to function effectively within the existing parameters of Scottish life, but also to be involved in the transformation of our society. For example, the objective focusing on the impact of ESOL on society requires that 'ESOL learners transform their lives and communities' and that learners 'get involved in their communities' (Education Scotland, 2015: 21). The objective describing the impact of ESOL on policy states that 'ESOL learners [should] effectively influence strategy and policy at local and national levels'.

These objectives go beyond the empowerment of individual ESOL students, and appear to be focused on the goal of emancipation. Inglis (1997: 4) distinguishes emancipation from empowerment in this way: 'empowerment involves people developing capacities to act successfully within the existing system and structures of power, while emancipation concerns critically analyzing, resisting and challenging structures of power'. The refreshed adult ESOL strategy does not use such words as 'resist' or 'challenge', but its objectives do imply an agenda that entails ESOL students engaging critically with existing power structures in Scotland, so that they may participate in their positive transformation.

Let us now examine how these policy objectives manifest themselves in practice. If, as the ESOL strategy suggests, we want an approach to education that raises awareness among vulnerable communities of existing power structures, with a view to encouraging these communities to have a transformative impact on society, a sensible place to seek ideas is in the work of Paulo Freire and the critical pedagogy movement that he inspired. Critical pedagogy, according to Giroux, is 'rooted in a project that is tied to the cultivation of an informed, critical citizenry capable of participating and governing in a democratic society' (Giroux, 2011: 7). Such a project fits rather nicely with the emancipatory aims implied within the adult ESOL strategy for Scotland. Similar programmes exist elsewhere in ESOL, for example the Reflect ESOL movement (Reflect Action, 2009), English for Action (EFA London, 2016) and the Action for ESOL campaign (Peutrell, 2015). These projects encourage students to develop English skills while engaging in political or developmental work.

ESOL policy in Scotland, then, is driven by a desire to improve the English language skills of immigrant communities so that they can participate in all aspects of society. Such a goal can be achieved through an approach to curriculum design and delivery which is underpinned by principles of critical pedagogy, so allowing the students to inform and influence curriculum content and take a transformative approach to education. It is surely a bold move for a government to advocate a policy that actively encourages students to engage with and transform existing hegemonies – a move that many ESOL practitioners would applaud. However, other contextual factors must also be considered. Around 80 per cent of ESOL provision in Scotland takes place in FE colleges (Rice *et al.*, 2005: 2), so factors affecting the FE sector make the implementation of the ESOL strategy rather less straightforward.

Policy drivers in FE

In recent years, Scottish FE colleges have undergone a major overhaul at the hands of the Scottish government. A decision was taken to reduce perceived inefficiencies by merging colleges through a process of 'regionalisation' (Scottish Government, 2013). The FE sector in England, which is also moving towards a more regionalized structure, would benefit from examining the outcomes of this process north of the border. Mergers in Scotland have resulted in the number of colleges being reduced by more than half, with each new college expected to take a regional approach to its provision. This has the obvious consequence of diminishing colleges' capacity to focus on the needs of local communities, and individual colleges' ability to specialize in particular subjects. The city of Edinburgh, for example, with a population of almost half a million, is now served by a single FE college. By contrast, Edinburgh has three universities, so that a far more comprehensive, wide-ranging and flexible range of programmes exists at higher-education level than at FE level.

A number of other changes have taken place in the Scottish FE sector, largely as a result of a policy document entitled *Education Working for All!* (Scottish Government, 2014), a report written by the Commission for Developing Scotland's Young Workforce (DYW). This report is now the key driver of Scottish FE policy, and it prioritizes the development of employability skills among young people to meet the needs of the Scottish economy. The impact of this report on FE provision is significant, as colleges have been encouraged to deliver highly instrumental full-time programmes to prepare students for areas of industry where there are skills gaps. The report has also encouraged colleges to focus provision on 16–24-year-olds.

The FE sector plays a critical role in preparing young people for work, and vocational programmes that lead directly towards employment are good for young people and good for employers. However, the ideology underpinning DYW and the SNP's approach to further education is clearly grounded in human capital theory (Schulz, 1961). Such an ideology, which regards people as commodities whose value lies in their ability to serve the economy, undermines any role that further education might play in the positive development of society. Rather than as people capable of making a contribution to Scottish life more generally, FE students are regarded primarily as a future workforce, who attend college to acquire specific skills to meet perceived industry needs. The exact nature of these industry needs can be difficult to predict, but such programmes tend to focus narrowly on skills for work at the expense of skills for other aspects of life.

The DYW commission was led by Sir Ian Wood, a leading figure in Scottish industry with no background in educational policy, which may help to explain why the policy is so directly focused on serving the needs of industry. Furthermore, the recommendations of the DYW report are in conflict with the socially just values embedded within the Adult ESOL Strategy. College ESOL managers, then, are receiving mixed messages; on one hand, their programmes should seek to emancipate ESOL students and engage them in projects that lead to the betterment of society, on the other they must address the other agendas that the DYW report requires all colleges to follow. Machiavelli discusses the question of populism over authoritarianism in his chapter entitled 'Concerning cruelty and clemency, and whether it is better to be loved than feared' (Machiavelli, 1908: 78–82). He concludes that, where possible, the prince should aspire to both. Perhaps, by using language that appears to promote liberal and socially just values, and then filtering the implementation of these policies through the neoliberal framework being imposed on the FE sector, this is what the SNP is trying to do.

Restrictions placed on the ESOL strategy

Of course, it is not impossible to find some common ground between the two policies and to design programmes that address the requirements of DYW while retaining some of the core values of the ESOL strategy. This is a key challenge for ESOL managers in the Scottish FE sector, namely to find common ground and identify aspects of each policy that can actually benefit ESOL students. The prioritization of full-time programmes has increased the number of class hours for students within the academic year. The focus on young people has facilitated the further development of courses such as Glasgow Clyde College's 16+ ESOL Programme, which caters primarily for unaccompanied minors entering the UK as asylum seekers or refugees, often as victims of human trafficking, and supports their integration into Scottish society (Education Scotland, 2015: 12).

The focus on accreditation has led colleges to increase the number and breadth of accredited outcomes attained by ESOL students. Nationally accredited units, in ESOL and in essential skills such as ICT, working with others and problem solving are being embedded into ESOL programmes across the FE sector, allowing students to gain qualifications while working on projects that address the needs of the ESOL strategy (e.g. Brown and Morgan-Thomas, 2016).

Figure 5.1: In 2015–16, ESOL students at West College Scotland raised a total of over £1500 through a range of fundraising activities for a number of charities that they themselves identified

The employability agenda and the resulting focus on workplace ESOL and career management facilitate the capacity of immigrants – many of whom already have high-level qualifications, experience or training from their own countries – to reach their full potential and increase their influence on a wide range of professions and areas of industry.

That said, the heavily instrumental focus of DYW makes it difficult for colleges to meet the needs of some ESOL students, diminishing their ability to achieve the objectives of the refreshed ESOL strategy. Before the publication of the DYW report, the preference among ESOL students – most of whom are mature adults – for part-time courses was reflected in the provision on offer: 84 per cent of ESOL students studied part-time (Education Scotland, 2014: 6). The increased emphasis on full-time programmes inevitably reduces the quantity of part-time provision. The 48 per cent reduction in part-time students in the college sector between 2008 and 2016 has raised concerns that programmes are now far less accessible to those in society who encounter the greatest barriers to learning. An Audit Scotland report states that most of the 'reductions in student numbers have been among women and people aged over 25' (Audit Scotland, 2016: 5). This is unsurprising as mature students are more likely to have childcare issues, work commitments or other responsibilities that prevent them from studying full-time.

A move towards full-time provision is therefore likely to make college ESOL provision inaccessible to a large number of potential students, often the ones who are already most marginalized. Of course, following Machiavelli's ideas that leadership is about gaining and maintaining power, then the needs of minorities who are unable to have their voice heard or influence public opinion are not relevant. The focus should instead be on appeasing powerful individuals and institutions – in this case the large corporations who control the economy.

While the employability agenda can serve to address some objectives of the refreshed ESOL Strategy, there is a blanket adherence to the DYW report that requires ESOL programmes to include features that lack relevance for many students of ESOL. One such requirement of the regional outcome agreement between a college and the Scottish Funding Council, which oversees funding provision to colleges, is that 'all full time courses include relevant, high quality work experience content' (Scottish Funding Council, 2016: 58). Such an objective is appropriate for school-leavers with no previous work experience, who are studying on vocational programmes with specific areas of industry in mind. However, building work experience into all programmes fails to acknowledge that many ESOL students are already in employment, or have previous work experience, or, in some cases, wish to learn English for completely different but no less important reasons. The requirement that college ESOL providers address the employability agenda takes the focus away from the benefits that ESOL can bring by facilitating successful integration in society.

Conclusions

The education policy of a country is very much a statement of intent about how that country's leaders envisage the long-term development of the nation and its people. The fact that Scotland has an ESOL strategy at all suggests that the government values the well-being of immigrant communities who, without English, risk marginalization. The transformative agenda embedded in the refreshed Adult ESOL Strategy and the critical and emancipatory approach to education that it appears to advocate imply that the SNP wishes to promote equality and social justice. However, the majority of ESOL provision in Scotland takes place in the FE sector, which is being driven by vaguely defined economic needs rather than a desire to emancipate college students. This significantly undermines college managers' ability to address the objectives of the ESOL strategy; access to provision is restricted to those who need it most, and content is dominated by agendas that are not always appropriate or relevant to ESOL students.

The publication of two parallel, but seemingly conflicting, educational policies raises questions about the SNP's underlying principles regarding the purpose of education. Does it really seek to use education as a means of emancipating its more disadvantaged citizens, or does it prefer to follow the neoliberal model of using education to serve the needs of big business? Does the SNP simply not realize what it is doing? Or is this an example of the duplicity advocated by Machiavelli (1908: 86), whereby the prince preaches one thing in order to please the people, even though he is 'most hostile' to it, and then takes other steps to ensure that those practices cannot be implemented? In any case, the potential of the ESOL strategy is compromised by the constrictions placed upon its main providers.

References

Audit Scotland (2016) *Scotland's Colleges 2016*. Edinburgh: Audit Scotland. Online. www.audit-scotland.gov.uk/uploads/docs/report/2016/nr_160825_scotlands_colleges.pdf (accessed 28 August 2016).

Brown, S. and Morgan-Thomas, A. (2016) 'Effective learning, teaching and assessment of ESOL through project-based learning'. Webinar, West College Scotland. Online. https://collegedevelopmentnetwork.adobeconnect.com/_a1043997050/p5zy0eygr3q/?launcher=false&fcsContent=true&pbMode=normal (accessed 28 August 2016).

Cooke, M. (2006) '"When I wake up I dream of electricity": The lives, aspirations and "needs" of adult ESOL learners'. *Linguistics and Education*, 17 (1), 56–73.

Education Scotland (2014) 'English for speakers of other languages in Scotland's colleges'. Online. https://education.gov.scot/Documents/ESOLScotlandsColleges.pdf (accessed 13 May 2017).

— (2015) 'Welcoming our learners: Scotland's ESOL strategy 2015–2020: The English for speakers of other languages (ESOL) strategy for adults in Scotland 2015'. Online. http://dera.ioe.ac.uk/22892/1/ESOLStrategy2015to2020_tcm4-855848.pdf (accessed 13 May 2017).

— (2016) 'What is Curriculum for Excellence?'. Online. https://education.gov.scot/scottish-education-system/policy-for-scottish-education/policy-drivers/cfe-(building-from-the-statement-appendix-incl-btc1-5)/What%20is%20Curriculum%20for%20Excellence? (accessed 13 May 2017).

EFA London (2016) English for Action: Learning language, making change. Online. www.efalondon.org/what-we-do/action (accessed 27 August 2016).

Giroux, H. (2011) *On Critical Pedagogy*. London: Continuum.

Guo, S. (2010) 'Lifelong learning in the age of transnational migration'. *International Journal of Lifelong Education*, 29 (2), 143–7.

Holligan, C. and Humes, W. (2009) 'The hidden politics of the Curriculum for Excellence'. *The Herald*, 17 September. Online. www.heraldscotland.com/news/12612261.The_hidden_politics_of_the_Curriculum_for_Excellence/ (accessed 28 August 2016).

Inglis, T. (1997) 'Empowerment and emancipation'. *Adult Education Quarterly,* 48 (1), 3–17.

Machiavelli, N. (1908) *The Prince*. Trans. Marriott, W.K. Originally 1515. Online. www.constitution.org/mac/prince.pdf (accessed 28 December 2016).

Peutrell, R. (2015) 'Action for ESOL: Pedagogy, professionalism and politics'. In Daley, M., Orr, K., and Petrie, J. (eds) *Further Education and the Twelve Dancing Princesses*. Stoke-on-Trent: Trentham Books, 139–56.

Reflect Action (2009) 'Reflect ESOL?' Online. www.reflect-action.org/reflectesol (accessed 27 August 2016).

Rice, C., McGregor, N., Thomson, H., and Udagawa, H. (2005) 'National "English for Speakers of Other Languages" (ESOL) Strategy: Mapping exercise and scoping study' (Research Findings 19). Edinburgh: Scottish Executive. Online. www.gov.scot/Resource/Doc/35596/0029540.pdf (accessed 27 August 2016).

Schultz, T.W. (1961) 'Investment in human capital'. *American Economic Review*, 51 (1), 1–17.

Scottish Executive (2002) 'The national debate on education: The best for all our children. Briefing pack'. Online. www.gov.scot/Resource/Doc/158359/0042897.pdf (accessed 30 August 2016).

— (2007) *The Adult ESOL Strategy for Scotland*. Edinburgh: Scottish Executive. Online. www.gov.scot/Resource/Doc/176977/0050036.pdf (accessed 27 August 2016).

Scottish Funding Council (2016) 'Regional outcome agreement: The west region. Update 2016–17'. Online. www.sfc.ac.uk/web/FILES/Outcome_Agreements_WestScotland1617/West_Scotland_Outcome_Agreement_2016-17.pdf (accessed 28 August 2016).

Scottish Government (2013) 'College regionalisation'. Online. www.gov.scot/Topics/Education/post16reform/college-regionalisation (accessed 30 August 2016).

Scottish Government (2014) 'Education Working For All! Commission for Developing Scotland's Young Workforce Final Report'. Edinburgh: The Scottish Government. Online. www.gov.scot/Publications/2014/06/4089 (accessed 6 June 2017).

UK Government (1999) Immigration and Asylum Act 1999: Chapter 33. London: The Stationery Office. Online. www.legislation.gov.uk/ukpga/1999/33/contents (accessed 24 July 2016).

Ward, J. (2007) *ESOL: The context for the UK today*. Leicester: NIACE.

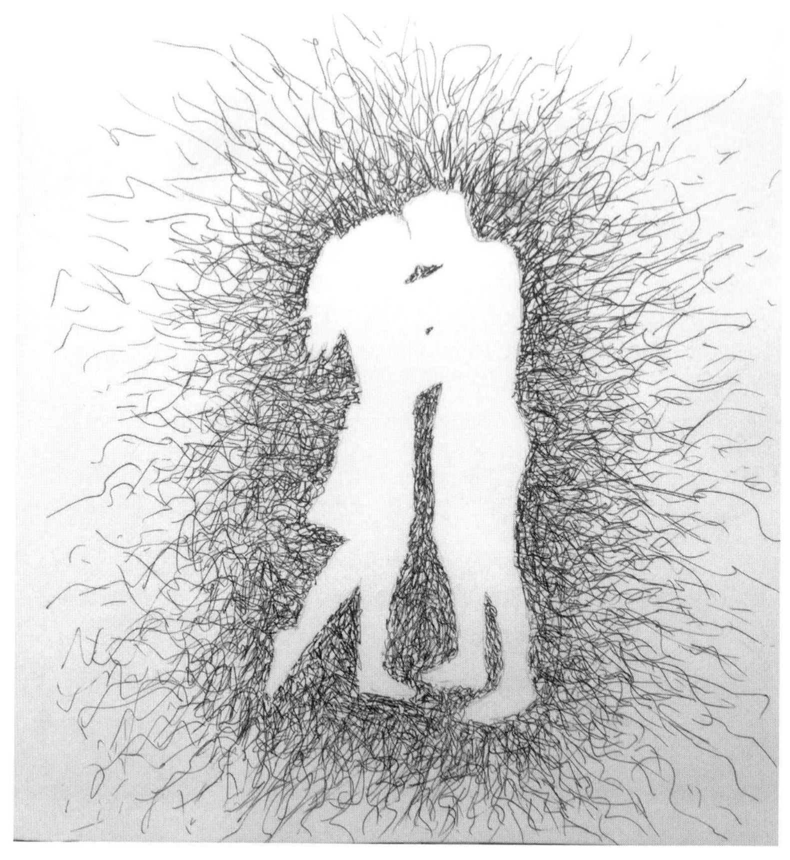

Aylin Hall

The purpose of getting power is to be able to give it away.

Aneurin Bevan

Chapter 6

No music in the principality of song: De-professionalization in Welsh FE

Peter Jones

Introduction

Devolution in 1999 has meant that education in Wales, including the further education (FE) sector, has become the responsibility of the Wales government. Trade union activists in Wales quickly realized that relationships with the government in Cardiff would be as crucial to their members as the relationship with Colegau Cymru, the Welsh college employers' association.

UCU Cymru (University and College Union Wales) was clear that two elements affecting the lecturers' role would be critical: the implementation of a common pay scale and the pursuit of a common contract. Without these, control over the teaching and learning process would move even further away from the lecturer. There was also an early realization that the intransigence of the employers meant that a long, hard fight lay ahead and that that fight would not be won without the members giving their support to the national negotiators. Unlike their English counterparts, these negotiators had, and continue to have, direct access to both the employers and the government. The negotiations in Wales focused on pay, funding mechanisms and the equality agenda, particularly the gender pay gap. Despite the redundancies of all three national union negotiators as well as of myself, then the Chair of UCU Cymru (which the different employers put down to coincidence), negotiations culminated in a national pay scheme and a common contract. This had been a manifesto promise of the Welsh Labour Party, which said it would 'introduce an all-Wales contract for FE lecturers' (Labour Party, 2011: 37).

In the early twenty-first century, relations between the national union and the Assembly Government in Cardiff were professional and, where possible, mutually supportive. The single pay scale and the common contract were agreed to be a benefit for Wales. There were, moreover, annual meetings between the union and the minister, in which UCU laid out thoughts about the future of FE, and the minister gave a keynote speech at the union's annual conference. As the years rolled on and ministers changed, however, the distance between the two parties grew, and in 2015 neither the minister nor his deputy attended the conference, which had the immediate effect of worsening relations. Meanwhile the colleges in Wales set about amalgamating and by 2015 the number of institutions had fallen from 22 to 14 because of mergers. As a result, the work of both the full-time trade union officials and the union's lay representatives increased as the colleges chose to make members redundant and to seek to harmonize contracts across the new institutions using their lowest common denominator.

The Education Workforce Council and the flight from democracy

> [I]n truth there is no safe way to retain them otherwise than by ruining them.
>
> Machiavelli (1908: 21)

The process

In its 2011 manifesto for the Wales Assembly elections, the Labour Party stated that it had 'long expressed its opposition to the incorporation of colleges of FE' (Labour Party, 2011: 37). It went on to state that 'colleges of FE, like every other publicly funded educational establishment in Wales, are public assets that belong to their local communities as well as its community of staff and learners' (ibid.). The manifesto continued by offering to reform FE along 'social enterprise lines' and to 'ensure that learner voice is central to strategic decision making in colleges' (ibid.). That same document rejected a return to local authority control.

In reality, those manifesto commitments led to the two-step drawing of the fangs of the FE unions under the provision of the Education (Wales) Act, which the Government in Wales passed in 2014 with the support of the Labour Party. Firstly, colleges were to be managed through non-profit institutions serving households (NPISH), which would mean a further distancing from the local control of colleges and a step nearer to privatization. Secondly, compulsory membership of the General Teaching Council Wales (GTCW) had previously been confined to school teachers, but under the 2014 Act membership of a new body, the Education Workforce Council (EWC), became compulsory for all teachers, including those working in FE.

The senior civil servant for education at the time held consultation meetings that were attended by college stakeholders, including members of corporations, senior managers and union representatives. The main meeting had UCU Cymru representation from full-time officials, officers, negotiators and TUC General Council members. From the start, however, senior union negotiators understood that this was less of a consultation and more of a 'this is what's going to happen' meeting, as every point raised by UCU Cymru and other campus unions was glossed over or ignored. The same government minister oversaw the change from the schools-based GTCW to the EWC. Lecturers in Wales had seen the rejection by FE lecturers in England of the Institute for Learning (IfL), but were not going to be allowed the same opportunity, and membership of the EWC would, by 1 April 2015, be a requirement (Llewellyn, 2015). The 2014 Act went further in that it placed upon colleges and supply agencies three duties:

1. Only employ registered staff (with pre-employment checks)
2. Refer cases to EWC where a member of staff is dismissed (or resigns in certain circumstances)
3. Deduct registration fee annually

While the unions would agree that all individuals who work with children and vulnerable adults should be subject to Disclosure and Barring Service (DBS) checks to help safeguard children and vulnerable adults, the Act placed an extra burden on the employer to ensure that every individual is also registered with the EWC. The employer is duty-bound to deduct the annual registration fee from each individual's salary, no matter how small that salary. However, the most contentious point for FE practitioners is referral to the EWC in disciplinary cases. The argument put by the unions is quite simple: it should be for the employer, and only the employer, to conduct disciplinary proceedings, not a third party.

Council

UCU Cymru had welcomed the creation of a body which supported and promoted the practices of the education workforce and which comprised a majority of registered or recently registered practitioners (Jones, 2010). The union felt it was crucial that standards should be set by education professionals, because it is they who have the necessary understanding and experience as classroom and workshop practitioners. With that in mind, the union proposed that the new Council should be made up of people elected by the education workforce. However, the minister rejected this and Council members are subject to ministerial appointment by nominating bodies. Indeed, of the fourteen Council members in 2017, only two have direct and recent experience of FE, and they are both nominees of Colegau Cymru.

At the same time, the Union's single nominee was rejected without explanation, which left UCU Cymru with no member on the Council.

Rather than deepening the professionalism of the FE lecturers' role, which is based on trust and autonomy, these decisions were informed by a managerial view of the teaching profession, which is alien to the experience of FE lecturers and which focused increasingly on the ability to meet targets (UCU, 2012). FE lecturers believed that their control of the teaching and learning process would quickly diminish.

Fees

Given the compulsory nature of membership of the EWC, UCU Cymru was keen to ensure that no member would suffer financial difficulties. It argued that if fees were to be compulsory, then the employer should be responsible for the payment of those fees. The Union also argued that any fees should be proportionate to salary. However, this too was rejected and a fixed fee (set at £45 in 2016) was levied irrespective of actual salary. This meant that a part-time associate lecturer teaching three hours a week at a normal hourly rate of £16.77 would need to work almost a whole week just to pay the fee.

Code of conduct

If the union were to concede that a professional body such as the EWC could have a disciplinary function to deal with matters of competence and conduct, that body would need the confidence of all parties, including the managers of 16+ provision and the Welsh Assembly government. Further, that confidence would have to be shared by the students and, importantly, the teaching staff. However, the union had two major concerns regarding the code of conduct: the public nature of any disciplinary process, and the permanent nature of any sanction.

As the hearings might be open to the public (as they have proved to be) there was concern that the case against any particular practitioner might be prejudiced by allegations made public during the process itself. Allegations brought before such a hearing could be untrue but still be highly damaging for the individual involved if the allegations were to be made public. A BBC investigation of similar procedures for school teachers in Wales had found that over 55 per cent of such allegations were 'false, unfounded or malicious' and that the 'allegations were later dropped' (Ryall, 2012).

A second, and serious, issue is that of permanency of exclusion from the teaching profession. There is widespread agreement among educationalists that there are instances where permanent exclusion from teaching is warranted and that in these cases the decision should be made public. The EWC, however, lists most of its suspensions as being the result of 'unacceptable professional behaviour', with little further detail. That catch-all phrase has meant that up to the summer of 2016, the GTCW/EWC had removed the licence to teach from 159 practitioners, with only six serving a time-limited suspension (EWC, n.d.). UCU Cymru have stated that 'it appears to our members that the EWC does nothing but give rise to public humiliation of colleagues' (UCU Wales, 2017: [5]). A further complication is that any appeal against the decision of the EWC is not to an appeal panel but only to the High Court. This is in complete disregard of the position of UCU Cymru, which, in its response to the proposed Bill, stated, 'With regard to registration appeals and disciplinary orders, it would also seem an opportune moment to introduce a right of appeal to the Council in the first instance, rather than having to go straight to the High Court' (UCU Wales, 2013: [5]). In drawing up the Education (Wales) Act 2014, the Labour-controlled Welsh Government demonstrated once again, however, its desire to distance itself from the unions by not allowing such a panel within the EWC.

Conclusion

Machiavelli (1908: 21) contends that in the case where principalities (in this instance, lecturers) have lived under their own laws (that is, a certain amount of academic freedom and control over the teaching and learning process), one of the options open to the new governors is to destroy the old state. Indeed, it seems that this is precisely what the Labour-controlled Welsh Government set about doing when it enacted the Education (Wales) Act 2014. Control has moved from the classroom out of the colleges altogether and has been placed with agents of the central state in the form of the EWC. This has also had the effect of reducing the power of the trade unions; because the EWC is not an employer, any industrial action against them might be interpreted by the court as illegal.

UCU Cymru, however, continues to fight for its members in Welsh FE institutions on two fronts: with the employer and with the EWC. The UCU Cymru office has come under increasing strain because of the number of cases it manages. The union's full-time officials were well used to dealing with employers and the issues that their members faced. Having to deal with the EWC has added to their workload especially because a typical EWC disciplinary hearing will have counsel representing the presenting officer and a legal adviser for the panel. This leads to the Union, too, requiring the services of counsel. Hearings then become mired in legalese, while the costs spiral upwards.

The EWC is not a democratic body and it certainly does not represent practitioners in the FE sector. The EWC's predecessor, the GTCW, had peer election as part of its selection process, but the Welsh Labour Government ensured that this practice would be discontinued in the EWC. The close working relationship that UCU Cymru had with the Welsh Labour Government has been lost as a direct result of the formation of the EWC. The Wales Government and the EWC have not heeded Machiavelli's (1908: 4) advice that 'in entering a province one has always need of the goodwill of the natives'. At every step, the union's proposals, ideas and nominations have been completely ignored. FE lecturers in Wales are now shackled to an organization that they did not want, that does not represent them and that has the power to remove their licence to practise. This has only served to increase the disgruntlement felt by many lecturers in the principality of Wales and to heighten opposition to the EWC. In particular, opposition to the compulsory nature of the fees is gathering momentum, which includes a Facebook page, Scrap the Welsh Teach Tax. However, a more telling point is the Union's view on the EWC's disciplinary function: 'Simply dealing with the consequences through the use of disciplinary panels will not enhance the quality and professional standards aspired to. We need to deal with the causes' (UCU Wales, 2017: [5]).

FE lecturers in Wales should continue to use the union's structures to mount a campaign against the registration fees of the EWC, and they should maintain pressure on the education minister to address their concerns. Unfortunately, there have been no signs from any of the opposition parties that the situation would change if they were in power. The union's fight for its members is one that it must fight alone.

> Adversity brings knowledge and knowledge wisdom.
>
> (Welsh proverb)

References

EWC (Education Workforce Council) (n.d.) Education Workforce Council homepage. Online. www.ewc.wales/site/index.php/en (accessed 16 April 2017).

Jones, P. (2010) 'Professional standards: Discussion paper'. Paper presented at UCU Cymru Annual Further Education Sector Conference.

Labour Party (2011) 'Welsh Labour manifesto 2011: Standing up for Wales'. Cardiff: Welsh Labour. Online. http://welshlabour.s3.amazonaws.com/welsh-labour-manifesto.pdf (accessed 16 April 2017).

Llewellyn, H. (2015) 'EWC Chief Executive's presentation'. Paper presented at UCU Cymru, January.

Machiavelli, N. (1908) *The Prince*. Trans. Marriott, W.K. Originally 1515. Online. www.constitution.org/mac/prince.pdf (accessed 25 April 2017).

Ryall, G. (2012) 'Most accusations against teachers in Wales are dropped'. *BBC News*, 27 February. Online. www.bbc.co.uk/news/uk-wales-16927479 (accessed 16 April 2017).

UCU (University and College Union) (2012) 'Initial submission from UCU to the Independent Review of Professionalism in the Further Education (FE) and Skills Sector'. Online. www.ucu.org.uk/media/4991/IfLCDP-review---initial-UCU-submission-Jan-12/pdf/ucu_initialsubiflirp_jan12.pdf (accessed 13 May 2017).

UCU Wales (University and College Union Wales) (2013) 'Response to: The Education (Wales) Bill consultation'. Online. www.ucu.org.uk/media/6019/Education-Wales-Bill-2014-UCU-Cymru-consultation-response-Sep-13/pdf/ucuwales_EducationWalesBill_sep13_.pdf (accessed 16 April 2016).

— (2017) 'Response to: Registration fees for the education workforce in Wales (2017)'. Online. www.ucu.org.uk/media/8443/Registration-fees-for-the-education-workforce-in-Wales-2017---UCU-Wales-consultation-response-Sep-16/pdf/UCUWales_finalregistrationfeesforEWC_sep16.pdf (accessed 16 April 2017).

Jake Wood

Power is no blessing in itself. ... But when it is employed to protect the innocent, ... it becomes a great blessing.

Jonathan Swift

Chapter 7

Under the sovereign's baleful gaze: Space, power and policy in the making of Irish further education and training

Fergal Finnegan

In the wake of the financial crisis the Irish government turned to education to provide a human capital fix for rising unemployment and a shrinking economy. The state surveyed the field of adult, community, vocational and further education and found it sorely wanting for the tasks ahead. The sovereign gaze could only see disorder and disarray and embarked on a reform project to make it a smoother and more integrated space that could better serve the economy. This attempt to redefine a busy and varied *field* as a unified *sector* is highly significant, and this chapter will offer a critical realist (Barnett, 2013; Bhaskar, 1979) reading of this policy turn in Irish adult education in which one can discern a shadow of Machiavelli's (1961) treatment of space and power in *The Prince*.

The making of the Irish further education and training sector

In 2011 the Irish state announced that it intended to embark on a major reform of adult education. This restructuring was led by a new body called SOLAS (this is an acronym for *An tSeirbhís Oideachais Leanúnaigh agus Scileanna*, the Further Education and Training Authority in the Irish language, which also means light in Gaelic). In 2014, SOLAS unveiled the *Further Education and Training Strategy*, and the publication of this document marked a major shift in the way adult education and lifelong learning are framed in Irish policy. A very diverse field – which has historically included a wide range of institutions such as community education centres, vocational training bodies, literacy projects and FE colleges as well as non-formal spaces – is being reshaped into a more tightly integrated sector (SOLAS, 2014). This has entailed changes in legislation and funding as well as the development of new management structures. As Murray (2014) also notes, the key terms and definitions used by policy-makers have changed: before the formation of SOLAS adult education was used as a preferred umbrella term for all work in the field (DES, 2000). But under the direction of SOLAS the work done across various institutions is commonly included in the further education and training (FET) sector. This change has been widely interpreted as a shift towards a more narrowly vocational conception of education.

The timing of these reforms is important. In 2009 senior management in FÁS (An Foras Áiseanna Saothair), the state's Training and Employment Authority, became embroiled in a major scandal that led to the organization's dissolution and the passing of the responsibility for training to the newly formed SOLAS. On a more global scale the Great Recession precipitated by the 2008 financial crisis had a severe impact on Ireland. Light-touch regulation of business and low corporate tax rates attracted significant flows of capital through Ireland in the 1990s and 2000s, and this fuelled the Celtic Tiger economy. But the Irish economy, which is very dependent on multinational investment and is highly financialized, was extremely vulnerable to any global downturn (McCabe, 2011). Consequently, the unravelling of the world economy that began in Lehman Brothers led in Ireland to an 85-billion-euro state-backed bailout of the banks, years of austerity, and the direct management of the Irish economy by the Troika (the European Union, the International Monetary Fund and the European Central Bank). A rapid rise in unemployment, from under 5 per cent in 2007 to 14 per cent in 2011, and the return of mass emigration meant that job creation quickly became the government's most pressing concern.

The redesignation of adult education as FET under these very particular circumstances is reflected in the priorities named in key policy documents. Tightening links between labour markets and FE, and job creation, are major concerns of the FET strategy document (SOLAS, 2014) and of state-commissioned research on FET (McGuinness *et al.*, 2014; Sweeney, 2013). In fact, formal links between FET institutions and social welfare agencies were established in order to promote 'labour activation'. Labour activation involves the close monitoring of job creation initiatives and the purpose and outcomes of education and training courses to assess whether they are successful in increasing the number of people in paid employment. Policy-makers also argued that the sector needed to gather far more detailed and timely data on progress made towards achieving policy goals. As a result, a national database has been created to track students' trajectories and outcomes and ensure that skill shortages in the labour market are filled. This is framed as an effort to be far more responsive to employers and also to become more student-centred (aims which policy-makers assume to be complementary). It is argued that, overall, these reforms will make FET more efficient, visible and mainstream.

Not all parts of the sector have been treated equally in this reform process, though. While the profile of FE colleges has risen, community education projects have been gutted through budget cuts (Harvey, 2012) as well as by the creation of quasi-markets in which organizations are forced to compete for funding to provide community development services. This downgrading is significant because community education, one of the main pillars in Irish adult education, has historically had close and organic links with grass-roots activism of various sorts. For example, community education centres and projects were established and run on a relatively autonomous basis by feminist groups, Irish Travellers and working-class activists in a wide variety of locations between the 1970s and the 2000s. Typically, such projects advocated participatory and collaborative approaches to education, and were often explicitly committed to social justice.

The rapidity of the changes, the new nomenclature of FET, the impact of budget cuts, the worsening of working conditions for tutors, the focus on immediate and readily measurable economic outcomes and the slow death of engaged community education have prompted discussion, and even heated argument, across Irish adult education. The enormous difference between how policy-makers and many practitioners view the field and its future has been a feature of public events and conferences since 2013, it surfaced as a defining theme in a landmark publication on Irish FE (Murray *et al.*, 2014).

Something old, something new

It is a mistake, though, to exaggerate the novelty of what has occurred, and in many respects the FET strategy marks the intensification of pre-existing trends rather than a complete break with the past. After all, human capital theory is a foundational discourse in modern Irish educational policy. Since the mid-1960s the modernization of the economy and the enhancement of the marketable skills of workers have been fundamental objectives of educational policy. Since the 1990s this idea has been most commonly articulated through the proposition, promoted by the Organisation for Economic Co-operation and Development (OECD) and the European Union (EU), that we now live in a knowledge-based economy in which education and knowledge are the key drivers of economic growth.

A utilitarian concern with outcomes in assessment and accreditation also pre-dates recent policy and legislative changes. This focus on outcomes reflects a much wider global trend towards standardization and transnational quality assurance; Allais (2014) noted that over the previous twenty years the number of countries using outcomes-based qualifications systems had mushroomed to 120. This 'extraordinary development' (Allais, 2014: 2) marks the emergence of a new educational order that is characterized by remarkably high expectations of education and of what might be achieved through the reform of curriculum and assessment. In Ireland, as elsewhere, this is underpinned by a dual faith in markets and managerialism that has characterized so much educational policy in the neoliberal era (Ball, 2007; Biesta, 2010). Features of this policy include an obsession with the role of education in fostering economic growth, the elaboration of new forms of public and private partnership, great store put on what is countable and predictable, the development of a panoply of targets and measures aimed at improving performance, and a distrust of non-standardized curricula and pedagogy. These are, however, part of a much bigger story of the rise of neoliberal ideas globally over the past forty years.

The Prince and 'seeing like a state'

Machiavelli also lived through a time of crisis and uncertainty, when the security and former glory of Florence had evaporated. Confronted by the flux of history he was above all a realist who counselled 'leaving aside imaginary things' (Machiavelli, 1961: 91) and concluded that 'the only sound, sure, and enduring methods of defence are those based on your own actions and prowess' (ibid.: 129). There is a boldness and perspicacity in this treatise that remains very striking indeed. He is a sort of 'Luther of secular power' as MacIntyre (1998: 127) remarked. It is this emphasis on agency and realism, the worldliness of his ideas, that has also made him such an influential thinker, including amongst radicals (Gramsci, 1971). But here I will offer a more partial, more oblique, and less sympathetic reading of *The Prince*, as it will help to foreground an aspect of recent educational policy in Ireland that deserves consideration – the precise way the field of adult education has been imagined and mapped as a FET sector.

Machiavelli (1961) begins *The Prince* with a discussion of how various types of principalities require diverse strategies of conquest and rule. There is a strong awareness of the spatial dimensions of power and how to stretch, extend and maintain power in a given situation through both military and political means. It invites the addressee of the book, the prince seeking glory and influence, to find, metaphorically, an elevated point from which to survey the world and puzzle out how best to direct events. Tellingly, this mapping exercise precedes Machiavelli's exploration of virtue, fortune and the necessary qualities and dispositions of a prince in a time of change. Just as tellingly, the inhabitants of the principalities are of little concern to him. Mapping space, Machiavelli suggests, makes the world legible and amenable to intervention.

The Prince is an exemplary, even foundational, text in the way it invites the reader to think about space, power and agency from above. Seeing from above with sharp-eyed purpose, and assuming that one has, or should have, the power to reshape what is surveyed in order to be able to act upon things and people, has since become so commonplace in politics and policy that it is now completely unremarkable. But the 'notion of the instrumental homogeneity of space' (Lefebvre, 1991: 285) on which this perspective is based, and of which Machiavelli offers an early example, was novel and revolutionary. New experiences, representations and conceptions of space emerged in the early modern period that were linked to urbanization, the changing role of markets and the development of the modern state (Lefebvre, 1991: see especially Chapter 4). Consequently, space became abstract and appears more homogeneous and unified. This notion of space as abstract, homogeneous and open to calculated intervention gave rise to simplified, synoptic accounts of the world that allow actors to see like a state, as the anthropologist James Scott (1998) puts it.

Reducing complexity in order to set priorities and organize the best use of resources is vital to the functioning of complicated and highly differentiated societies and is commonly seen as the defining purpose of policy (Sum and Jessop, 2013). I am not objecting to these mapping exercises *per se*, and nor do I wish to seek refuge from the realities of the world in a comforting fug of postmodern theory. Rather, the point is to recall that such princely visions are only simplifications developed from a particular set of interests and social experiences, and thus limited. These 'abridged maps ... did not successfully represent the actual activity of the society they depicted, nor were they intended to; they represented only that slice of it that interested an official observer' (Scott, 1998: 3). A greater degree of wariness is needed: policy descriptions are only types of maps, and we cannot rely too heavily on such thin simplifications, as this can easily lead us to miss or misrepresent what is truly important in a field of practice.

Princely visions and the missing history of Irish adult education

This brings me back to the current policy context in Ireland. Put simply, the current FET strategy offers a much too smooth and featureless map of adult education. In other words, the thin simplifications are a little *too* thin; signs have been taken for wonders and basic maps are taken as solid descriptions of present reality. To a large extent this is because recent policy is marked by an absence of historical imagination and to a striking degree shows no awareness of the socio-historical formation of the field. Perhaps a zeal for reform has made policy-makers impatient with the past. Consequently, the complexities, contradictions and possibilities that have been, and remain, central to, and even constitutive of, the field are entirely overlooked.

As Murray (2014) notes, adult education/FET is largely understood in these documents in negative terms and defined in relation to what it is not – it is not school and it is not HE – or viewed as a lowly waystation, that is, as the institutions tasked with bringing adults through the intermediate levels of the National Framework of Qualifications. The haziness of existing definitions of FET has given rise to considerable frustration, and to complaints that it lacks an identity or brand (McGuinness *et al.*, 2014; Sweeney, 2013). One of the most common tropes used in these documents is to highlight fragmentation and disorder in the field and to pitch current policy initiatives as a panacea (McGuinness *et al.*, 2014; SOLAS, 2014; Sweeney, 2013). Through more careful management and more clearly defined outcomes FET will flourish; what is needed above all, it seems, is the prince's unifying vision and willingness to take bold and decisive action. However, both the prognosis and the remedy are threadbare and unconvincing.

It is more accurate to say that Irish adult education has historically been a loosely bounded and contested space – a type of res publica – shaped by multiple professional and non-professional actors, including the state and diverse social movements. Tracing its layered formation, one can point to (and this is an indicative rather than an exhaustive list) the impact religious, nationalist and socialist groups have had on institutions and practices and to how community groups, agricultural organizations and feminists have all shaped the field. This openness and this collaboration inside and outside established educational institutions have led to a good deal of messiness and sometimes incoherence. But this should not mean that we then overlook how it has also served as a space for innovation in pedagogy, a seedbed of new ideas and knowledge in education and craft, and as a space of political experiment and democratic practice. From a historical perspective, instead of the spatial homogeneity of princely visions we can discern the 'interpenetration and superimposition of [various types of] social spaces' (Lefebvre, 1991: 88) in this field through time. The work of community groups, the activity of social movements, extra-mural initiatives aimed at widening access to young and mature working-class students, the development of accredited apprenticeships and so forth have all resulted in the creation of new types of educational and social spaces. These have sedimented in the ideas, practices and values within a shared field. This lends Irish adult education a fuzzy and layered quality that partly stems from the messy business of negotiating the meaning of freedom and knowledge amongst various groups and organizations. This layered messy quality, its multiplicity, is precisely what makes much of adult education innovative and politically important. But this sort of understanding often eludes princes who assume that in an age of measurement their sole task is to map, marshal and master the world below them.

References

Allais, S. (2014) *Selling Out Education: National qualifications frameworks and the neglect of knowledge*. Rotterdam: Sense Publishers.

Ball, S.J. (2007) *Education plc: Understanding private sector participation in public sector education*. London: Routledge.

Barnett, R. (2013) *Imagining the University*. Abingdon: Routledge.

Bhaskar, R. (1979) *The Possibility of Naturalism: A philosophical critique of the contemporary human sciences*. Atlantic Highlands, NJ: Humanities Press.

Biesta, G.J.J. (2010) *Good Education in an Age of Measurement: Ethics, politics, democracy*. Boulder, CO: Paradigm Publishers.

DES (Department of Education and Science) (2000) *Learning for Life: White Paper on Adult Education*. Dublin: The Stationery Office.

Gramsci, A. (1971) *Selections from the Prison Notebooks of Antonio Gramsci*. Ed. and trans. Hoare, Q. and Nowell Smith, G. London: Lawrence and Wishart.

Harvey, B. (2012) *Downsizing the Community Sector: Changes in employment and services in the voluntary and community sector in Ireland, 2008–2012*. Dublin: Irish Congress of Trade Unions.

Lefebvre, H. (1991) *The Production of Space*. Trans. Nicholson-Smith, D. Oxford: Basil Blackwell.

Machiavelli, N. (1961) *The Prince*. Trans. Bull, G. Harmondsworth: Penguin Books.

MacIntyre, A. (1998) *A Short History of Ethics: A history of moral philosophy from the Homeric age to the twentieth century*. 2nd ed. London: Routledge.

McCabe, C. (2011) *Sins of the Father: Tracing the decisions that shaped the Irish economy*. Dublin: History Press.

McGuinness, S., Bergin, A., Kelly, E., McCoy, S., Smyth, E., Whelan, A., and Banks, J. (2014) *Further Education and Training in Ireland: Past, present and future* (Research Series 35). Dublin: Economic and Social Research Institute.

Murray, M. (2014) 'What's in a name? Terminology, power and contestation. In Murray, M., Grummell, B., and Ryan, A. (eds) *Further Education and Training: History, politics, practice*. Maynooth: MACE Press (102–21).

Murray, M., Grummell, B., and Ryan, A. (eds) (2014) *Further Education and Training: History, politics, practice*. Maynooth: MACE Press.

Scott, J.C. (1998) *Seeing like a State: How certain schemes to improve the human condition have failed.* New Haven: Yale University Press.

SOLAS (2014) *Further Education and Training Strategy 2014–2019.* Dublin: SOLAS.

Sum, N.-L. and Jessop, B. (2013) *Towards a Cultural Political Economy: Putting culture in its place in political economy.* Cheltenham: Edward Elgar.

Sweeney, J. (2013) *A Strategic Review of Further Education and Training and the Unemployed.* Dublin: National Economic and Social Council.

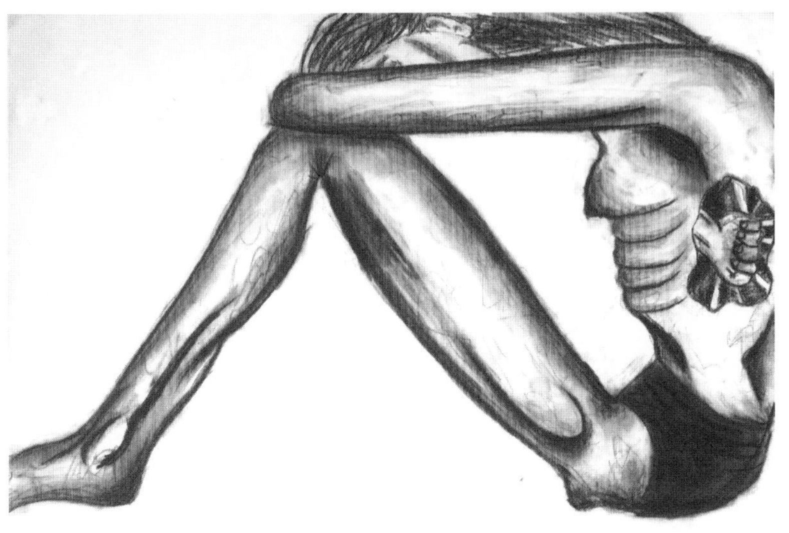

Bethany Williams

Only a man who knows what it is like to be defeated can reach down to the bottom of his soul and come up with the extra ounce of power it takes to win.

Muhammad Ali

Chapter 8

The Prince and English apprenticeships

Simon Reddy

This chapter will explore the British government's aim to establish three million apprenticeships by 2020 in relation to Machiavelli's notion of the ends justifying the means. It focuses on both full-time courses and apprenticeships in plumbing to interrogate how the apprenticeship deal is degraded by the government's socio-economic strategies as well as the deceptive marketing of training (Ball, 2008; Reddy, 2014).

> [M]en are so simple, and so subject to present necessities, that he who seeks to deceive will always find someone who will allow himself to be deceived.
>
> (Machiavelli, 1908: 84)

Apprenticeship may be understood as an explicit agreement between a worker and an employer; the apprentice agrees to work on low wages for a long period of time, which benefits the employer. In return, the apprentice acquires the skills, knowledge and experience demanded by the employer and the economy. At the end of the apprenticeship (which is 48 months in the case of plumbing apprenticeships), there is an implicit promise of something better for apprentices – a settlement by way of job progression, higher wages and improved status (Snell, 1996; BIS, 2012; Reddy, 2015). However, deception is afoot in English apprenticeships, and apprentices may be obstructed from capitalizing on the apprenticeship riches they have been promised (City and Guilds, 2012).

Following the English riots of 1981, the government was keen to encourage unemployed young people into college and onto youth training schemes or apprenticeships. However, the significant decline of English apprenticeships by the early 1990s gave rise to a new concern about how the nation's stock of workers with intermediate qualifications compared with those of other successful European countries, such as Germany, which had relatively high levels of these technician-level workers (Gospel, 1995; Steedman, 1998; Barnett, 2004). Consequently, the official Leitch Review of skills (Leitch, 2006) championed 'increasing the supply of skills and qualifications as a monocausal prescription for economic success' (Coffield, 2004: 284–5).

Before Leitch's review, Steedman, Gospel and Ryan had identified a need to address the growing problem of youth unemployment by advocating high-quality preparatory training and an expansion in the number of apprenticeships. They highlighted the 'serious skill shortages and enduring skills gaps at the skilled crafts, technician and associate professional level', and warned that skills shortages had a number of macro-economic consequences in 'contributing to wage inflation and making macro-economic policy management more difficult by pushing up wages and lowering productivity growth in the longer term', and that the 'strategy for growth' they drafted aimed to address inflationary wage pressures caused by skills shortages in sectors such as construction by exploiting the potential of apprenticeships (Steedman *et al.*, 1998: 7). Steedman *et al.* suggested 'limiting apprentice pay' to 'reduce the costs of training to employers and facilitate the offer of more places' (1998: 13). They proposed that increasing the number of apprenticeships would contribute to the nation's stock of intermediate qualifications and in turn increase productivity, lowering youth unemployment and deflating craft wages to reduce the risk of macro-inflation in the wider economy.

Increasing the number of apprenticeships offered construction industry employers a large selection of partially trained, available workers, but apprenticeships were generally perceived as having low status in England, resulting in low demand. With a view to raising the status of and demand for apprenticeships in England, Sir Michael Wilshaw, the chief of the Office for Standards in Education (Ofsted), set out his priorities, which included the following:

> Apprenticeships must have parity of esteem with A levels. They must be sold aggressively to schools, parents and young people.
>
> (Michael Wilshaw, speech to the CBI on 18 November 2014, cited in Hughes, 2014)

Therefore, in order to get many young people interested in low-status, low-paid apprenticeships, some institutions relied on Machiavellian marketing of vocational courses, which was sometimes judged to be irresponsible. Yet, the deceiver will always find someone ready to be deceived. In one instance in 2006, the Advertising Standards Authority (ASA) investigated claims made by a private training provider known as OLCI Practical Training, which delivered recognized City and Guilds qualifications. OLCI had made misleading claims in the national press regarding plumbers' earnings and career opportunities; in particular, a complaint to the ASA contested the rate of £130 per hour that was mentioned in the ad. The ASA (2006) upheld the complaint, and its adjudication document reported that OLCI's advertisement 'was likely to mislead', breaching clauses for substantiation and truthfulness in regard to employment and business opportunities. Despite heavy criticism of such unethical marketing, a decade later similar campaigns are still being used aggressively by reputable institutions to entice young people, unemployed adults and career switchers onto plumbing courses. One such was reported in a local newspaper:

> [O]ne of the UK's top accredited providers of compliance, technical and safety training in the utility sector ... has warned that gas, water and electricity workers could demand Premier League-level salaries if the skills shortage in the utilities sector isn't dealt with by the government and employers.
>
> (Vergnault, 2016)

The prospects of steady employment and better pay have been key selling points for apprenticeships, with respected organizations such as City and Guilds (2012) touting its own 'Rich List' and the idea that vocational learning is a gateway to wealth regardless of the student's background. Regrettably, this list consists of a relatively small selection of very successful, high-earning celebrities who undertook apprenticeships but who are not representative of the general population. Nevertheless, supporting growth in apprenticeships and pre-apprenticeships, the Conservative Party manifesto in 2015 set a clear target to deliver three million apprenticeships by 2020 (Richmond and Simons, 2016: 6–7). Even before this target was set, however, successive governments have provided support to employers to provide apprenticeships. For example, in 2008, the Department for Innovation, Universities and Skills (DIUS) and the Department for Children, Schools and Families (DCSF) stated:

> [W]e believe that there is scope for moderate growth in Apprenticeship numbers by offering similar direct payment incentives to large companies, so that they can recruit more Apprentices than they need.
>
> (DIUS and DCSF, 2008: 38)

Reddy (2014) argues that government-sponsored supply-side growth in pre-apprenticeships and apprenticeships in plumbing was significantly increased by the number of unemployed adults and adult career switchers entering the occupation. This empirical study of full-time courses and apprenticeships in plumbing found that apprentices were outnumbered at least ten to one by a combination of full-time 16–19-year-old students and adult career switchers on vocational courses not associated with apprenticeships. In contrast to many of our European neighbours, English plumbers do not have to serve an apprenticeship to qualify, owing to a lack both of workforce regulation and of protectionism. In Germany, plumbers have to achieve Meister [Master] status in order to set up an enterprise. The lack of such regulation in England has created an 'anything goes' culture generating excessive competition for apprenticeships in the workforce from adult students and career switchers (who can attend full-time college courses to train to become self-employed plumbers) as well as from migrant labour within the European labour market (Fuller and Unwin, 2013: 3). Because of the growth in apprenticeships and other types of preparatory vocational training, colleges complained of being unable to find work experience or apprenticeship placements for all of their students within the construction industry. Indeed, the lack of progression into the construction industry for pre-apprenticeship trainees and adult career switchers entering the plumbing trade is a critical concern. In addressing this issue, at least one further education (FE) institution has opted for an apparently innovative solution of buying a house for students to use for construction simulations, so they can gain much-needed work experience. Managers at this college claimed that many employers were reluctant to take students on work placements because of obvious safety concerns and insurance issues relating to having inexperienced and unskilled workers on site (Simons, 2016). The college did not, however, mention that there was little, if any, demand from industry to sponsor work experience opportunities for students. Nevertheless, the provision of a house to simulate work experience has been a great success for the college, which stated that a hundred people had qualified as a result and profits from the sales of the newly refurbished houses would be reinvested in the project:

> It could get very big very quickly. ... There's great appetite for this to be an even bigger cross-college project and there are so many ways for different students to benefit from it. The sky's the limit, really.
>
> (Simons, 2016)

The house 'was run exactly as a commercial construction site would be, so punctuality, attendance and professional behaviour are key themes drummed into learners' (ibid.), but there is no mention of the wages or any payments that students could have expected if the project had indeed been a real construction site.

While this appears to be a legitimate and laudable strategy from a pedagogical point of view, and while it may please external inspectors, there are some serious practical implications in the scaling up of this initiative for full-time, traineeship and pre-apprenticeship students that may not have been considered. A comparative study of plumbing education and training in Hong Kong and England (Reddy, 2017) uncovered a similar initiative in Hong Kong. This revealed a conflict of interests when colleges purchase real properties for the purpose of training students. Using free labour presents colleges with an unfair advantage over local construction workers, who are required by law to be paid for their services.

Another possible implication of this new initiative is that it creates an artificial demand. Work experience is most likely difficult to secure for construction students because there is little or no demand for work experience candidates from within the construction industry. If there were, then they would probably be strongly sponsored by employers, as is the case with apprenticeships. However, in this situation, the demand for workers does not come from employers but rather from the college institution. The outcome of creating an artificial demand is greater competition among students for jobs, which arguably diminishes progression opportunities while driving down pay. The comparative study found that competition for work placements was fierce and a small minority of students were even found to be working unpaid for long periods of time in order to secure or continue into an apprenticeship (Reddy, 2014). Such a process stands to breach the implicit contract within the traditional apprenticeship agreement:

> Paying a lower wage than for a fully qualified worker while a person receives training is a long-standing principle of traditional Apprenticeships. In the UK there is an implicit contract that the individual learner is making a contribution to their human capital that will pay future dividends in terms of better pay and employment prospects on completion of their training.
>
> (BIS, 2012: 9)

As this quotation from a government document makes clear, a deal is being done when full-time students or apprentices work for low or, as in some instances, no wages (Reddy, 2015). The apprenticeship deal means that in return for the apprentices' long period of low-wage employment, something better has to come at the end of the toil. The same is the case for those working unpaid on simulated construction sites such as the college house mentioned above. However, the Trade Union Congress (TUC) found that between 2007 and 2015 in the UK:

> [R]eal wages – income from work adjusted for inflation – fell by 10.4%. That drop was equalled only by Greece in a list of 29 countries in the Organisation for Economic Cooperation and Development (OECD).
>
> (Allen and Elliott, 2016)

When this is considered in the light of *The Prince* (Machiavelli, 1908), a prudent ruler cannot and must not honour his word when it places him at a disadvantage. The conditions for apprentices may degenerate as a consequence of government interventions that subordinate education to economics, while rendering education itself into a commodity that can, in turn, be made subordinate to profit (Ball, 2008). Educational processes play their part in the creation of the enterprise culture and the cultivation of enterprising subjects (Ball, 2008; BIS, 2009). In keeping with this, the current UK apprenticeship strategy highlights skills shortages and skills gaps, giving the impression that work is easily available and highly paid. Highly convincing but misleading marketing campaigns that entice those interested in potentially lucrative apprenticeships or other types of vocational training have become commonplace in the construction sector. Reddy (2014) reports that many unemployed adult students and career switchers were responding to media hype by attending full-time college courses with an entrepreneurial view of becoming self-employed in the belief they would earn lots of money.

To conclude, a case can be made that the current government strategy has led to higher levels of employment in the overall population and has driven down wages and consequently lowered macro-economic inflation; Steedman *et al.*'s (1998) strategy for growth was robust. So, government may ignore or even connive in the peddling of inflated accounts of skills shortages in construction and elsewhere, because achieving success in policy for vocational education is now based on achieving high numbers of apprentices. Thousands of misguided young people and adults from the poorest backgrounds are competing for apprenticeships that they thought would be abundant and easy to attain. But, as Machiavelli knew, the ends justify the means:

> [O]ne judges by the result. For that reason, let a prince have the credit of conquering and holding his state, the means will always be considered honest, and he will be praised by everybody

> because the vulgar are always taken by what a thing seems to be and by what comes of it.
>
> (Machiavelli, 1908: 86)

References

Advertising Standards Authority (ASA) (2006) 'ETSE Ltd t/a OLCI Practical Training'. 22 November. Online. http://webarchive.nationalarchives.gov.uk/20080728115738/http://www.cap.org.uk/asa/adjudications/Public/TF_ADJ_41966.htm (accessed 7 June 2017).

Allen, K. and Elliott, L. (2016) 'UK joins Greece at bottom of wage growth league'. *The Guardian*, 27 July. Online. www.theguardian.com/money/2016/jul/27/uk-joins-greece-at-bottom-of-wage-growth-league-tuc-oecd (accessed 20 November 2016).

Ball, S.J. (2008) *The Education Debate*. Bristol: Policy Press.

Barnett, C. (2004) 'Education for industrial defeat: The post-war British record'. Paper presented at the 2nd City and Guilds Annual Fellowship Lecture.

BIS (Department for Business, Innovation and Skills) (2009) 'Skills for growth: The national skills strategy: Executive summary'. Department for Business, Innovation and Skills. Online. http://webarchive.nationalarchives.gov.uk/+/http://web.bis.gov.uk/assets/biscore/corporate/docs/s/skills-strategy-summary.pdf (accessed 25 April 2017).

— (2012) 'Apprenticeship pay Survey 2011 (BIS Research Paper 64). Department for Business, Innovation and Skills. Online. https://core.ac.uk/download/pdf/4159566.pdf (accessed 25 April 2016).

City and Guilds (2012) 'City and Guilds Vocational Rich List 2011'. Online. www.cityandguilds.com/news/April-2012/news/vocational-rich-list#.WP9FK1KZNE4 (accessed 25 April 2017).

Coffield, F. (2004) 'Evidence-based policy or policy-based evidence? The struggle over new policy for workforce development in England'. In Rainbird, H., Fuller, A., and Munro, A. (eds) *Workplace Learning in Context*. London: Routledge, 279–98.

DIUS (Department for Innovation, Universities and Skills) and DCSF (Department for Children, Schools and Families) (2008) 'World-class apprenticeships: Unlocking talent, building skills for all: The Government's strategy for the future of apprenticeships in England'. Department for Innovation, Universities and Skills. Online. http://webarchive.nationalarchives.gov.uk/tna/+/http:/www.dius.gov.uk/publications/world_class_apprenticeships.pdf/ (accessed 25 April 2017).

Fuller, A. and Unwin, L. (2013) 'Apprenticeship and the concept of occupation'. Briefing Paper. Gatsby Charitable Foundation, London. Online. www.gatsby.org.uk/uploads/education/reports/pdf/apprenticeship-and-the-concept-of-occupation.pdf (accessed 16 January 2017).

Gospel, H.F. (1995) 'The decline of apprenticeship training in Britain'. *Industrial Relations Journal*, 26 (1), 32–44.

Hughes, D. (2014) 'Employers, vocational education and parity of esteem'. Blog, 19 November. Online. http://deirdrehughes.org/2014/11/employers-vocational-education-parity-of-esteem/ (accessed 15 January 2017).

Leitch, A. (Sandy) (2006) *Prosperity for All in the Global Economy: World class skills. Final report* (Leitch Review of Skills). Norwich: HMSO.

Machiavelli, N. (1908) *The Prince*. Trans. Marriott, W.K. Originally 1515. Online. www.constitution.org/mac/prince.pdf (accessed 15 January 2017).

Reddy, S. (2014) 'A study of tutors' and students' perceptions and experiences of full-time college courses and apprenticeships in plumbing'. PhD thesis, University of Exeter. Online. https://ore.exeter.ac.uk/repository/bitstream/handle/10871/15728/ReddyS.pdf?sequence=1&isAllowed=y (accessed 13 May 2017).

— (2015) 'Rethinking the apprenticeship settlement'. *FE News*, 16 June. Online. www.fenews.co.uk/fe-news/11569-rethinking-the-apprenticeship-settlement (accessed 7 June 2017).

— (2017) 'A comparative study of plumbing and training education: England and Hong Kong' (World Plumbing Council Scholarship Report). World Plumbing Council. Online. http://worldplumbing.org/assets/uploads/2016/11/2015-WPC-education-and-training-scholarship-report-Simon-Reddy.pdf (accessed 17 July 2017).

Richmond, T. and Simons, J. (2016) *The Skills We Need, and Why We Don't Have Them: How apprenticeships should be reformed to make the UK compete on the global stage*. London: Policy Exchange. Online. https://policyexchange.org.uk/wp-content/uploads/2016/11/Apprenticeships.pdf (accessed 23 December 2016).

Simons, S. (2016) 'A house where learners can build their careers'. *TES*, 31 July. Online. www.tes.com/news/further-education/breaking-news/a-house-where-learners-can-build-their-careers (accessed 1 September 2016).

Snell, K.D.M. (1996) 'The apprenticeship system in British history: The fragmentation of a cultural institution'. *History of Education*, 25 (4), 303–21.

Steedman, H. (1998) 'A decade of skill formation in Britain and Germany'. *Journal of Education and Work*, 11 (1), 77–94.

Steedman, H., Gospel, H., and Ryan, P. (1998) 'Apprenticeship: A strategy for growth'. Centre for Economic Performance, London School of Economics and Political Science. Online. https://core.ac.uk/download/pdf/94631.pdf (accessed 26 September 2016).

Vergnault, O. (2016) 'Why plumbers and electricians could earn Premier League wages'. *Plymouth Herald*, 6 June. Online. www.plymouthherald.co.uk/plumbers-electricians-earn-premier-league-wages/story-29366542-detail/story.html (accessed 26 September 2016).

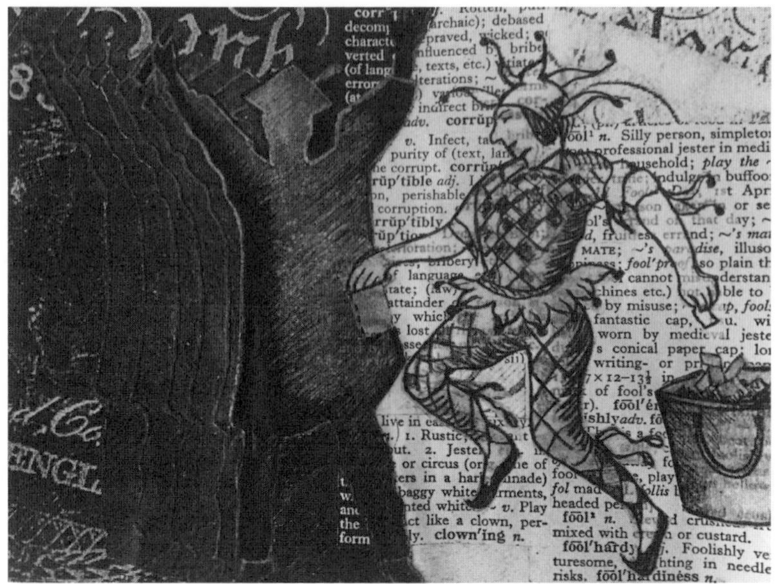

Linda Stephens

Power does not corrupt men; fools, however, if they get into a position of power, corrupt power.

George Bernard Shaw

Chapter 9

The former principal–agent problem in Victorian technical and further education: Principals with principles

Gavin Moodie

> I can add colours to the chameleon,
> Change shapes with Proteus for advantages,
> And set the murderous Machiavel to school.
>
> (William Shakespeare, *Henry VI, Part 3*)

'Up to 10 Victorian TAFE board chairs have been "sacked" amid claims of political payback against institutes that have protested against state government budget cuts', reported Australia's national daily newspaper in 2013 (Ross, 2013b). Victoria is Australia's second-biggest state, with a population of 6 million. TAFE is the acronym for technical and further education, and now refers in Australia to public providers of vocational education and training. At the time Victoria had 18 TAFE institutes, 288 community education providers, and 420 private providers of publicly funded vocational education (NCVER, 2014). The sudden budget cut of around 30 per cent of TAFEs' institutional grants resulted in the closure of several programmes, the disposal of facilities, the closure of campuses, the dismissal of around 1,000 staff, the quadrupling of some student fees and the amalgamation of three institutes, and it sent many of the state's institutes into deep deficits (Preiss, 2015). The then Conservative Coalition Government lost power at the next election, at least partly because of its damage to TAFE institutes (Noonan, 2014).

This chapter recounts the circumstances that led to the dismissal of over half of Victoria's TAFE board chairs, which the government and its officials treated as an instance of the classic principal–agent problem, where the government as principal exercised its powers to ensure that its interests were served by its institutes as agents. This is contrasted with the Australian government's treatment of the very prominent opposition of (lamentably few) vice-chancellors to its contentious proposal in 2014 to deregulate university fees as an issue of institutional autonomy and accountability. This shows that the divide between vocational and higher education is just as deep in the institutionalization of power as it is in curriculum, quality assurance, financing, funding levels and other more commonly observed features of the sectoral divide.

Boring legal stuff

Victorian TAFE institutes are corporations established by the Victorian government pursuant to the Education and Training Reform Act 2006 (Victoria). Institutes are governed by a board. Before 2012 the board comprised nine to fifteen directors of whom at least half were appointed by the government. The chair of the board was elected by the board. In 2010 the then Labor Government proposed to amend the Act to provide for the chair of each TAFE board to be appointed by the government. This was opposed by the Conservative Coalition. The shadow minister Peter Hall said in the second reading debate opposing the amendment:

> This is an unnecessary grab for power. It is an expression of the minister's wish to centralise all these appointments. It is typical of this Labor government, the members of which feel they must have their hands on absolutely everything. The minister suggested there needed to be more lines of accountability because these institutes are engaging in commercial activities and as they receive significant funding from the taxpayer they need to be accountable to the taxpayer. They are already accountable, and they are already engaging in significant commercial activity.
>
> (Parliament of Victoria, 2010: 4867)

The amendment failed to pass that parliament. However, in 2012 the Coalition was in government and Peter Hall, now Minister for Higher Education and Skills, proposed that the Act be amended to provide for the chair of each TAFE board to be appointed by the government. Hall used the same justification the former Labor Government used, and which he had opposed in opposition, that government needed the power to ensure that TAFE institutes were sufficiently commercially accountable (Ross, 2013a). This time Labor opposed the move. The Labor spokesperson Jenny Mikakos said in the second reading debate:

> What does this really tell us? It is telling us that this government wants to silence dissent and wants to stifle criticism at a time when the sector is very alarmed about its future. It is giving the minister complete control over board appointments and centralising a lot more power in his hands. The bill is going to lead to the politicisation of board appointments at a crucial time for TAFEs – at the beginning of next year.
>
> (Parliament of Victoria, 2012: 5143)

Those amendments passed Parliament, giving the government the power to reconstitute TAFE boards and replace their chairs, which the government exercised in the following year.

Victorian, and indeed all Australian, universities are constituted very differently; they have far greater capacity, right and obligation to govern themselves than do TAFE institutes. Each public university in Victoria is established under its own Act, though they follow a common pattern. The government appoints a minority of members of the body governing the university, and the university governing body appoints its own chair.

Cry 'Havoc!' and let slip the dogs of neoliberalism

In Shakespeare's *Julius Caesar* (2012) Mark Antony closes his first soliloquy, over Caesar's corpse on the floor of the Senate, by presaging vengeance for Caesar's assassination:

> And Caesar's spirit ranging for revenge,
> With Atè by his side come hot from hell,
> Shall in these confines, with a monarch's voice,
> Cry havoc and let slip the dogs of war,
> That this foul deed shall smell above the earth
> With carrion men, groaning for burial.
>
> (Shakespeare, 2012: III.i.295–300)

Atè is the classical spirit of vengeful bloodlust. 'Cry havoc' is the order given for pillaging after a battle (Shakespeare, 2012: note on l. 1501, 'Cry havoc'). In Shakespeare's tragedy the demise of the head of state was followed by a battle and then pillaging; in TAFE's tragedy pillaging was followed by a battle and then the demise of heads of TAFE.

The havoc and pillaging of TAFE originated with the policy introduced by the then (2008) Labor Victorian government that it called 'Securing jobs for your future: skills for Victoria'. This phased in, from 2009 to 2012, three big changes to vocational education in the state.

First, the government introduced an entitlement to vocational education that it subsidized. Prospective students had to meet conditions to be eligible for the training entitlement, but otherwise the government's commitment was uncapped or open-ended (Victorian Government, 2008: 15). Second, the government allowed providers to supplement its subsidy with fees that were initially in a band between the minimum and maximum fees it set (ibid.: 23), and later the Coalition Government removed minimum fees (Ross, 2011) so that providers could offer programmes just for the government subsidy. Third, the government made training subsidies available equally to public TAFEs and to registered private for-profit providers of vocational education (ibid.: 22).

This had numerous effects, five of which caused most havoc. First, standards plunged, which persists. Australian vocational education is based on job competencies. Since competency-based training is evaluated only by outcomes, until recently there was little if any evaluation of inputs such as curriculum and hours of instruction or of processes such as pedagogy. Assessment is by the provider, which means that there is no external assessment, or even moderation, for almost all programmes. So, many providers maximized their profits by offering programmes of one-tenth of the duration they were notionally funded to provide and with only token and in some cases no assessment (Strong, 2012; Sheehan, 2012).

Second, a crisis of quality emerged, which also persists. Quality assurance in Australian vocational education is wholly inadequate in volume, since there are far too few auditors, and it is wholly inadequate in form, so that even were there enough auditors, quality still would not be assured. So, many providers maximize their profits by having grossly inadequate and in some cases no facilities, by employing teachers who are inadequately qualified, and by providing either no practical classes and work experience, or only unstructured and incidental training on the job.

Third, unscrupulous practices proliferated. Providers paid agents on commission to recruit students. Recruiters recruited students in shopping malls (Strong, 2012), students were recruited by offers of inducements such as free iPads, providers or their agents paid sports clubs commissions to enrol their members in their programmes (Tomazin, 2012), families sitting around their kitchen table were enrolled in a programme and providers claimed government subsidies for a higher-level programme than the one they actually offered to groups of students, a practice known as 'multi-layering' (Strong, 2012).

Fourth, the number of private for-profit providers taking advantage of the government funding increased by 29 per cent and enrolments in private providers exploded by 308 per cent from 2008 to 2011 (Dunckley and Mather, 2012: 10). One private for-profit provider increased its enrolments by 4,000 per cent in one year (Sheehan, 2012) to become the largest provider in Victoria in 2011 with 1,400 enrolments (Ross, 2012).

Fifth, and most importantly for the government, this whole enterprise resulted in 2011–12 in the payment of subsidies 56 per cent greater than the government had expected (Dunckley and Mather, 2012: 10).

In 2011 the newly elected Coalition Government maintained the obviously flawed market in vocational education that the previous Labor Government had created, but cut its subsidies for the fastest-growing fields, including business studies, hospitality and fitness training, and cut by 25 per cent government payments for community service obligations at the big metropolitan TAFEs (Sheehan, 2012; Ross, 2011). As Sheehan (2012) observed, the government cut its funding for public TAFE institutes to compensate for the explosion in subsidies for private providers.

The changes in 2011 did not fix any of the problems that had arisen or become manifest since 2008, and in particular they did not stop the increase in government subsidies of private vocational education. The government responded to the problems caused by the big expansion in the training market by marketizing it even further in 2012, introducing what advocates for the training market call improved 'market design'. The government cut even further its subsidies for programmes that were expanding quickly and introduced what it called full 'contestability' of all government funding of vocational education: it removed all government support for TAFEs' community service obligations and made the same government subsidies available equally to public TAFEs and private for-profit providers. TAFEs were losing enrolments to private for-profit providers that were undercutting them on standards, quality and fees, government support for some of their biggest programmes was cut substantially again, and they also lost the funding that supported their community services and facilities such as libraries, student services and facilities, and community outreach.

The accumulation of the government's cuts in 2011 and its deeper cuts in 2012 led to the outcomes we opened with: TAFEs cut several programmes, facilities, campuses and staff; and TAFEs increased their fees substantially, by four times for some programmes. This in turn led to several big demonstrations and substantial negative publicity (Norling, 2012). There was a battle to reverse the government's policy, or at least its latest cuts to TAFE. Directors of TAFE institutes stated clearly the extent of and reasons for cuts (Mackenzie, 2012), informed the media of the effects of the cuts on their institutes and the problems they caused (Strong, 2012), and at least one director wrote an article for the national media discussing the flaws in the government's policy and their consequences (Griffiths, 2012). But the objectors substantially lost the immediate battle and the government retained its policy and budget cuts with only a token concession to the objections that had been pressed vigorously and loudly.

Two years later, in 2014, the Commonwealth Conservative Coalition Government proposed its own neoliberal changes to higher education, which were remarkably similar to the flawed changes the Victorian government had introduced in vocational education five years earlier. ('The Commonwealth' is the shorthand for the federal government provided in the Commonwealth of Australia Constitution Act, 1901. It was first proposed as the term for the federation of the six Australian crown colonies at the 1891 constitutional convention to describe the nation as a political as well as a geographic entity. The name was initially controversial, because of its association with Cromwell's 'Commonwealth of England' (Irving, n.d.; Wikipedia, n.d.).)

Amongst several other proposals, the Commonwealth sought to extend government subsidies for higher education to all registered providers, including private for-profit providers (Australian Government, 2014: 63). The Labor Commonwealth Government had progressively from 2009 to 2012 removed caps on the number of domestic bachelor students it subsidized at public universities (Commonwealth of Australia, 2009: 17), and the Conservative Commonwealth Government also proposed that private providers could also offer unlimited numbers of undergraduate places subsidized by the government (Australian Government, 2014: 63). The government proposed removing the caps on the fees that universities could charge, so that they could charge unlimited fees backed by income-contingent loans financed, subsidized and guaranteed by the Australian government (Commonwealth of Australia, 2014: 85).

These proposals were criticized extensively in the media (Gittins, 2014; Moodie, 2014a; Quiggin, 2014; Byron, 2015) (including by drawing lessons from the earlier failures in vocational education (Higgins, 2016)), in the grey literature (Kniest, 2014; Ryan, 2014), in a parliamentary inquiry (Parliament of Australia, 2014) and in the general community. There were several noisy demonstrations against the proposals, many of which were covered extensively in the media (Moodie, 2014b). While most vice-chancellors of elite and highly selective universities strongly supported the removal of fee caps (Quiggin, 2014), it was opposed by some (Kristjanson, 2014; Vann, 2014), and vigorously by one, Stephen Parker (Parker, 2014a, 2014b, 2015; Macdonald, 2014). The proposals failed to pass the upper house, and after persisting for three years the Coalition dropped its proposals in this form in 2016.

Et tu Brute? – Then fall, Caesar!

As we noted at the outset, the Victorian government reconstituted the boards of TAFE institutes in 2013, replacing the chairs of the boards whose directors had opposed the government's changes most vigorously. The minister said that this was to make the boards more 'commercially focused' (Ross, 2013b), because the sacked chairs lacked 'the ability to lead "a large and complex government business"' (Ross, 2013a), exactly the grounds that the minister had said were unnecessary three years previously as shadow minister (Parliament of Victoria, 2010: 4867). Yet the board chairs replaced by the government were successful leaders and owners of substantial businesses (Ross, 2013a; Sheehan, 2013). The new board chairs obtained the resignations of the TAFE directors who had criticized government policy openly, yet the outgoing director of Holmesglen Institute, Bruce Mackenzie, had 'more commercial flare in his little finger than those who would want to govern the sector going forward' according to his outgoing board chair, who had founded Kane Constructions when he was 27 in the 1970s and which in 2013 had 'an annual turnover of between $400m and $500m' (Ross, 2013a).

The Victorian government's dismissal of TAFE chairs and ultimately directors was thus attacked for being hypocritical and dishonest, but no one questioned its legitimacy. TAFE institutes were considered extensions if not parts of the relevant government department by the ministers and officials who were insisting that the institutes compete as if they were autonomous private bodies. The public agreed that the government was directly responsible for TAFE institutes, for it held the government accountable for institutes' decisions to close programmes and campuses, rather than regarding them as the independent decisions of autonomous bodies.

In contrast, the Australian government made no move to dismiss or even discipline the chairs, governing boards or vice-chancellors who had criticized and campaigned against the government's policy of deregulating fees. Of course, any move to do so would have been met with outrage as an illegitimate infringement on universities' institutional autonomy and vice-chancellors' intellectual freedom, two concepts that are largely foreign to vocational education in Australia, and perhaps elsewhere.

Principals and agency

This chapter illustrates that in Victoria, and perhaps other jurisdictions, power in public vocational education is retained by the government and its officials, and that heads of institutes and chairs of boards have authority only to implement government policy without publicly questioning its efficacy, let alone its wisdom. The government and its officials treated the issue as an instance of the classic principal–agent problem, where the government as principal exercised its powers to ensure that its interests were served by the institutes as agents.

The Australian government took the opposite position with universities. The dispute over fee deregulation extended over years rather than the months that the TAFE cuts occupied, and unlike the Victorian government in 2012, the Australian government did not have a majority in both Houses of Parliament and had to persuade several cross-benchers in the upper house to get its legislation passed. The course of the public debate was therefore crucial for the Australian government's proposals to be legislated. Yet the Australian government and its ministers made no overt move against the vice-chancellors who so actively opposed its policies.

This story illustrates that the divide between vocational and higher education is just as deep in the institutionalization of power as it is in curriculum, quality assurance, financing, funding levels and other, more commonly observed, features of the sectoral divide (Wheelahan, 2000).

References

Australian Government (2014) 'Department of Education budget statements. Outcome 3: Higher education, research and international'. Canberra: Department of Education. Online. http://education.gov.au/portfolio-budget-statements-2014-15 (accessed 25 April 2017).

Byron, J. (2015) 'What next on uni deregulation, Mr Pyne: A horse's head? *The Australian*, 11 March. Online. www.theaustralian.com.au/higher-education/opinion/what-next-on-uni-deregulation-mr-pyne-a-horses-head/news-story/3dcb18767efe4a4f64678f735138bc84 (accessed 25 August 2016).

Commonwealth of Australia (2009) 'Transforming Australia's higher education system'. Canberra: Department of Education, Employment and Workplace Relations. Online. www.voced.edu.au/content/ngv%3A14895 (accessed 4 May 2016).

— (2014) 'Budget 2014–15: Budget measures. Budget paper no. 2: 2014–15. expense measures: education. Canberra: Commonwealth of Australia. Online. www.budget.gov.au/2014-15/content/bp2/html/index.htm (accessed 25 April 2017).

Dunckley, M. and Mather, J. (2012) 'Gillard's training reform hit by blowout'. *Australian Financial Review*, 2 July, 1–10.

Gittins, R. (2014) 'Why "competition" means university fees will rise'. *Sydney Morning Herald*, 31 May. Online. www.smh.com.au/business/why-competition-means-university-fees-will-rise-20140530-399pd.html (accessed 13 May 2017).

Griffiths, R. (2012) 'Market failure caused TAFE disaster'. *The Australian*, 16 May. Online. www.theaustralian.com.au/higher-education/opinion/market-failure-caused-tafe-disaster/story-e6frgcko-1226356632503 (accessed 22 May 2012).

Higgins, T. (2016) 'Fee deregulation won't save taxpayers a cent in the long run'. *The Australian*, 13 April. Online. www.theaustralian.com.au/higher-education/opinion/fee-deregulation-wont-save-taxpayers-a-cent-in-the-long-run/news-story/7b204e14fadc069b438da34246557543 (accessed 25 August 2016).

Irving, H. (n.d.) 'Australian federation'. Civics and Citizenship Education website. Online. www.civicsandcitizenship.edu.au/cce/helen_irving,9939.html (accessed 23 November 2016).

Kniest, P. (2014) 'How much will a uni degree cost?' National Tertiary Education Union. 27 May. Online. www.nteu.org.au/article/How-much-will-a-uni-degree-cost%3F-16333 (accessed 25 April 2017).

Kristjanson, L. (2014) 'V-C slams fee deregulation'. *The Scan*, 27 May. Online. http://the-scan.com/2014/05/29/22509/ (accessed 9 June 2014).

Macdonald, E. (2014) 'Vice-chancellor gets backing for tough stance over reforms'. *Canberra Times*, 4 December, 4.

Mackenzie, B. (2012) 'Message to all staff: State budget impact on Holmesglen'. MS, Holmesglen Institute of TAFE, Melbourne.

Moodie, G. (2014a) 'More expensive, more elite: Higher education in five years'. *The Conversation*, 14 May. Online. https://theconversation.com/more-expensive-more-elite-higher-education-in-five-years-26641 (accessed 13 May 2017).

— (2014b) 'Sorry Tony, the student demo on Q&A was democracy in action'. *The Conversation*, 6 May. Online. https://theconversation.com/sorry-tony-the-student-demo-on-qanda-was-democracy-in-action-26321 (accessed 13 May 2017).

NCVER (National Centre for Vocational Education Research) (2014) 'Australian vocational education and training statistics: Students and courses 2013: Publicly funded training providers'. Adelaide: National Centre for Vocational Education Research. Online. www.voced.edu.au/content/ngv%3A62832 (accessed 19 August 2016).

Noonan, P. (2014) 'Learning from Victoria's TAFE mistakes'. *The Conversation*, 7 December. Online. https://theconversation.com/learning-from-victorias-tafe-mistakes-34646 (accessed 13 May 2017).

Norling, K. (2012) 'Media coverage of TAFE cuts to June 5'. National Tertiary Education Union website. 5 June. Online. http://www.nteu.org.au/women/article/Media-Coverage-of-TAFE-Cuts-to-June-5-12870 (accessed 13 May 2017).

Parker, S. (2014a) 'Letting the market rip will suck the soul out of universities'. *Conversation*, 2 May. Online. https://theconversation.edu.au/article-26216 (accessed 25 August 2016).

— (2014b) 'Stephen Parker: Higher education changes a "fraud on the electorate"'. *The Conversation*, 2 December. Online. https://theconversation.com/stephen-parker-higher-education-changes-a-fraud-on-the-electorate-34909. Online. https://theconversation.edu.au/article-34909 (accessed 13 May 2017).

— (2015) 'Drawing positives from negatives: Looking back at the higher education reforms'. *The Conversation*, 17 March. Online. https://theconversation.com/drawing-positives-from-negatives-looking-back-at-the-higher-education-reforms-38890 (accessed 13 May 2017).

Parliament of Australia (2014) Committee Hansard, Senate Education and Employment Legislation Committee, Friday, 10 October: Higher Education and Research Reform Amendment Bill 2014. Online. http://parlinfo.aph.gov.au/parlInfo/search/display/display.w3p;db=COMMITTEES;id=committees%2Fcommsen%2F7634a65f-301e-4ee9-8932-99d7e5efd482%2F0001;query=Id%3A%22committees%2Fcommsen%2F7634a65f-301e-4ee9-8-932-99d7e5efd482%2F0000%22 (accessed 25 April 2017).

Parliament of Victoria (2010) Parliamentary debates (Hansard), Legislative Council, 56th Parliament, 1st session, Thursday, 16 September (extract from book 14). Online. www.parliament.vic.gov.au/images/stories/daily-hansard/Council_Feb-Jun_2010/Council_Daily_Extract_16_September_2010_from_Book_14.pdf (accessed 13 May 2017).

— (2012) Parliamentary debates (Hansard), Legislative Council, 57th Parliament, 1st session, Tuesday, 27 November (extract from book 19). Online. www.parliament.vic.gov.au/images/stories/daily-hansard/Council_2012/Council_Daily_Extract_Tuesday_27_November_2012_from_Book_19.pdf (accessed 13 May 2017).

Preiss, B. (2015) 'Victorian TAFEs record estimated $50 million loss'. *The Age*, 16 April. Online. www.theage.com.au/victoria/victorian-tafes-record-estimated-50-million-loss-20150416-1mm68v.html (accessed 20 August 2016).

Quiggin, J. (2014) 'Three misguided beliefs of the Group of Eight universities'. *The Conversation*, 11 September. Online. https://theconversation.com/three-misguided-beliefs-of-the-group-of-eight-universities-31334 (accessed 13 May 2017).

Ross, J. (2011) 'Skills reform stoush'. *The Australian*, 21 October. Online. www.theaustralian.com.au/higher-education/skill-reform-stoush/story-e6frgcjx-1226172111688 (accessed 23 October 2011).

— (2012) '"Rip-off" college corners education market'. *The Australian*, 22 March. Online. www.theaustralian.com.au/higher-education/rip-off-college-corners-education-market/story-e6frgcjx-1226306500387 (accessed 24 August 2016).

— (2013a) 'Business chiefs not qualified for TAFE'. *The Australian*, 3 April. Online. www.theaustralian.com.au/higher-education/business-chiefs-not-qualified-for-tafe/story-e6frgcjx-1226611209714 (accessed 3 April 2013).

— (2013b) 'Victorian TAFE chairs "sacked"'. *The Australian*, 28 March. Online. www.theaustralian.com.au/higher-education/victorian-tafe-chairs-sacked/story-e6frgcjx-1226608521445 (accessed 30 March 2013).

Ryan, C. (2014) 'Impact of the Australian higher education funding reforms'. Melbourne Institute Policy Brief 2/14, University of Melbourne. Online. http://melbourneinstitute.unimelb.edu.au/__data/assets/pdf_file/0010/2168191/pb2014n02.pdf (accessed 13 May 2017).

Shakespeare, W. (2012) *Julius Caesar*. Ed. Cox, J.D. Peterborough, Ontario: Broadview/Internet Shakespeare Editions. Online. http://internetshakespeare.uvic.ca/doc/JC_M/scene/3.1/ (accessed 22 August 2016).

Sheehan, B. (2012) 'Once was TAFE'. *The Scan*, 29 April. Online. https://the-scan.com/2012/04/29/once-was-tafe/ (accessed 22 August 2016).

— (2013) 'Excuses for heavy-handed TAFE sackings don't hold up'. *The Conversation*, 3 April. Online. https://theconversation.com/excuses-for-heavy-handed-tafe-sackings-dont-hold-up-13178 (accessed 13 May 2017).

Strong, G. (2012) 'Lessons to be learnt'. *The Age*, 25 May. Online. www.theage.com.au/national/education/lessons-to-be-learnt-20120524-1z7v0.html (accessed 24 May 2012).

Tomazin, F. (2012) 'Minister rages against rorts for courses'. *The Age*, 27 May. Online. www.theage.com.au/victoria/minister-rages-against-rorts-for-courses-20120526-1zbzq.html (accessed 27 May 2012).

Vann, A. (2014) 'Federal budget update'. Charles Sturt University blog, 28 May. Online. http://blog.csu.edu.au/2014/05/28/federal-budget-update/ (accessed 15 April 2015).

Victorian Government (2008) 'Securing jobs for your future: Skills for Victoria'. Melbourne: Department of Innovation, Industry and Regional Development. Online. www.education.vic.gov.au/Documents/training/providers/rto/securjobsfuture.pdf (accessed 24 August 2016).

Wheelahan, L. (2000) *Bridging the Divide: Developing the institutional structures that most effectively deliver cross-sectoral education and training*. Leabrook, South Australia: National Centre for Vocational Education Research. Online. www.ncver.edu.au/publications/509.html (accessed 25 August 2016).

Wikipedia (n.d.) 'Commonwealth'. Online. https://en.wikipedia.org/wiki/Commonwealth#Australia (accessed 23 November 2016).

Part Three

Introduction: The Body Politic: Citizenship, Community and Professionalism

Maire Daley

Mary Dietz suggested that Machiavelli's intention in writing *The Prince* was to deceive Lorenzo de' Medici, to trap him into acting in such a way as would destroy him; in contrast, John Langton argued that Machiavelli sought to teach the prince how to govern so that the autocratic state could evolve into a republic (Langton and Dietz, 1987). This is a classic argument that illustrates how profoundly different conclusions can be drawn from the same piece. Dietz (Langton and Dietz, 1987) concedes that to truly know Machiavelli's intention you probably would have to have been there, but that too is arguable.

Perhaps some difficulties in reading arise because of his teaching style. We might call his approach didactic, which might have limitations as a methodology, and we don't know the extent to which his advice was heeded by the prince, but the process Machiavelli engages us in and offers the prince is an education.

While Machiavelli's intention and methodology (and gendered language) may be problematic, his description of the character of a good leader is relevant to a modern teacher:

> It makes him contemptible to be considered fickle, frivolous, effeminate, mean-spirited, irresolute, from all of which a prince should guard himself as from a rock; and he should endeavour to show in his actions greatness, courage, gravity, and fortitude; and in his private dealings with his subjects let him show that his judgments are irrevocable, and maintain himself in such reputation that no one can hope either to deceive him or to get round him.
>
> (Machiavelli, 1908: 87–8)

The central theme of the need for courage and intelligence is straightforward advice for a prince or a teacher today.

This part of our Machiavellian project invites colleagues to enter into an exploration of power and professionalism in FE by offering space for practitioners to consider how they experience professionalism, how their professionalism is supported or diminished by practices in the sector, and how that impacts on teaching and learning. At the heart of the debate on professionalism in the sector is the place of trust; Machiavelli cautions the prince, 'too much distrust render[s] him intolerable' (ibid.: 79).

Gary Husband starts by questioning the place of innovation within colleges, particularly where it is used as a measure for assessing effective teaching and good educational experiences. Exploring the effects of performativity, he argues that Machiavelli would not be surprised or shocked by what he might find in FE colleges today, and links, in part, the narrowing of what education has come to mean in the sector to a focus on innovation as a method of teaching at the expense of a focus on deeper knowledge, skills and critical thinking.

Jim Crawley argues that groups of teachers, if they connect with each other, will make a difference to their own professionalism and to the experience of their students. Exploring theories of Dewey and Freire around collective activity and the value of collaboration in the process of learning, he asks, 'where are energies best placed?' Crawley proposes that 'we should organise, plot and prepare for drawing together acts of connection into principalities of people', and suggests that we need to work together as connected professionals in order to do that.

David Powell, while offering an explanation for the 'mess we are in' – with a teacher educators' enthusiasm – encourages teachers to collaborate and find ways to take control of and strengthen their professional exchanges. He explores Kemmis *et al.*'s (2014) concepts of ecologies of practices and supports their call to set up 'genuinely democratic, communicative space(s) for dialogue with leaders, students and co-workers'. He offers strategies and practical ideas that could empower individual teachers through collective actions and shows how strong professionals can make significant differences to the quality of the educational experiences of students.

Rajiv Khosla illustrates the frustrations to professional autonomy that both Ofsted and mocksteds can cause teachers in colleges. He uses his own experience of being a teacher educator and a trainee inspector, together with his research in a further education college (FEC), to illustrate how debilitating it can be for teachers not to feel valued. He suggests that, even if inspectors are effective, the inspection process is not. Mistrust in college managers overspills to include inspectors, and the greatest effect of current quality management systems in colleges is not improvements in teaching and learning but the continued diminution of the professional autonomy of teachers.

Alex Dunedin exposes the strength of gate-keeping processes and the assumptions that are made about what constitutes education when opportunities for learning are offered outside the academy. He outlines a process in which obstacles are met, and sidestepped, one after another in the development of the Ragged University project. The passion behind the venture comes across, together with the determination to hold on to key principals, and makes for an intriguing account. Dunedin concludes, 'The resources which are needed are found amongst us. We carry on because it is our life, our collective experiences, where memories and learnings are shared like bread.'

Vicky Duckworth, with an eye on the importance of critical education, provides insight into the barriers that some students face; she shows how systems and practices support or discourage students, and exposes the power relations in the classroom. She argues that education has the power to transform lives and highlights the impact on individuals of a deeply unequal society. She argues that teachers play a key role in challenging inequality, and concludes that the way we educate teachers is of critical importance, as they carry a golden opportunity to promote social justice and challenge inequality both 'in and out of the classroom'.

Like Machiavelli, the writers here offer an education through a critical process that is contextualized and uses cautionary tales, practical examples and learning from experience and scholarship – methods that have held for five centuries.

References

Kemmis, S., Wilkinson, J., Edwards-Groves, C., Hardy, I., Grootenboer, P., and Bristol, L. (2014) *Changing Practices, Changing Education*. Singapore: Springer.

Langton, J. and Dietz, M.G. (1987) 'Machiavelli's Paradox: Trapping or teaching the prince'. *American Political Science Review*, 81 (4), 1277–88.

Machiavelli, N. (1908) *The Prince*. Trans. Marriott, W.K. Originally 1515. Online. www.constitution.org/mac/prince.pdf (accessed 1 April 2017).

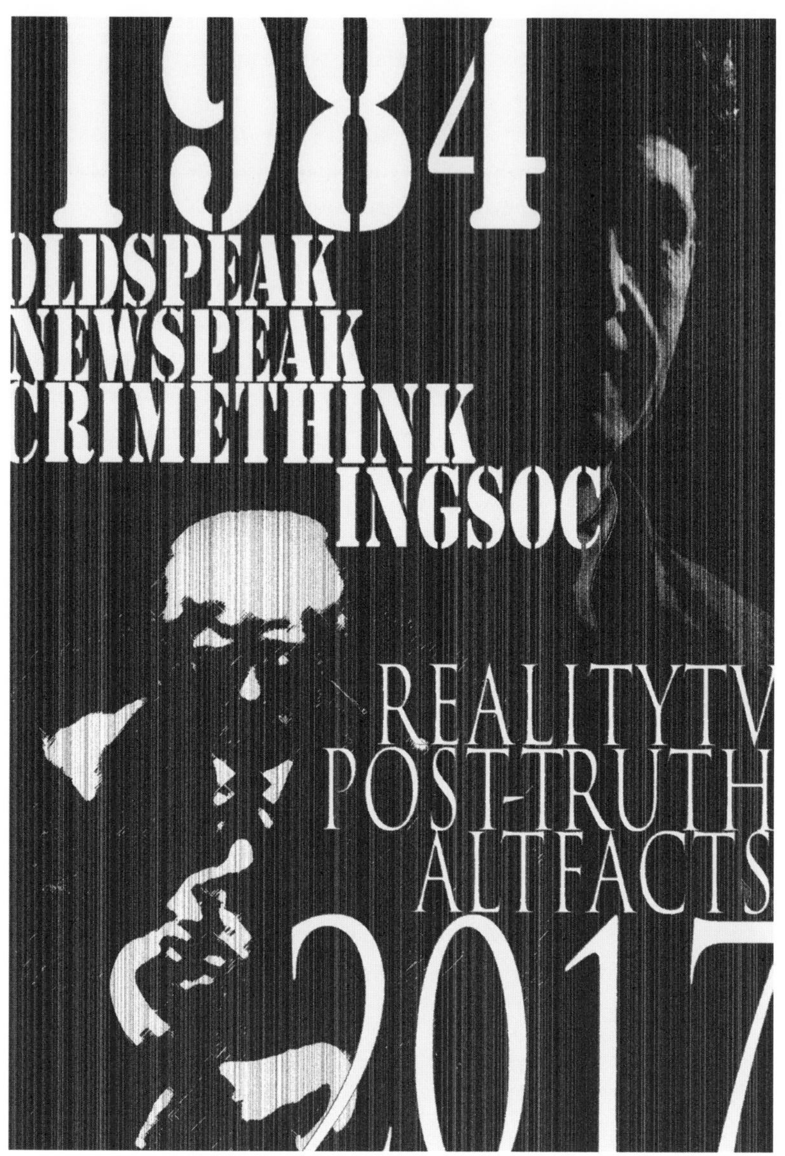

Bronek Kram

Power is not a means; it is an end. One does not establish a dictatorship in order to safeguard a revolution; one makes the revolution in order to establish the dictatorship. The object of persecution is persecution. The object of torture is torture. The object of power is power.

George Orwell, *1984*

Chapter 10

The renovation of Machiavellian innovation: A return to a celebration of the good

Gary Husband

Introduction

In the time between the writing of *The Prince* (Machiavelli, 1908) and of *Discourses* (Machiavelli, 1975), Machiavelli's stance on the source and meaning of innovation in leadership and power develops and changes significantly. In *The Prince*, Machiavelli represents the notion of innovation as development in government or the law, implemented by a new 'prince' in order to bring about change and maintain power. Later, in *Discourses*, a shift in the representation of innovation occurs: innovation comes to be presented as a return to original founding principles of kingdoms and empires that have become corrupted over time. Machiavelli turns to Rome as an example of a great republic and argues for a 'restoration' of the proven and successful. In contrast to the interpretation presented by Machiavelli, the term 'innovation' in educational nomenclature has come to mean a continual creative and revolutionary approach to teaching, where anything seen to fall short of arbitrary measures of excellence is frequently devalued and labelled inadequate or insufficient. A Machiavellian interpretation of innovation, as a founding principle based on the great work of predecessors, provides us with an opportunity to return to a celebration of what is good and to value consistency and quality. As Machiavelli himself asserts, '[a] wise man ought always to follow the paths beaten by great men, and to imitate those who have been supreme' (Machiavelli, 1908: 22). This is, however, not to say that creativity, design and experimentation have no place within further education (FE). Quite the contrary – there is no better place for such endeavours.

It is not that long ago that I sat in a meeting room in (what will remain) an anonymous further education college in the UK. The discussion was heated and had been going for some time. The basic assertion by the chief protagonist was that 'we [the college] need to measure innovation, we need to assess the innovation of staff and record it in the annual review process'. When my initial shock and anger had subsided enough for me to trust my mouth not to say what I was actually thinking, I managed to stutter something about it being a ridiculous plan. I tried in vain to convince the assembled senior executive staff that it was in fact not just a bad idea, but in the international rankings of bad ideas it was seeded. I gave up protesting, (perhaps smugly) safe in the knowledge that it just wasn't realistically possible and in all likelihood would fizzle out at first contact with the poor individual who would have to try and implement it, which is of course what happened. However, this set me thinking about the language, behaviours and practices in college environments and the seemingly widening divide between teaching and learning and the strategic positioning of the neoliberal management of colleges.

It could be argued that Machiavelli was the original neoliberal, or the first, at least, to write a manual for neoliberalism's associated practices. However, Machiavelli has been much lauded but equally maligned in the centuries since his treatises on leadership were written. A student of history, Machiavelli was able to paint a colourful and detailed picture of his theories and ideas, drawing on the experiences of those he admired and also of those he did not. Given the many interpretations and philosophical analyses of Machiavelli's work, it is in some ways very easy to understand how his name has become associated with negative connotations and aspects of the didactic and soulless seizing and wielding of power. However, if read as satire or as a polemic interpretation of the actions of his peers and forefathers, Machiavelli's work takes on a different and more nuanced perspective, perhaps a commentary provided to secure his own position and future while barely disguising his distaste. Although such a portrait does not exist, I cannot help but imagine Machiavelli being represented in the finest oils of his time with his tongue pressed firmly in his cheek.

Literal translation of the depicted actions of despots and the descriptions of heartless or self-serving princes shields the reader from the underlying subtleties of language and nuance evident in both of Machiavelli's prominent works. Even when he is openly critiquing poor decisions, and offering warning or encouragement in rehearsing the actions of the more despicable characters portrayed (Pope Julius, Cesare Borgia and Alexander the Great, to name but a few), it is possible to detect an admiration coming through in the language and style of the descriptions. In his writing, Machiavelli only just manages to veil the frustrations so strikingly evident to him, as they must have been to him as a high-ranking official in the weakened state of Florence, while those around him, such as Cesare Borgia, carved out new states with a brash and forceful boldness that only having an army at your back could sustain. The methods of leadership depicted in *The Prince* are often distasteful to modern sensibilities, but such were the times that the actions taken by the successful leaders of the day were risky, decisive, imaginative and, in the literal sense of the word (which I will come back to later in this chapter), innovative. Although Machiavelli concentrated his attention and analysis on the upper echelons of the military and the ruling classes, his work also served as a series of allegories intended to inform many different types and situations of leadership. A friend recently confided that she had read *The Prince* in preparation for parenthood!

When applying a relatively light analysis of much of the practice of management and leadership within current FE contexts across the UK, it is easy to draw parallels with Machiavelli's work. Much of what is described in *The Prince* offers an easy and relatively simple metaphor for the current and continued policy drive towards regionalization and merger, quality-driven accountability, performance indicator-based review and the more hegemonic practices from business and industry prevalent in senior management suites. I am sure that, given the opportunity to review much current practice, Machiavelli would find nothing new or surprising. However, I believe there is one distinct difference in practice that would cause a raised eyebrow to the already distorted imaginary portrait of Machiavelli described previously, namely language, or, more accurately, the changing subtext and nuance associated with many common phrases in further education.

As translators have made successive and successful attempts at modernizing the original text and teasing out Machiavelli's meaning, they must have been keenly aware of the author's disposition to clarity and direct language. Machiavelli's work is so important because he was an ardent student of the classics, and he communicated these stories without feeling the need to embellish them with subtlety or intrigue. A rich and vibrant history forms the backdrop to *The Prince*, which is precisely, concisely and accurately conveyed. In contrast, when reading policy documents or college strategic plans or attending meetings in FE colleges you might be forgiven for believing that you had fallen into some sort of Orwellian *1984*-esque nightmare where all are communicating in Newspeak. Abbreviations and acronyms abound and almost everything is said to be synergistic or pump-primed. Sentences are often needlessly extended with words that express little. More has become less in the language of FE, and as a sector FE is the poorer for it. Abstruse language, however, is itself not the most troubling factor. Most troubling are the underlying beliefs and related actions that this new form of language is trying to express: performativity in accountability, quantification as a driver for pedagogy, and the narrowing of what constitutes education.

A short time perusing the websites of colleges will amass a fine collection of mission, vision and value statements. On close inspection, very few stand out as different or meaningful, because they largely say the same things. The words 'excellence', 'collaboration', 'enterprising' and 'innovative' all appear regularly and prominently. The desire to deliver on these public promises is evident, but these statements descend into little more than rhetoric. What do they actually mean? Taking 'excellence' as an example, it can mean so many things (excellent teaching, excellent buildings, excellent students, *ad infinitum*), and it is very contextually dependent. In short, it means many things but is often used to give the impression of considered action. The use of the word 'innovation', however, has become increasingly pervasive and embedded in further education. Few ideas are presented without the addition of being innovative or generating innovation or supporting innovative synergies. Innovation has seemingly become the ubiquitous measure of everything in FE. There are statements calling for innovative teaching, innovative learning, innovative enterprise and innovative business practice, but what consequences are related to these behaviours and actions? As Silver (1999: 145) highlights, 'to stimulate innovation' invites us to ask not only 'What kind of innovation?', but also 'Whose innovation and in whose interests?' These considerations are sadly and frequently lost within the current rhetoric and discourse in FE.

Innovation in teaching and professional practice is now so universally lauded, expected and demanded that it has almost come to mean something entirely different. Statements appear that require 'innovation in practice', where simply substituting 'good' or 'imaginative' would yield more meaning. Innovation is now measured and has caused a shift in both expectation and experience. Related language has been downgraded in the process of elevating innovation. A simplistic but interesting comparison is provided by considering the meaning of the word 'satisfactory'. In general, everyday discourse 'satisfactory' has come to mean something less than good or not as good as it could be. How would being described as a satisfactory parent or lover make you feel? The point here is that although education, and specifically further education, may not be the cause of language value shifts, they are victims of it.

New descriptor	**Old descriptor**
Satisfactory	Poor
Good	Satisfactory
Innovative	Good
World-changing (Well done!)	Excellent

Figure 10.1: The changing meaning of descriptors (slightly tongue in cheek)

Extending and escalating the previous example using 'satisfactory', consider Figure 10.1. The expectation that teaching and learning will be good has now been supplanted in the language of public-facing documents and of policy and shared-values statements by the use of innovation. The problem with this approach is not that innovation is bad, but rather that being good (at teaching, support, admin ... insert anything you like here) is no longer good enough. The expectation that practice must somehow be eternally changing, reinventing, repositioning and indeed innovating is, however, not sustainable. This position is exhausting and adds to the lie that somehow innovation is quantifiable and related to performance. This is also where we return once more to Machiavelli. Although he did not use any word related directly to innovation he certainly commented on invention, reinvention and change and on political acts of innovative leadership, and his own position also shifted.

Godin (2014) highlights how Machiavelli's views changed over the years between *The Prince* and *Discourses* and how he came to view innovation (political and military manoeuvring, and wisdom in leadership) not as the pursuit of the new and always untested, but as the ability to adapt the successful practice of others into a new arena, that is, as imagination in adaptation and not necessarily in creation. Although Machiavelli was seemingly an admirer of innovation, he did not see it as a constant process of renewal or of endlessly seeking new ways of achieving the same end. He would have seen that as wasteful, inefficient and an unnecessary expenditure of time and resources. Instead, he drew on the valuable, proven and successful (if not always savoury) practices of ancient Rome, contemporary Italy and the wider arena of Europe. A slightly more modern example that illustrates this point comes from Henry Ford, who famously quipped, 'I see no advantage in these new clocks. They run no faster than the ones made 100 years ago' (Kirov, 2016: 28)

This has interesting parallels with the current discourse in further education. If assessed, measured and inspected educators stopped trying to create innovative methods to replace tried and tested practice, they may start to focus on refinement, detail, and depth. This requires an emphasis on high-quality, well-planned and robust teaching instead of a drive for constant innovation in which the vehicle of delivery becomes more important than the subject matter itself; that is to say, it is all form and no substance. In summary, then, Machiavelli teaches us more about language and clarity of expression than about leadership and management practices, in FE as elsewhere. My reservations, however, should not be misunderstood. There is nothing wrong with innovative teaching practice; it should be commended, shared and celebrated. But should it be measured, demanded and inspected? Probably not, or, to be more Machiavellian, definitely not.

References

Godin, B. (2014) 'The politics of innovation: Machiavelli and political innovation, or, How to stabilize a changing world' (Working Paper 17). Project on the Intellectual History of Innovation, Montreal.

Kirov, B. (2016) *Henry Ford: Quotes and Facts*. North Charleston, SC: CreateSpace Independent Publishing Platform.

Machiavelli, N. (1908) *The Prince*. Trans. Marriott, W.K. Originally 1515. Online. www.constitution.org/mac/prince.pdf (accessed 1 April 2017).

— (1975) *The Discourses of Niccolò Machiavelli*. Trans. Walker, L.J. Originally 1531. London: Routledge and Kegan Paul.

Silver, H. (1999) 'Managing to innovate in higher education'. *British Journal of Educational Studies*, 47 (2), 145–56.

Mia Moore

The more powerful the class, the more it claims not to exist.

Guy Debord, trans. Ken Knabb,
The Society of the Spectacle

Chapter 11

The prince and the paupers: The mean end of the stick

Alex Dunedin

Introduction

Machiavelli's writing has shaped many managerial perspectives and practices. Whatever you make of it, whether you see it as a manual on taking and holding power in a state or as a satire, it articulates how duplicity and amorality can be key organizational practices. This chapter argues that the ascendant managerial and bureaucratic governing structures in our culture create a gulf between public policy and practice, leaving people stranded both within and without institutions. Furthermore, when communities attempt to develop civic and educational activities, barriers are put in place that preclude their progress. To illustrate this argument, ideas from *The Prince* will be contrasted with others drawn from Mark Twain's *The Prince and the Pauper*, demonstrating the latter's more empathetic and humane values and suggesting different ways we can engage with the world.

I run a free, open and informal educational project called Ragged University. Inspired by Victorian communities that created their own ragged schools, it is an initiative in which everyone is respected as having valuable knowledge that can be shared to promote learning outside of institutional spaces. However, running a grass-roots community organization comes with hidden problems, so a model has developed that can operate without budget, equipment or fixed premises and utilizes available infrastructure and common technology to facilitate public events. The following vignettes illustrate some of the common experiences of a community of people trying to organize individual-led education. The dominant rhetoric of policy holds high its aspirational ends to justify its means, and in the process practices are governed and ultimately controlled with a disregard for the collateral damage at the grass-roots level. Power can blind those who wield it and limit perspectives. A failure to learn from the experience that others live through results in a mean, homogenized end that reproduces the existing landscape, one in which policy leads to the knowledge and skills of passionate intelligent people being peripheralized and unvalued.

Permission to exist

> Let us change the tense for convenience.
>
> (Twain, 2006: 100)

The inspiration for the Ragged University project emerged from the needs and aspirations of its participants, recognizing that the knowledge and skills people have are a vital part of a society in which everyone can find belonging and a part to play. Without these opportunities people may be marginalized and exploited. This ethos is evident in Thomas Guthrie's pamphlet 'A plea for the ragged schools; or Prevention better than cure', which rehearsed the effects of marginalization: 'These neglected children, whom we have left in ignorance, and starved into crime, must grow up into criminals, – the pest, the shame, the burden, the punishment of society' (Guthrie, 1847: 15). A form of this marginalization exists still and triggered the establishment of the current project, which drew on the history and principles that had previously brought about free primary school education in the UK. Calling this project 'Ragged University' was powerful because it conferred a common ownership of the concept of knowledge and community. However, here we met a problem: we were told to get permission from the Secretary of State for Business Innovation and Skills to use the term 'university'.

'University' can only be used in a name by a body that satisfies governmental criteria; these relate to student numbers, good governance and degree-awarding powers. The words 'association', 'group' and 'co-operative' all fall under the same Act, and also require authorization. This bureaucratization and its associated administrative burden became significant obstacles. We explained that we were alluding to a concept that 'everybody is a Ragged University, a unique and distinct body of knowledge accredited with their life experience and with a membership of one' (Ragged University, 2011). The problem then moved into one of deferral, and even though we were informed it was a laudable project we needed to continue to pursue authorization for using the word before we used the name. The identity of the project was being controlled by decision-makers far from the community: instantly, the network of people involved started to feel the costs associated with the formalization of the project. Machiavelli writes:

> Such a government, having been established by the new prince, knows that it cannot maintain itself without the support of his power and friendship, and it becomes its interest therefore to sustain him.
>
> (Machiavelli, 1998: 18)

Displacement of volunteers

> Particularly new comers – such as small husbandmen turned shiftless and hungry upon the world because their farms were taken from them to be changed to sheep ranges.
>
> (Twain, 2006: 580)

We persisted, and by encouraging people who loved what they do to share their knowledge for free in social spaces like pubs, cafés and libraries we managed to create public events that were open to everyone. The first events happened in a London pub, and quickly we saw that people were getting something valuable from them. The plan was to let happenstance decide who was to talk about what and resist the idea of gate-keeping. Learning and knowledge were to be respected as embedded in dialogue and eclecticism. Other routes result in a progressive narrowing of what becomes valued and who gets to take part; instead our aim was to democratize the experience as much as possible: anyone can contribute as a speaker (so long as any talk is consistent with the Universal Declaration of Human Rights).

Soon people got in touch from other cities: in Glasgow and Manchester groups asked if they could arrange an event of their own. We started to build a networked organization which offered mutual support so that the project could grow, with broader activities. It was exciting, the talks were interesting and mixed, the audiences were a range of people who could not be pinned down to reductive demographics. The project had reached a certain size; we had identified some needs and we developed and put into practice a model that could meet those needs. There was a demand for regular events in all the cities; we just had to work out the logistics that made more possible.

In our native spaces, amongst our friendships, so much learning and teaching takes place. Surely we could list ourselves as an opportunity for people to volunteer. Surely it would be easy to tap into the multi-million-pound-resourced volunteer organizations set up to provide community and charitably oriented activities. Quickly we were to find that to be a part of volunteer provision we needed to have in place certain features such as insurance policies, often charitable status, and usually money enough to pay for a membership. That the voluntary sector's financial and legal mode of operation may impede the agency of communities to organize is of concern. Machiavelli writes:

> A prince, moreover, who wishes to keep possession of a country that is separate and unlike his own, must make himself the chief

> and protector of the smaller neighbouring powers. ... He has merely to see to it that they do not assume too much authority, or acquire too much power.
>
> (Machiavelli, 1998: 10)

Charity registration

> Kings cannot ennoble thee, thou good, great soul, for One who is higher than kings hath done that for thee; but a king can confirm thy nobility to men.
>
> (Twain, 2006: 93)

We persisted, and under our own steam ran events at which people shared their knowledge. It was becoming clear, however, that we needed to have some formal bureaucracies in place before a whole wider infrastructure could be accessed, in terms of volunteering, resources, support and finance to build upon what we had achieved. We started to look at formalizing as a charity and made attempts to register (perhaps ironically, formal universities are charities and function under charitable law). Without gathering £5,000, in England we could not become a registered charity. A policy to get communities to start their own businesses to fund any charitable activities was pushed. However, the rhetoric of becoming a social enterprise was problematic. This presents opportunity costs: running a business is one thing, developing a free education project is another; the danger was that the creation of a business was to take primacy. Thus, we looked at registering as a charity in Scotland, but the process of responding to subsequent questions aimed at ensuring the charitable nature of the project became too onerous for us as volunteers.

A further challenge was that in describing the project as education-based we met with the stipulations that only trained teachers could do talks and that learning outcomes needed to be demonstrated for each and every person who attended events. Our argument that education can mean other things – backed up by published and peer-reviewed educational research – was not seen as pertinent. We received advice elsewhere that we should form a board of trustees different from those we had nominated. We were advised to form a board from people with status and wealth if we wanted to be successful, but the chasing of celebrity or privilege seemed antithetical to the very principles of the informal communities from which the Ragged University had emerged. The response from the charity regulator appeared to amount to a type of twelve-step plan to replicate what formal education already does, and does well. Our project never had the intention of setting exams and recasting the informal in the image of the formal. It is a complementary space situated in communities where everyone – teacher or not – can participate in knowledge sharing and building. Ultimately, unless registered charitable status is conferred, access to funding becomes severely restricted for a project and limits its potential reach and impact. Machiavelli writes:

> In those states that are governed by an absolute prince and slaves, the prince has far more power and authority; for in his entire dominion no one recognizes any other superior but him.
>
> (Machiavelli, 1998: 15)

Access to funding

> And when he awoke in the morning and looked upon the wretchedness about him, his dream had had its usual effect – it had intensified the sordidness of his surroundings a thousandfold.
>
> (Twain, 2006: 5)

It was dawning on us that formalizing as a charity was too problematic, as it would bring the danger of changing the nature of the project from what the communities created to what the regulations stipulated. We continued to look for other routes for resourcing our community activities. Seeking corporate funding was quickly ruled out, as corporations insist on branding as well as various open-ended legal stipulations. We looked at a grant from the Co-operative Group, but the Group insisted that they had legal access to all the paperwork of the organization. This was unacceptable, as we had drawn up non-disclosure agreements with people who had shared their work. We looked at other grants and started to think through what was left. To get funding we had to produce measurements of outcomes, but introducing this kind of bureaucracy into the community setting was unacceptable: very quickly there was strong and clearly worded feedback from members of the community that this was not what people had signed up for. Measuring what goes on in these interpersonal spaces discourages many people from attending, leaving a narrow bandwidth of the usual suspects: predominantly people who are familiar with and understand the nature of the outcomes and measurements culture, usually formally educated, financially better off, middle-class sections of society that work with such bureaucracies. Imposition of these measures would change the role of the coordinators of the events from stewarding amongst the community to data-mining for policy-makers and accountants. Many conversations were had and it was clear that if the soul of the project was to remain intact a focus on measurements and outcomes should not be entertained. Such a shift might significantly intimidate and exclude people who lack literacy skills from taking active and valid participatory roles in organizing community events. Fundamentally, we understood that managing the paperwork would displace the community activity itself. Projects become encumbered with bureaucracies and with values that serve those bureaucracies, like cuckoos imposing themselves on communities. The message is 'no engagement, no provisioning', and thus activities and communities are controlled. Machiavelli writes:

> Colonies are not very expensive to the prince; they can be established and maintained at little, if any, cost to him. ... And as those who are thus injured by him become dispersed and poor, they can never do him any harm, whilst all the other inhabitants remain on the one hand uninjured, and therefore easily kept quiet, and on the other hand they are afraid to stir, lest they should be despoiled as the others have been.
>
> (Machiavelli, 1998: 9)

Who's allowed to make what meaning?

> He had ceased to ask questions of anyone, since they brought him only insult instead of information.
>
> (Twain, 2006: 11)

Formalized bureaucracies have a talent for demarcating who gets to make what meaning, reflecting their tendency to create gate-keeping behaviours within the politics of knowledge. Once I was invited to present at a conference on 'Inequalities in Historical Perspective'. I gave a talk on research I had read on social capital. I argued that inclusive forms tend to have positive externalities and exclusive forms tend to have negative externalities. A visiting academic said to me, 'Do you think you should be using this academic language?' I replied that I didn't think they would understand the vernacular of the sink estate where I lived; a 'Tower of Babel' conversation ensued. On another occasion, two eminent thinkers who were interested in the project proffered me their thoughts: 'Maybe you might get traction somewhere in the fringes of the humanities, but certainly not in the STEM subjects.' The implications of this are huge – that one cannot have something valuable to offer if one comes from outside of the academic context. My response was that these traditions of thinking belong to us all and it is absurd to suggest that all learning and discovery is located within the formal halls of education. Participants of the Ragged University project have encountered many excellent thinkers who have created brilliant work that had been overlooked because they lack formal education. Inside informal spaces people can have these conversations and be valued for the working knowledge they demonstrate through interaction. A robust and accessible means of realizing the accreditation of prior learning would allow this knowledge to come to the fore; failing to allow this sets up the traditional regimes of truth which have come to represent how our world is ordered. Machiavelli writes:

> There should not be a free debate, for that is the principal instrument of sedition, but in the people's council only those who are invited by the magistrates to speak should do so, and only on the subject entrusted to them.
>
> (Machiavelli, 1998: 143)

Conclusion

And so the project continues; the communities still exist, people share and learn, events happen without any funding through people's involvement. It is a project born of passion for open education. Many people take part: professors talk alongside people without formal qualifications and enjoy the informal settings where they can explore ideas together. The resources that are needed are found amongst us. We carry on because it is our life – our collective experiences – where memories and learning are shared like bread. In those spaces everyone is welcome and everyone is valued as having something to share. The doors are always open, the events are always free. There it is safe to talk and safe to be true to our varied experiences. It is a space of conversation and mutual building. It is a concept of education in which authority is not invested in a person but located in a subject that we collectively negotiate with a sense of play. Held in such social spaces is a hope for a wider conversation, for a broader sense of participation in what we call knowledge.

References

Guthrie, T. (1847) 'A plea for the ragged schools; or, Prevention better than cure. 9th ed. Edinburgh: J. Elder. Online. https://archive.org/details/apleaforraggeds01guthgoog (accessed 9 March 2017).

Machiavelli, N. (1998) *The Prince*. Trans. Detmold, C.E. Ware: Wordsworth Editions.

Ragged University (2011) 'A rose is ragged by any other name ...'. The Eclectic, 10 April. Online. www.raggeduniversity.co.uk/2011/04/10/ragged-rebrand (accessed 9 March 2017).

Twain, M. (2006) *The Prince and the Pauper*. Originally 1882. Online. www.gutenberg.org/files/1837/1837-h/1837-h.htm (accessed 9 March 2017).

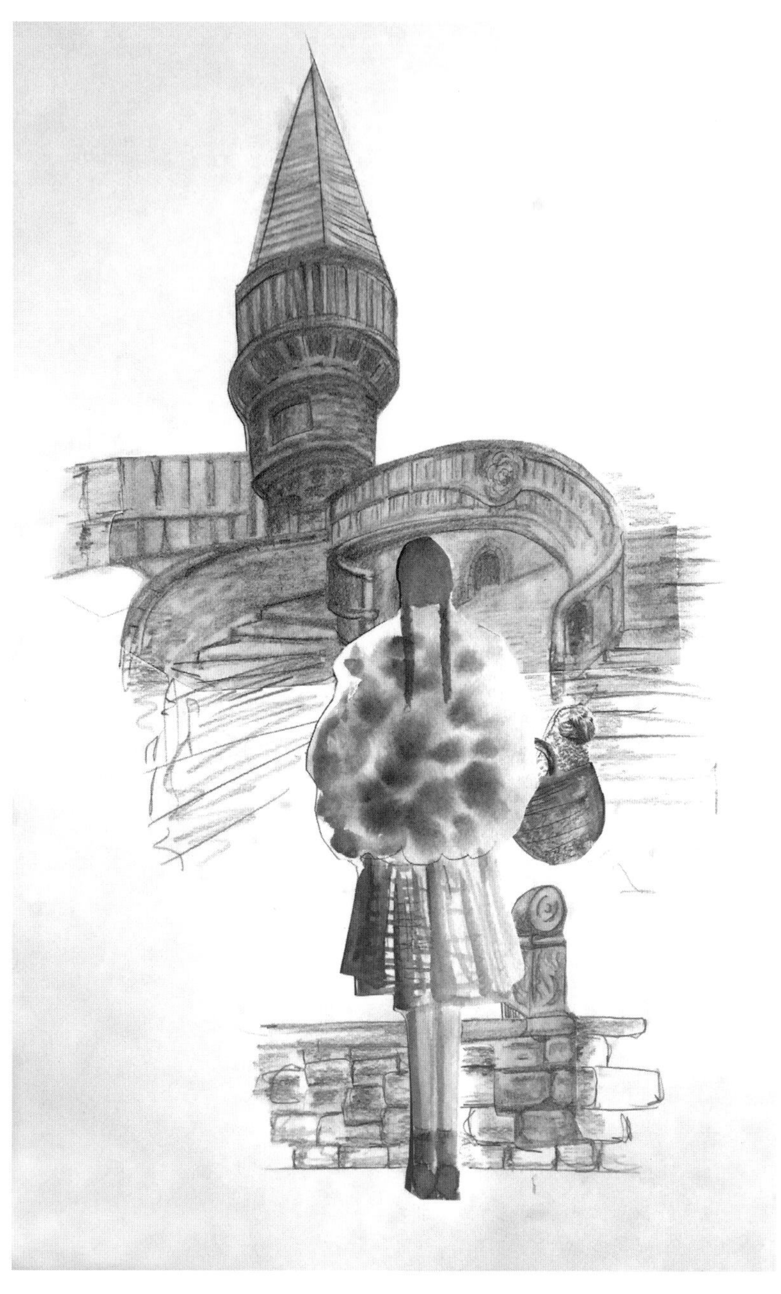

Gabi Clarke

'You've always had the power my dear, you just had to learn it for yourself.'

Glinda, the Good Witch of the North
(*The Wizard of Oz*)

Chapter 12

Principalities of people: Destabilizing the prince's power through acts of connection

Jim Crawley

Overthrow? ... Get connected!

Machiavelli (1908: 7) argued that those who remain 'poor and scattered ... are never able to injure' the prince. 'Poor and scattered' is a description which just about sums up the professional situation of many working in further education (FE). Machiavelli also believed that a prince who had held power for some time was more likely to have loyal and well-disposed subjects than a new prince. Even if that is true, the difficulty with FE is that princes (or princesses) rarely stay in power for very long. During the thirty years before the 2015 election 61 secretaries of state had been responsible for skills policy in Britain (City and Guilds, 2014: 2). That is a stunning number of different princes. Princes and princesses of the principal and senior manager variety may stay in post for longer than secretaries of state, but in an ever-changing sector many staff (including princes) have to cope with a new person in power every few years. Machiavelli recognizes that ruling by absolute power is often the approach taken when principalities are unstable, although he understands that this is unlikely to gain the goodwill of the people, and he doesn't advance it as the best strategy. The use of absolute power has been the favoured approach of governments and often that of local princes or princesses (principals), though few would admit this.

This chapter argues that overthrowing or overpowering the princes, their principalities and their absolute power would be exhausting, unlikely to achieve anything, potentially fatal (at least professionally), and more damaging to many than helpful to some. Not wishing to dampen spirits, however, the chapter proposes that there is another way which is far more likely to achieve some success and may even help practitioners to find more enjoyment and potentially empowerment as professionals working in FE.

In a nutshell, the idea is based on groups of FE teachers coming together to carry out small acts of connection – in *Dancing Princesses* terms they could be described as 'acts of resistance' (Ball and Olmedo, 2013: 94) – which they have agreed and planned themselves and which they think could make a difference to their teaching and their students' learning. If these acts of connection and those carrying them out could be further linked to others, they could build into larger connections or even a principality of people. This constitutes not so much a revolution as a process of recapturing and rebuilding localized pride and autonomy. Encouraging and positive results instil a feeling in participants that ownership has been gained of a small corner of their particular principality, and this can lead to a natural desire for more acts of connection and developing networks.

Acts of connection

The idea of people combining to carry out meaningful acts in education is not new. John Dewey (1916: 16) describes life as most 'educative' when 'an individual shares or participates in some conjoint activity', and that participation 'on equal terms' and 'fullness and freedom of interaction' are parts of education in 'a desirable society' (ibid.: 63). He argues for education to be part of society's democratic openness and believes that connecting with others in a 'shared learning experience' (ibid.: 12) is a crucial part of learning. Paulo Freire (1972) argues that education is a conversational process that takes place when people work together with a common aim, and that this can result in meaningful education that liberates rather than oppresses. One of his clearest statements of philosophy is contained in the sentence 'Knowledge emerges only through invention and re-invention, through the restless, impatient, continuing, hopeful inquiry human beings pursue in the world, with the world, and with each other' (Freire, 1972: 72). More recently, communities of practice have been advocated as opportunities for professionals to join together and participate in activities as a group over a period of time to solve problems. It is argued that this can lead to shared 'understandings concerning what they are doing and what this means in their lives and for their communities' (Lave and Wenger, 1991: 98).

What links these three examples to acts of connection is an emphasis on human interactions leading to a world where learning is constructed by humans from those interactions.

A more recent technical idea that can also be linked to acts of connection is that of marginal learning gains, an approach that has been part of British cycling, with great success in the 2008, 2012 and 2016 Olympics.

Marginal learning gains theory involves seeking small improvements in a number of different elements. Aggregating those small gains leads to a significant overall improvement (Rienzo *et al.*, 2016). Key components of this approach are participant buy-in and high-quality teamwork. The approach is appearing in educational contexts but has not yet become widely embedded in practice. It does, however, offer a further reinforcement of the potential of acts of connection to make a real difference.

Growing connections

It is not difficult to see how acts of connection would bring benefits for small groups of teachers in a local situation. It may not need to go beyond that, but it is important for a chapter such as this to suggest how further connections could build into something with more significance. Two examples of acts of connection in practice are described below.

The Sharing Innovation in Teacher Education (SITE) project

In 2011–12, a group of expert teacher educators from the South West Centre for Excellence in Teacher Training (SWCETT) conceived a project that involved sharing innovatory teacher education activities. A selection that the team had utilized and evaluated as successful in their own programmes was agreed, and the activities were placed in a project catalogue. In one or two cases the activities had also been commented on favourably by Ofsted during inspections of teacher education. The 'innovation catalogue' was then made available to teacher education teams from two universities, two FE colleges, one private training provider, and one regional infrastructure support organization, all in the south-west of England. Practitioners in these colleges selected two items from the catalogue, made use of them, then contributed in a number of ways to a project evaluation of their usefulness or otherwise. The project involved 16 teacher educators and more than 150 teacher trainees. The results suggested these acts of connection worked. Participants felt that:

- a significant majority of the innovations worked well and they would use them again
- their teacher education programmes could be improved by the use of such activities, and the process of project networking and evaluation helped participants actively engage.

The project's final report found that the collaborative, step-by-step, bottom-up approach was particularly welcomed by participants and that they would both use the innovation activities again and seek out further opportunities for such collaboration. Overall, it was concluded that this was 'an approach that could generally work well in many other aspects of the professional life of teachers in the [FE] sector' (Crawley, 2012: 11).

The Learning Design Support Environment project
This Economic and Social Research Council (ESRC) project ran from 2008 to 2011 and was aimed at 'enabling teachers to collaborate on how to plan and design their teaching' (Laurillard, 2012: 1). The project activity was focused on modelling 'learning designs' for higher-education (HE) lecturers in the use of, and through the medium of, technology. The project was based on the pedagogical principle that, if teachers are to adopt an innovation, whether by using technology, or in any other way, they need to believe it will be useful and they need to understand why. The project developed and made use of a specially tailored software environment that would support teachers in their development and construction of learning designs. Over one hundred HE academics engaged with different aspects of the project and its evaluation. The project evaluation reported that 'by [the teaching community's] adopting, adapting, trialling, and sharing their learning designs' and as a result of small changes and familiar pedagogies and technologies, signs of seeding innovation could be identified. It was argued that 'the teaching community' could 'develop a collective intelligence of what makes effective learning designs' (Laurillard, 2012: 5) from the approach of this project.

The presence of acts of connection (both technical and human), including practitioners working together to enhance teaching and learning through their joint efforts, is clearly visible across these two examples.

Connecting the connections

Machiavelli (1908) warned that people who have previously enjoyed liberty in their city or country will have 'greater hatred, and more desire for vengeance' when a new ruler arrives. With typical directness, he suggests that 'the safest way is to destroy them' (21). Although applying this reference may seem like exaggeration, I have been working in the sector long enough to remember enjoying a period of professional (and practical) liberty in the course of the 1970s and 1980s. There were also some generously funded initiatives and policies which at the time did make a real difference to many adults and young adults. Since FE college incorporation in 1993 and the imposition of managerial approaches that follow business principles, there is evidence of a gradual destruction of some of what had been so positive as prince after prince applies absolute power. We are now also entering a period of time when some of the components of FE (such as adult and community education) are experiencing a more rapid process of destruction (Crawley, 2015). Teachers responding to this destruction with 'hatred' and 'vengeance' is unlikely, however, to lead anywhere except to further destruction, and is not in the nature of most teachers, in any case.

As is often suggested in the precursor to this book (Daley *et al.*, 2015), resistance in some way to acts of managerial vandalism is essential. Hargreaves (2003: 24) argues that teachers can move from being casualties to being the catalysts that society demands that they are, but they must take ownership of their profession and 'build a new professionalism'. Gleeson *et al.* (2005) have described this as the making and taking of professionalism.

Having explored cunning plans and simple techniques associated with the concept of acts of connection, the chapter now moves on to propose that we should organize, plot and prepare for drawing together acts of connection into principalities of people, and that we need to work together as connected professionals in order to do that.

Firstly, this is not yet another fashion or fad and it is not an idea that has been made up during an afternoon coffee break. The ideas derive from a doctoral study (Crawley, 2014) that included a detailed examination of teacher professionalism in FE. A number of models of professionalism were critiqued, and this new model built from careful research combined with experience of over thirty years of working in the FE sector. Secondly, this is not an easy route to autonomy and improvement. It is a challenging and wide-ranging idea, and it will not be easy to achieve. Starting to move towards it through acts of connection, however, will be a worthwhile enterprise and on its own should build a strong foundation. The framework draws from a wide range of ideas and principles about teaching, learning and professionalism and blends them in a particular way. Writers including Dewey (1916), Dzur (2008), Freire (1972), Fuller and Unwin (2003), Hillier (2012), Lave and Wenger (1991), Rogers (1961), Sachs (2000) and Schön (1983) have all contributed their thinking to this model. How then does the model of the connected professional work?

There are four connections that combine to make a connected professional:

1. The Practical Connection – the practical underpinning of the teaching skills, knowledge, understanding and application that are essential for all teachers to be able to carry out their role.

2. The Democratic Connection – the active involvement in democratic action where practitioners work with other colleagues towards achieving agreed common goals.
3. The Civic Connection – the active engagement in civic action with the wider community to support and enact development with and for that community. This involves moving outside of the day-to-day interactions of education, and pursuing goals, activities and developments for and with the broader community.
4. The Networked Connection – the cultivation, involvement and sustaining of the means of active engagement with other professionals and the wider community.

One aspect of this model which is rarely present in others is the civic connection. Machiavelli (1908: 43) describes what he calls a 'civil principality', in which a 'leading citizen becomes the prince of his country, not by wickedness or any intolerable violence, but by the favour of his fellow citizens'. I am not arguing that a single prince finding favour is the solution, but that FE should reconnect with the broader community as part of a civic principality where the people have the say rather than the prince. By community I mean everyone from businesses to community groups to public and private services to local individuals. FE professionals could contribute in simple, small ways, such as by providing community taster sessions, revived adult and continuing education, community events, volunteering and joint work on local services. These civic acts of connection would help the sector and its professionals remember how they can help the community more fully and directly. By working with others than their own immediate colleagues, FE professionals can reclaim their true place as a central part of that community, rather than as a business alongside many others competing for funding and contracts.

The fourth, networked connection is the means by which a community of connected professionals will develop and grow, and is the crucial connection that helps it to work. The networked connection is the key to the other three, which are unlikely to become widely valued unless they are switched on and connected, and that connection sustained. Ideas that feature in research from Hargreaves (2003) and Veugelers and O'Hair (2005) support this approach, which starts with the development of what has been called network learning.

Network learning

Veugelers and O'Hair (2005) describe network learning as a process that helps teaching professionals learn and teach together more effectively. Network learning is characterized by sharing, critiquing and planning together, which helps to 'learn across cultures to identify, analyse and solve pertinent problems impacting teaching and learning' (Veugelers and O'Hair, 2005: 2). The idea of network learning draws on traditions of technology and computer networking, and argues that the use of learning technology should help learning to become more accessible and successful. As is often the case, the technology is not a mandatory component, but rather a tool for helping connections happen (Crawley, 2010; Garrison and Anderson, 2003; Selwyn, 2008). From a review of literature of examples of network learning, Veugelers and O'Hair (2005) found evidence of positive contributions to school improvement, facilitating professional development, developing and sharing resources and establishing international networks and relationships. Network learning can make acts of connection stronger, and help them to build. If the switch to activate the networked connection cannot be found, professionals will remain disconnected.

Building principalities of people

Since the route to becoming a connected professional is challenging and multi-faceted, and adds expectations of the work of FE teachers beyond what they already have in their overworked and overloaded lives, why would anyone want to move in that direction?

In the precursor to this book (Daley *et al.*, 2015), Joel Petrie (2015: 7) argues that 'to reclaim what has been lost in FE we may need to create stories, invisible spaces, and an FE sector of the mind'. The active, collaborative, bottom-up form of professionalism I am proposing in this chapter could create a sector of the mind, and the connected professionals involved could form principalities of people. Small acts of connection can make a difference and they do not involve a great deal of risk. They should be possible for most, if not all, who work in the sector. The building of principalities of people, or something very similar, will add value to our work in FE.

Pragmatically, of course, no one is likely to operate fully within all of the connections of the connected professional all the time, in just the same way that no teacher can be outstanding in every way all the time. Most will operate somewhere within the network of the four connections at any given time, with many connections on very good days and with just a few on less good days.

The key focus of the ideas in this chapter has been that we should seek to establish the strongest connections possible between groups of FE professionals so that they can stand and work together for the benefit of their students, their professional identity and the good of the greater community. That is why the groupings concerned deserve the title principalities of people. The princes and princesses may find this somewhat more connected set of people to be more troublesome, but they should also appreciate that the acts of connection will lead to both marginal gains and, potentially, major improvements. Throughout *The Prince*, Machiavelli himself (1908: 46) recognizes the value of having the people on the prince's side; he argues, 'it is necessary for a prince to have the people friendly, otherwise he has no security in adversity'.

If we do not try to move towards acts of connection, towards being connected professionals and building principalities of people, however, our future will continue to be disconnected and unfulfilled, and ultimately we will be unable to serve our students in the way they deserve.

References

Ball, S.J. and Olmedo, A. (2013) 'Care of the self, resistance and subjectivity under neoliberal governmentalities'. *Critical Studies in Education*, 54 (1), 85–96.

City and Guilds (2014) *Sense and Instability: Three decades of skills and employment policy*. London: City and Guilds.

Crawley, J. (2010) *In at the Deep End: A survival guide for teachers in post-compulsory education*. 2nd ed. London: Routledge.

— (2012) 'South West Centre for Excellence in Teacher Training (SWCETT): Sharing Innovation in Teacher Education (SITE) project evaluation report'. Online. http://teachereducatoruk.wikispaces.com/file/view/SITE%20Final%20 Report%20v2.pdf/443018608/SITE%20Final%20Report%20v2.pdf (accessed 21 June 2017).

— Crawley, J. (2014) 'How can a deeper understanding of the professional situation of LLS teacher educators enhance their future support, professional development and working context?' PhD Thesis, Bath Spa University of Bath.

— (2015) 'Adult education needs an urgent and radical rethink'. *The Conversation*, 30 March. Online. https://theconversation.com/adult-education-needs-an-urgent-and-radical-rethink-39391 (accessed 28 August 2016).

Daley, M., Orr, K., and Petrie, J. (eds) (2015) *Further Education and the Twelve Dancing Princesses*. Stoke-on-Trent: Trentham Books.

Dewey, J. (1916) *Democracy and Education: An introduction to the philosophy of education*. New York: Macmillan.

Dzur, A.W. (2008) *Democratic Professionalism: Citizen participation and the reconstruction of professional ethics, identity, and practice*. University Park, PA: Pennsylvania State University Press.

Freire, P. (1972) *Pedagogy of the Oppressed.* New York: Herder and Herder.

Fuller, A. and Unwin, L. (2003) 'Fostering workplace learning: Looking through the lens of apprenticeship'. *European Educational Research Journal*, 2 (1), 41–55.

Garrison, D.R. and Anderson, T. (2003) *E-Learning in the 21st Century: A framework for research and practice.* London: RoutledgeFalmer.

Gleeson, D., Davies, J., and Wheeler, E. (2005) 'On the making and taking of professionalism in the further education workplace'. *British Journal of Sociology of Education*, 26 (4), 445–60.

Hargreaves, A. (2003) *Teaching in the Knowledge Society: Education in the age of insecurity.* New York: Teachers College Press.

Hillier, Y. (2012) *Reflective Teaching in Further and Adult Education.* 3rd ed. London: Continuum.

Laurillard, D. (2012) A Learning Design Support Environment (LDSE) for teachers and lecturers: ESRC end of award report' (RES-139-25-0406). Swindon: Economic and Social Research Council.

Lave, J. and Wenger, E. (1991) *Situated Learning: Legitimate peripheral participation.* New York: Cambridge University Press.

Machiavelli, N. (1908) *The Prince.* Trans. Marriott, W.K. Originally 1513. New York: E.P. Dutton and Co.

Petrie, J. (2015) 'Introduction: How Grimm is FE?' In Daley, M., Orr, K., and Petrie, J. (eds) *Further Education and the Twelve Dancing Princesses.* Stoke-on-Trent: Trentham Books, 1–12.

Rienzo, C., Rolfe, H., and Wilkinson, D. (2016) 'Powerful learning conversations: Evaluation report and executive summary'. London: Education Endowment Foundation. Online. https://educationendowmentfoundation.org.uk/public/files/Projects/Evaluation_Reports/EEF_Project_Report_PowerfulLearningConversations (accessed 10 June 2017).

Rogers, C.R. (1961) *On Becoming a Person: A therapist's view of psychotherapy.* Boston: Houghton Mifflin.

Sachs, J. (2000) 'The activist professional'. *Journal of Educational Change*, 1 (1), 77–95.

Schön, D.A. (1983) *The Reflective Practitioner: How professionals think in action.* New York: Basic Books.

Selwyn, N. (2008) 'Realising the potential of new technology? Assessing the legacy of New Labour's ICT agenda 1997–2007'. *Oxford Review of Education*, 34 (6), 701–12.

Veugelers, W. and O'Hair, M.J. (eds) (2005) *Network Learning for Educational Change.* Maidenhead: Open University Press.

Lexie Cave

The greater the power, the more dangerous the abuse.

Edmund Burke, Speech on Middlesex Election

Chapter 13

Better to be feared than loved? The terrors of performativity in FE

Rajiv Khosla

> Upon this a question arises: whether it be better to be loved than feared or feared than loved? It may be answered that one should wish to be both, but, because it is difficult to unite them in one person, it is much safer to be feared than loved, when, of the two, either must be dispensed with.
>
> (Niccolò Machiavelli, *The Prince*)

This chapter investigates the impact of performance management systems on further education (FE) practitioners, by providing a unique insight into Ofsted from the point of view of a teacher and an additional inspector and combining it with the findings of research undertaken within a large FE college in the north of England.

As a practitioner in the FE sector since 2001, I have witnessed and experienced at first hand many changes and their implications. Ofsted's influence within the FE sector has grown, as have feelings of fear and resentment amongst some practitioners, leading to calls for the reform, and even the abolition, of the inspectorate (UCU, 2013). Changes in government policy, and the increasing impact and alleged politicization of the inspectorate (Coffield, 2013), have led to a shift from quality assurance to quality improvement and to increased use of performance management systems. Performance management is not new in colleges, but the use of such systems and the stress and direct threat perceived by staff are increasing.

Coffield (2012) is particularly critical of the politicization of Ofsted: applying its own grades, he gives the latest version of the Common Inspection Framework (CIF) a grade 3: requires improvement. O'Leary (2013) shows that Ofsted has had a major influence on the establishment and use of graded systems of observation of teaching and learning (OTL) within the sector. My experience as a practitioner and with Ofsted has shown me how the outcome of an OTL, whether as part of an Ofsted visit or as a quality improvement exercise, can have major implications for a practitioner and their career, as discussed later in this chapter.

Systems of OTL and quality improvement have evolved within colleges over the past few years. I undertook a study within a large FE college, which investigated the impact of targeted mini-inspections which took place within the college during the academic year 2011–12. Designed to mirror an Ofsted inspection within a concentrated area of the college, these inspections were commissioned and run by the college but were led by an external consultant (an Ofsted-trained inspector), accompanied by both external observers and internal college managers.

Key findings of the research showed that having an external Ofsted-trained consultant, appointed by senior management to lead the process, resulted in staff, including some managers, viewing the inspection process with cynicism and mistrust. Many participants in the interviews carried out as part of the study commented upon the aggressive, abrasive and hard approach adopted by the lead inspector, who they felt had a preconceived and senior- and management-led agenda. One interviewee stated that staff felt vulnerable throughout the week of the inspection and believed that what they said to the inspection team would be 'twisted and skewed' so that the process was not impartial. The use of external observers was viewed by some interviewees as deliberately intrusive and as adding to the pressure imposed by the process. Further feelings of mistrust were expressed as some interviewees commented that what was reported by the lead inspector in the final inspection reports was inaccurate and had a clear management bias designed to undermine teaching staff. There was also a feeling amongst some participants that they had been lured into a false sense of security and into being too open with inspection teams and not preparing as thoroughly as they would for an Ofsted inspection. One interviewee (a manager) stated that there was an honest and open attitude, with no attempt to cover anything up as managers wanted the inspection team to find weaknesses and to see the department as it was. The manager commented that in hindsight the department team was too honest and too open.

The targeted nature of the inspections was also perceived as a threat: some interviewees commented that staff felt their jobs were under threat. Feelings of vulnerability, apprehension, anxiety, stress, tension and devastation were attributed to the inspection week. These feelings mirror the feelings of staff during Ofsted inspections found by Rennie (2003). One manager commented that the process had destroyed staff morale, which resonates with a quote from Sir Michael Wilshaw, the then head of Ofsted. 'If anyone says to you that staff morale is at an all-time low, you know you are doing something right' (Abrams, 2012). Little wonder that Coffield suggested that Wilshaw 'has some idiosyncratic ideas about motivating staff' (Coffield, 2013: 11). Overall, the mini-inspection process was perceived by the majority of participants in the study as yet another attack on a teacher's professional autonomy. This echoes the concept of 'the terrors of performativity' (Ball, 2003) and supports Coffield's (2013) suggestion that staff are becoming resources that can be managed and changed.

The rationale for the mini-inspection process from a management perspective was the drive from quality assurance to quality improvement. This has been heavily influenced by Ofsted and can be evidenced from a variety of Ofsted reports since about 2007. The drive for the continual improvement of teaching and learning has led to developments in the college OTL system as well as in other systems of performance management. Labelled 'mocksteds', these mini-inspections, designed to be dry runs for inspection, usually bring the whole organization under the spotlight. An interview with a senior manager revealed that the use of an external Ofsted inspector to lead the inspections and to train the inspection teams was designed to give the process credibility; the use of external observers had, according to that manager, been seen as good practice in the sector. The senior manager said the rationale for focusing inspections on underperforming areas of the college was that they would identify key areas for development in preparation for the real Ofsted inspection, and prepare staff, by providing a better understanding of the process, so that they would not be afraid of inspection. It was stressed a number of times in the interview that this was not intended as a punitive exercise to target areas of the college and staff for redundancies; rather, it was designed to be a supportive and developmental exercise that would end by formulating action plans for improvement.

Senior Manager and Lead Inspector clearly indicated in interviews that they perceived that the process complemented an Ofsted inspection. The interviews with ordinary staff provided a different view. While some staff did comment that the process was a useful exercise in preparation for an Ofsted inspection, the overall view was that it was unfair and unclear and had a hidden agenda. Middle managers, however, generally stated that the exercise did complement the Ofsted process, although some did voice the concerns raised by staff, particularly the concern about targeting certain areas of the college.

During the interviews with staff emotions ran high on several occasions. One interviewee said that there was 'an alternative agenda', found the whole experience 'scary' and said that there was a sense of 'panic' amongst staff. Their negative experience of the inspection had clearly wounded some staff, and the damage inflicted by the process had clearly not healed. The experience of inspection, along with cynicism about the process, had had an impact on staff perception of senior management, and in some cases had brought about a reduction of faith in the inspection process. Analysis of the comments received through the study makes it clear that staff found that the process had no beneficial impact on teaching and learning, and some were critical of the lack of post-inspection support. Managers provided a completely opposite view, arguing that improvements had been made as awareness was raised of what needed to be done to improve the quality of teaching and learning.

From another standpoint, my personal experience as a trainee additional inspector with one of the now defunct inspection service providers (ISP) provides insight into the relationships – often perceived as complex – between Ofsted, organizations and staff. The inspectors with whom I worked were highly trained, knowledgeable and extremely hard-working. The inspection teams were professional and conducted inspection duties with integrity and honesty, and in accordance with the code of conduct for inspectors. Staff in the inspected organizations unsurprisingly demonstrated a mixture of emotions – anxiety, nervousness, apprehension and (over-) excitement – all wanting to show their organizations in the best possible light. What surprised me the most was that inspectors wanted organizations to do well and demonstrate improvements; inspectors focused throughout on the positive aspects of the organization.

So why are so many staff so fearful of inspectors and inspections? From my interviews with staff, many of these fears and anxieties appear to be rooted in messages from management. The fear of the outcome of inspection has been engrained in organizations along with the myths and legends of inspections and inspectors from hell that emerge as the dreaded phone call from the Lead Inspector to announce the inspection is anticipated. Managers have often been instructed by their superiors to make teachers ready and prepared for battle with the Inspectorate by ensuring that they are fully armed with lesson plans, student profiles and assessment records (all of which are time-consuming to produce and rarely looked at). Endless compulsory staff development sessions are arranged so that staff are clear on how to act and perform during the inspection. Conversations with staff have revealed that some managers motivate their staff by reminding them that a poor inspection will almost inevitably result in job losses within their department.

Any organization requires motivated, committed and valued staff if it is to maximize performance. If, however, staff feel that performance management systems are punitive and offer no support, they will naturally feel targeted and threatened. Where management styles are predominantly autocratic, staff morale is affected, and staff question their level of professional autonomy. Moreover, industrial relations between unions and management are strained in many organizations when little or no consultation takes place over key proposed changes.

Better to be feared than loved?

From my own and others' research within the sector it appears that some college principals and other senior managers favour the instillation of a culture of terror and fear. This does not improve teaching and learning, and nor does it reduce levels of staff turnover or sickness and stress levels. It is most likely to result in a negative impact on student experience. Coffield's advice to Amanda Spielman (the head of Ofsted from January 2017) should be extended to college principals:

> The focus of inspection [should] change from arithmetical targets to improvements in quality, which is not something 'assured' by management, but a desire for tutors to get better at teaching just for the sake of doing a more professional job.
>
> (Coffield, 2017)

Finally, from my own standpoint with over a decade of experience in teacher education, where the professional development of the teachers is of paramount importance, the grading of trainee teachers remains highly contested. The removal of grades for individual lessons that has been adopted by Ofsted is welcome, but many organizations still insist on a system of individual lesson grading and an observation policy linked to performance management. Until observation of teaching is completely detached from performance management the process will be largely viewed as punitive.

In the spirit of Machiavelli, I would offer the following advice:

- **Principals:** adopt a coaching-style system of ungraded classroom observations, led by subject specialists; promote professionalism via the use of reflective accounts and reflective discussions among staff.
- **Ofsted:** heed the advice offered to Spielman by Coffield (2017) to remove all forms of grading from inspection.
- **Tutors:** continue to challenge the unfair, punitive and very often demoralizing observation systems in your workplaces, and be empowered by embracing developmental measures such as peer observations.

References

Abrams, F. (2012) 'Is the new chief inspector of schools just an instrument of government?' *The Guardian*, 23 February. Online. www.theguardian.com/education/2012/jan/23/chief-inspector-schools-michael-wilshaw (accessed 1 April 2017).

Ball, S.J. (2003) 'The teacher's soul and the terrors of performativity'. *Journal of Education Policy*, 18 (2), 215–28.

Coffield, F. (2012) 'Ofsted re-inspected'. *Adults Learning*, 24 (2) (Winter), 20–1.

— (2013) 'Can we transform classrooms and colleges without transforming the role of the state?' Paper presented at the Newbubbles Annual Further Education Conference, Guildford, 22 March.

— (2017) 'An open letter to the new chief inspector: "Let's make Ofsted a force for good"'. *TES*, 21 January. Online. www.tes.com/news/further-education/breaking-views/open-letter-new-chief-inspector-lets-make-ofsted-a-force-good (accessed 13 May 2017).

O'Leary, M. (2013) 'Surveillance, performativity and normalised practice: The use and impact of graded lesson observations in further education colleges'. *Journal of Further and Higher Education*, 37 (5), 694–714.

Rennie, S. (2003) 'Stories from the front line: The impact of inspection on practitioners'. London: Learning and Skills Development Agency.

UCU (University and College Union) (2013) 'UCU Congress Report 2013'. Online. http://uculondonregion.wordpress.com/reports/congress-report-fe2013/ (accessed 20 August 2016).

Eryn Hadrill

I'll protect you from the hooded claw,
Keep the vampires from your door.

Frankie Goes To Hollywood ('The Power of Love')

Chapter 14

The Prince, principals and their principalities

David Powell

> Sign o' the times mess with your mind.
>
> (Prince, 1987)

The contents of the two typical newspaper articles on education that follow remind us of the performative and managerialist context for leaders of schools and their staff (Ball, 2003) and, it might be argued, for principals who lead colleges in the further education (FE) and skills sector, and their staff as well.

'And this year I have absolutely no idea what my students will get in their GCSEs – neither as a teacher of a GCSE class nor the head of 180 children in that year' (Anonymous, 2016: 34).

'Should parents be able to sue over poor results?' was the provocative headline in the Education section of *The Guardian* on Tuesday 30 August, 2016. The sub-heading explained that a father, whose son achieved just one GCSE at his private school, was suing the school for £28,000 and discussed whether this was justified.

It makes you wonder how things have become so messy. A.L. Kennedy (2015), speaking on BBC Radio 4's *A Point of View*, also reached the conclusion that education was in a mess, adding, 'but in many ways a quiet mess'. This chapter is aimed at those who are interested in learning more about how colleges work, and how they can become part of a democratic movement that changes the practices of their further education college (FEC) and thus transform the lives of their students and their co-workers. It examines the mess we're in by using a case study of a recent Ofsted inspection, and more specifically the contribution princes and princesses, as principals and leaders, can make to ameliorating or worsening a FEC's predicament. The examination in this chapter has five elements.

1. It introduces Kemmis *et al.*'s (2014) concepts of ecologies of practices and practice architectures, which are contemporary theories of practice for a college or school or other educational provider, to explain how a principal's 'sayings, doings and relatings' (ibid.: 31) can 'sustain or

suffocate' (ibid.: 51) the other college practices, involving teachers, students' learning, the professional learning of staff and the research and evaluation at the FEC.

2. It considers the semantic space, the physical space, in terms of work and activity, and the social space, at a FEC, and how these arrangements 'hang together' (ibid.: 4) as well as their impact on the ecologies of practices and practice architectures.
3. It examines how the policy landscape shapes the elaborate and fragile ecosystem of a FEC.
4. It provides a conceptual lens through which to analyse the practices and practice architectures through a self-assessment activity on the 'sayings, doings and relatings' (ibid.: 31) and consider their impact on your institution's practices.
5. It invites princes and princesses and their staff to 'be the change they want to see in this world' and engage in the Habermasian idea of 'productive dialogue' (Coffield, 2014: 84). Through this, they may reach agreement on how, together, they can deal with the messiness they face.

In 2014–15 Ofsted judged just 44 per cent of the leadership in general FECs to be good or outstanding. A recent survey of 240 senior leaders in colleges by City and Guilds (2016) indicated a mismatch between challenges to the sector and the stated priorities of the sector's leaders. FE leaders face greater uncertainty than ever because of regionalization of FE provision through area reviews, changing demographics that affect their intake, and increased competition from schools and universities. The National Audit Office (2015: 6) has, moreover, warned that 'the financial health of the FE college sector has been declining since 2010/11'. Given this context, the fact that leaders are distracted from curriculum issues, including the quality of teaching, learning and assessment (TLA), is understandable, but not excusable. A plethora of organizations, including the Department for Education, consistently criticize FECs and their leadership for the absence of robust debate or pedagogically informed thinking about the nature and practice of TLA. Marvin Gaye might well have asked: 'What's going on?' (1971).

My father worked at Stafford College between 1964 and 1994, and recently asked me what was going on at the college after I told him that their most recent Ofsted inspection judged them to be 'Inadequate' (Ofsted, 2016). After I'd explained the Ofsted regime – all Dad knows is the more benign, supportive Her Majesty's Inspectorate (HMI) – he asked, 'How has that happened at Stafford [College]?' What has happened provides a way to introduce Kemmis *et al.*'s concept of ecologies of practices, because colleges are constantly subject to mutable government policy and, after that, it is what happens at the site that dictates how well the college does. Kemmis *et al.*'s (2014: v) argument is that 'education always transpires in particular places ... and its transformation [is] a matter of reconfiguring [the] practices [of the site]' (Kemmis and his team call colleges and schools 'a site' (ibid.: 143)). What are the five practices of the ecology? Leadership, students' learning, teachers' teaching, professional learning, which includes continuing professional development (CPD) and initial teacher education (ITE), and research (ibid.: 51). These practices hang together within an elaborate ecosystem in which any one of the practices can destabilize the others. Kemmis *et al.* (ibid.) posit that each college is unique because of the practices that exist there, and that what works at one college may not work at another because of how these practices interrelate at each college.

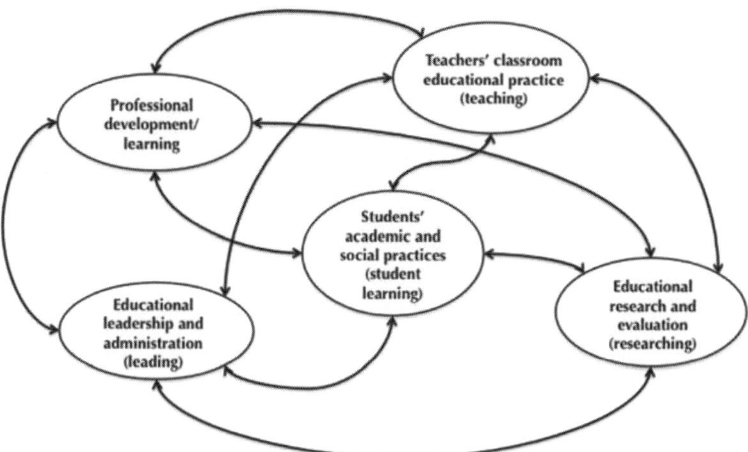

Figure 14.1: The theory of ecologies of practice

These five practices consist of 'sayings, doings and relatings' (ibid.: 31) of the practice, i.e., what a teacher says in their conversations with students, colleagues and so on; what a teacher does (and what they say and do are not always congruent) in the classroom, the staffroom and so on; and a teacher's relationships with their students, their colleagues and their college leaders, as well as their engagement with research, both at their own site and in published work. The 'practice architectures ... are ... the arrangements that support particular practices at particular sites' (ibid.: vi). Each practice is '*enmeshed* with' (ibid.: 38) the practice architectures of the site. (They may be as likely to stifle such practices as to support them.)

These practice architectures are themselves shaped by a set of arrangements: the semantic space defined by the language we use when communicating at the college, the physical space where we are expected to do our jobs, the social space determined by power and solidarity. These three arrangements also 'hang together' and can 'support practices and prefigure their development' (ibid.: v). (Again, the arrangements may stifle as well as support.)

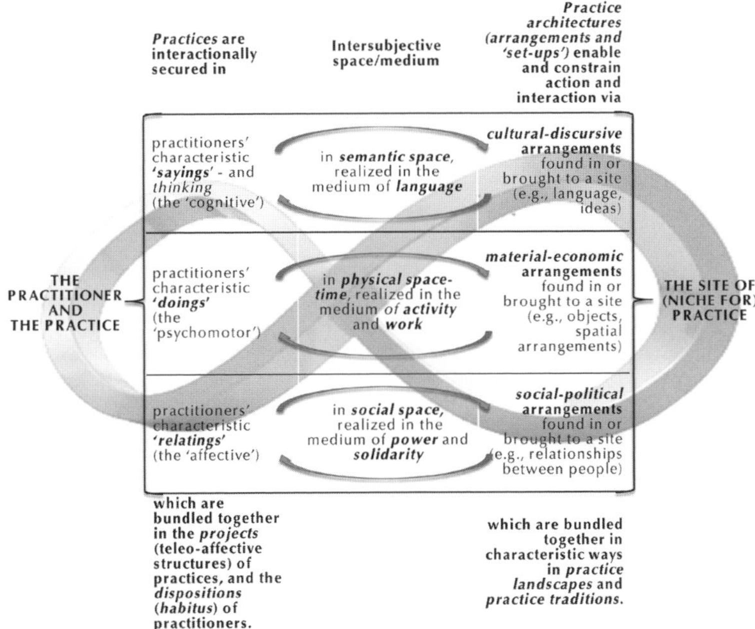

Figure 14.2: The theory of practice architectures

So, Dad, what has happened at Stafford is that the ecologies of practices are not in harmony. Ofsted's judgement that leadership and management are inadequate and the quality of teaching, learning and assessment requires improvement (Ofsted, 2016) suggest to me as a researcher, teacher educator and former member of staff at Stafford College that the leadership and teaching practices were suffocating students' learning.

Here's a short recap and an exercise to see what you have learned so far about ecologies of practices and practice architectures. The following statement is taken directly from Ofsted's report on Stafford College. Read it and then answer the questions that follow it.

> Leaders have not been successful in reducing differences in attainment between groups of students since the previous inspection. While leaders and managers analyse most equality and diversity data well to identify trends in outcomes for different groups and any areas of concern, actions taken were not successful and too many of the targets set in the 2014/15 equality and diversity action plan were not achieved.
>
> (ibid.: 3)

1. Which of the ecologies of practices are hanging together in this statement?
2. Which of the practice architectures of the practices are present in this statement?

Read the following statements on teaching, learning and assessment and answer the questions at the end of it.

> Teaching, learning and assessment are still not consistently good across all subject areas. Attendance is low in some areas and, despite improvement, is too low in English and mathematics classes. The pace of learning is too slow in adult lessons and a few lessons for learners on study programmes, resulting in students being disengaged and not making good progress.
>
> (ibid.: 4)

1. Which of the ecologies of practices are hanging together in this statement?
2. Which of the practice architectures of the practices are present in this statement?

Ah but, I hear you say, what about Ofsted and education policy? Well, whatever we think of Ofsted and government policy, there has been a degree of consistency for the colleges caught up in the 'policy amnesia' (Higham and Yeomans, 2007: 33) and the 'failures of policy learning' (Raffe and Spours, 2007: 1). It is how the college responds that matters, and the princes (or princesses) are the architects of the response, aren't they? The transformation of a college and its practices starts with us adopting a 'critical' (ibid.) approach to our own practice. To start with, we need to understand our behaviours and self-limiting assumptions and transform them, then we can join in a 'productive dialogue' (Coffield, 2014: 84) with our students, our co-workers, including the professional learning team, and our prince (or princess) and their senior leadership team.

Little princes and princesses: Judge yourselves before you judge others

'It is far more difficult to judge oneself than to judge others. If you succeed in judging yourself correctly, then you are truly a [wo]man of wisdom' (Saint-Exupéry, 2009: 37).

Gandhi is reported to have said, 'My life is my message', and our 'sayings, doings and relatings' are our message to those we meet and work with, whether they are students, colleagues, support staff, cleaners, or the prince or princess of the college. Our 'sayings, doings and relatings' affect the ecology of practices, too, and will suffocate or sustain our co-workers' practices. Our use of email is an example of a contemporary practice that can give us an insight into who we are and what we have become. Our (mis) use of email is indeed a 'sign o' the times'. Have a look at your email 'sent' box for the last seven days and answer the following questions:

1. How many emails did you send?
2. Which days of the week did you send them? When during the day did you send the emails?
3. Why are you sending the emails?
4. Who are you sending these emails to? How close to your work space are the recipient(s) of your emails? What is stopping you speaking to the person?
5. What are you assuming when you send the email?
6. How do you greet the recipient(s)? What type of message is it? What language do you use?
7. Is a response required? If so, how much time have you given the person to respond?
8. What impact will this email have on the recipient(s)?
9. When you receive an email, how quickly do you respond?
10. In a conversation, how often do you say 'put it in an email' or 'email that to me'?
11. How has email become part of your practice?
12. Have you been on a course about managing your email inbox?

Being the change you want to see in this world

> What have I become, my sweetest friend?
>
> (Cash, 2002)

I remember Monica Box, who was principal at Calderdale College at the time, quoting Ghandi, 'Be the change you want to see in this world', and it struck a note with me. This final section of the chapter invites you to join others in a sincere and genuine 'conversation' (Kemmis *et al.*, 2014: 8) about the changes you would like to see in your college. Kemmis *et al.* remind us not to succumb to the ritualistic, formulaic and imposed consultation conversations that characterize so much of the 'New Public Management "re-engineering" of organisations and procedures'. They call us instead to set up genuinely democratic, communicative spaces for dialogue with leaders, students and co-workers to debate and reach a consensus about the 'sayings, doings and relatings' (ibid.: 31) of a good education, and then to commit to forms of 'communicative action' (ibid.: 9) that change the practices that need to be changed. I want to go back to a song I first heard in late 2010 to conclude this chapter. The song is taken from the album *Wake Up!* by John Legend and The Roots (2010), which includes covers of less well-known protest and political songs from the 1960s. The song is called 'Our generation (the hope of the world)' and I invite you to be part of our generation:

> Hope of the world is in our generation
> (let's straighten it out).
> It's all left up to us to change this present situation
> (let's straighten it out).
>
> (Leon Moore and C.L. Smooth)

References

Anonymous (2016) 'Secret headteacher: "After Thursday's GCSE results, will I still have a job?"' *The Guardian*, 23 August 2016, p. 34. Online. www.theguardian.com/education/2016/aug/23/secret-headteacher-gcse-results-students-exams-worry (accessed 10 June 2017).

Ball, S.J. (2003) 'The teacher's soul and the terrors of performativity'. *Journal of Education Policy*, 18 (2), 215–28.

Cash, J. (2002) 'Hurt'. *The Man Comes Around*, track 2 (American Recordings IV). Louisville, KY: American Recording Company.

City and Guilds (2016) 'Further education: New challenges, new opportunities'. London: City and Guilds of London Institute.

Coffield, F. (2014) '"Facts alone are wanted in life": The unwelcome return of Mr Gradgrind'. In Coffield, F., Costa, C., Müller, W., and Webber, J. *Beyond Bulimic Learning: Improving teaching in further education*. London: Institute of Education Press, 64–88.

Gaye, M. (1971) 'What's going on'. *What's Going On*, track 1. Detroit: Tamla Records.

Higham, J. and Yeomans, D. (2007) 'Policy memory and policy amnesia in 14–19 education: Learning from the past?' In Raffe, D. and Spours, K. (eds) *Policy-Making and Policy Learning in 14–19 Education*. London: Institute of Education Press, 33–60.

Kemmis, S. (2016) 'Theorising education as practice.' Paper presented at the College of Education, University of Kentucky, 17 October.

Kemmis, S., Wilkinson, J., Edwards-Groves, C., Hardy, I., Grootenboer, P., and Bristol, L. (2014) *Changing Practices, Changing Education*. Singapore: Springer.

Kennedy, A.L. (2015) 'The worth of education'. *A Point of View*. BBC Radio 4. 14 June.

Legend, J. and The Roots (2010) 'Our Generation'. *Wake Up!*, track 4. New York: GOOD Music.

National Audit Office (2015) *Overseeing financial sustainability in the further education sector*. London: National Audit Office HC 270 July 2015.

Ofsted (Office for Standards in Education, Children's Services and Skills) (2016) *Stafford College Inspection Report, 9–12 February 2016*. Manchester: Ofsted. Online. https://reports.ofsted.gov.uk/inspection-reports/find-inspection-report/provider/ELS/130813 (accessed 1 September 2016).

Prince (1987) 'Sign o' the Times'. *Sign o' the Times*, disc 1, track 1. Chanhassen, MN and Burbank, CA: Paisley Park Records/Warner Bros.

Raffe, D. and Spours, K. (2007) 'Three models of policy learning and policy-making in 14–19 education'. In Raffe, D. and Spours, K. (eds) *Policy-Making and Policy Learning in 14–19 Education*. London: Institute of Education Press, 1–32.

Saint-Exupéry, A. de (2009) *The Little Prince*. London: Egmont.

Siobhan Carmichael

We still think of a powerful man as a born leader and a powerful woman as an anomaly.

Margaret Atwood

Chapter 15

Transforming *The Prince* to a Prince of Hope: Emancipatory adult education empowering students and communities

Vicky Duckworth

Read the words below closely:

> We have not seen great things done in our time except by those who have been considered mean; the rest have failed.
>
> (Machiavelli, 1908: 75)

The new Prince of Hope that I propose will challenge this, reclaiming the notion of 'great things' as one of virtue and positioning emancipatory education at its helm:

> We have seen great things done in our time by those who have been considered socially just, brave, prepared to step out from the mean corners of individuality to the centre of humanity; the rest have failed. Indeed, I say that the adult students, finding themselves now sufficiently powerful through transformative and emancipatory education, and partly secured from the immediate dangers of structural inequalities by having armed themselves in their own way, and having in a great measure crushed those forces in their vicinity that could injure them if they wished to proceed with their conquest, had next to consider their future, for they knew that the appointed politicians, who too late were aware of their mistakes, would not support them. And from this time they began to seek new alliances and not to temporize with the community in the expedition which they were making in pursuit of freedom of thought and empowerment, and this they have accomplished because they had passion, hope, and importantly had been part of critical education.
>
> (Prince of Hope, 2017)

Ruptures

Critical education creates ruptures where a more level playing field can be established for those from marginalized and disadvantaged backgrounds. Critical education recognizes that transformative learning does not happen exclusively in traditional settings, and acknowledges alternative literacies and languages such as art, poetry, music and dance, as well as other forms of expressing meaning. Learning can happen in both small steps and seismic strides that are not necessarily bound to a straight path, but may spiral (Duckworth and Ade-Ojo, 2015). Critical education acknowledges that historical and contemporary disparities, such as class, gender and ethnicity, exist in students' lives. These disparities can shape students' choices (or lack of choices) as well as their experiences. Critical educators recognize and value the cultural dimensions the students bring with them, and they work with students to breathe life into teaching as a model for social justice.

Paths

Women and men carry with them ability and desire that stem from and lead to many pathways in the personal and public domains of their lives. These routes can have a strong influence on the shape and experiences of families, communities and society. Whatever the journey, every person should be encouraged and challenged to live and experience life fully; they should have a path of hope and justness that sees them pursue and express their desires and goals passionately to accomplish them. The chains of oppression, once broken, raise questions that can leave educators looking for a lens of hope, for example how culture impacts teaching in a culturally diverse classroom (Robinson-Pant, 2016). A difference stands between a culturally diverse session and one sensitive to ethnicity. A culturally diverse class is one in which students and teachers represent a variety of different backgrounds but which does not particularly presume an ethnically sensitive environment. A class that is sensitive to ethnicity is multicultural and intentionally incorporates a lens on ethnic sensitivity. But do not assume that culture is easy to recognize in learning spaces; it can be hidden beneath words spoken and garments worn. Dialogically engaging with students, sharing their interests and passions, can help us to resist hegemony and cross boundaries of language and culture, opening our eyes to discover, celebrate and share our lived experiences of resistance and empowerment (Duckworth and Smith, 2017).

The new Prince of Hope recognizes

We must be aware that students come with many traditions and world pictures that are very different from those of the dominant culture.

My own northern princely clothes of hope

I was born, brought up and live in the same emotional and geographical landscape and community as my students in North Manchester. This immersion allows me to have, as a practitioner and researcher, a critical positioning whereby I have insider knowledge of their lives, motivations, pressures, hopes and dreams (see Giroux, 1997; Macedo, 1994; Shor 1992; Ade-Ojo and Duckworth, 2016). From this insider position the critical model of education can move towards the student being the co-producer of knowledge. The generation of this powerful knowledge shifts away from teacher-directed, top-down, standardized assessments that prescribe the same for all students regardless of their ability, values, ethnicity, history, community requirements or specific contexts (Ade-Ojo and Duckworth, 2015). Instead it takes an egalitarian approach, in which there is a sharing of power, and of knowledge in its many forms, between the teacher and the student through the curriculum, its contents and its methods. Freire (2005) proposed to do this via 'culture circles' – discussion groups in which educators and students participate in dialectic engagement for consciousness raising, liberation, empowerment and transformation. Education for liberation provides a forum for the development of those skills and competencies without which empowerment of students, teachers and the community would be impossible.

Poverty and schooling

Stella was a mature student, a mother, a wife, a sister, a niece, a daughter and a woman with a goal when she commenced the literacy night class I was teaching in order to move from being a cleaner to being a carer. She told of her experiences of learning and home life as a child, experiences that shaped the choices she had. Stella shares her story with you to illuminate the impact of poverty on learning, to challenge notions of a meritocratic society and the associated negative stereotypes that bruise and batter self-esteem and confidence.

For Stella being poor meant her parents did not have enough money to heat the house. Stella felt different to the others when she went to school and thought that being poor left her open and vulnerable:

> You felt ashamed somehow, that people were looking down at you – like if you was hungry it was your fault and had nowt to do with not having enough money. You kept everything in so no one singled you out. My husband says that I still worry rather than sharing it with him. I try to make out all's well even if sometimes it's not. At least now you can knock up a decent meal for under three quid.

Being poor did not stop Stella from describing her childhood as happy. However, going to school hungry, she found it hard to concentrate. And seeing her mother and father struggle over money made her sad.

> Yeah. That's where your energy went – on surviving, not school work. It's like you were expected just to get on with it at school no matter what was happening at home or in your belly for that matter. Try concentrating when you're mad hungry – no chance. The teacher would be speaking and you'd be imagining some lovely meal – it's odd now people have too much to eat, then there wasn't enough, no cheap frozen food. It must be a nice feeling to be a child and have nowt to think about but learning. Still, I've got a bit of a chance to do that now, more than me mum had.

> Ah, er, my mum and dad they did struggle – I've seen my mum and dad go without food to feed us. Now she – my mum – had a hard life, then my dad had an accident at British Rail. He was in hospital for a long time. He crushed his ribs and he was on sickness benefit and I can always remember we'd moved to Oil Avenue at the time, at Primrose Bank, and they hadn't sent his sick pay and it were February and it were really really bad weather and the icicles run on the inside of the window. … It was absolutely freezing and she'd no coal left and my dad went all round the house and got all the old shoes and burnt them on the coal fire. She made a pan of hash on the fire because there weren't gas for the gas cooker. By the end of the weekend he'd burnt everything he could burn and my mum had this beautiful, I mean it must have been worth a fortune today, highly polished sideboard left off my grandma and he had to chop it up, I mean I can remember my mum going in the kitchen absolutely heartbroken, but he had to keep us warm and we had to bring all the mattresses downstairs. We thought it were brilliant and then the electric went and they had candles and my dad was making

> us shadows on the wall and he played the mouth organ to keep us occupied because there were no telly. We'd be singing Christmas carols in February. [Laughs]
>
> There were seven of us. But you know – and them are my memories – they're good memories. My mum and dad could have just put us in care and I can always remember that we couldn't go to school on the Monday morning because there was no hot water for a bath and the house was too cold to go upstairs for a bath, so she went into school and told the headmaster what had gone on and the headmaster phoned the social services, they came down and they'd been paying my dad fourteen pounds a week short in his benefits and that's why my mum was struggling. In fact if it weren't for – er – this lady called Vera and John her husband – they had the off-licence and they ticked my mum potatoes and bread and things to get us over the weekend and corned beef – she made this big pan of corned beef hash. And she never ticked cigarettes and my dad smoked Woodbines and John come round to the house and give my dad forty Woodbine and said, 'Here Danny don't be telling our Vera them are off me'. I always have that memory because he really realized my dad always worked up till this accident, my mum and dad were never on benefits you see and they never knew and, er, we survived that weekend but we thought it were brilliant.
>
> Downstairs sleeping on mattresses ...
>
> Playing the Christmas carols and we were all singing them. And when I look back now and I always say, when I'm having a laugh with my mum, you know when my dad chopped that sideboard up you should have told him to burn one of the kids — there were seven kids and only one sideboard. [Laughs]

The influence of a child's background and their experience of inequality is significant for their experience of schooling. Teachers are in a position to legitimate or denigrate the culture, community and values exhibited by their students, by accepting or rejecting them. The way that teachers (and indeed fellow students) communicate this acceptance or rejection of what students bring, which is very often associated with the latter's economic situation, can have a profound effect on students' learning journeys (Duckworth, 2014). Rejection may cause stigma and shame. Stella also had dyslexia; she described how:

> *Stella:* With me being dyslexic and them not recognizing it, I was just made to feel I was useless, so I didn't go in.
>
> *Interviewer:* How old were you when you left school, when you decided not to go back?
>
> *Stella:* I just used to go in and get my mark and then just come out. If I played truant my mum would find out so I used to just go in and get my mark and slip off. And I was that important to the school I did it for three years and nobody realized I wasn't there. That's 'cause I was thick and I was on the outskirts like I said, the teachers were more focused on the children who could get on with their work.
>
> *Interviewer:* Did you have any support from anyone, any friends at school?
>
> *Stella:* Oh yeah, there was a girl called Doreen who I still very much like. She used to say if she was asked that I'd gone to the dentist. She knew what I was like, and Doreen, bless her, even helped me to read and she did it and that's why I can read, 'cause my best friend taught me to read.

This labelling as 'useless' and 'thick' impacted on her experience of school and how she viewed herself. However, the notion that students are determined by poverty and exclusion needs to be challenged by critical adult education. Through effective support along their trajectory, in the private and public domains of their lives, including home, the community, school, college and the workplace, they can build a better future, a princely future in which agency and choices shift them from the margins of poverty and oppression to the centre of empowerment. It is by returning to adult basic education that the students in my study turned their and their families' lives around (Duckworth, 2014).

Stella – her own prince – swirls her life towards the sun

Stella stayed in the area where she was born and brought up; she left school, married and has a family of three. Arriving at college in her fifties she wanted to read and write better so that she could leave the relentless cleaning jobs behind and pursue her dream to work as a care assistant. With grit and determination, she grabbed hold of her future with both hands, took agency in reaching her goals and gained the confidence and skills to read and write. She describes how:

> getting an education and doing my NVQ in health has given me other options, not just cleaning. I can care for the elderly. Having these choices is empowering, it makes me feel good.

Stella is one prince among many, who presents us with a picture of how transformative education has made a real difference to her life; it has brought her joy, fulfilment and choices.

Treading the land of hope

Women and men in lifelong learning have demonstrated that people given the opportunities and choices to pursue the power of transformative education are equal to women and men who boast of great accomplishments, having been born into the wealth and privilege that steered their way. Those who are forced to make their way through hardship with their own resilience are more than capable of achieving the same heights. These people, often marginalized and silenced, are in the majority. They tread on most of the land, but that does not position them with humanity, dignity, equity and equality. The society in which we live is characterized by deep inequality between those born into wealth and those born into a cycle of deprivation from their first cry in the world.

And so, the way of the new Prince of Hope must be to embrace golden opportunities for grass-roots inclusion and collective action that can truly be realized through educating our teachers to become critical educators and 'organic intellectuals' (Gramsci, 1971: 3), who promote social justice and who challenge inequality in and out of the classroom.

References

Ade-Ojo, G. and Duckworth, V. (2015) *Adult Literacy Policy and Practice: From intrinsic values to instrumentalism*. Basingstoke: Palgrave Macmillan.

— (2016) 'Of cultural dissonance: The UK's adult literacy policies and the creation of democratic learning spaces'. *International Journal of Lifelong Education*, 1–18.

Duckworth, V. (2014) *Learning Trajectories, Violence and Empowerment amongst Adult Basic Skills Learners*. London: Routledge.

Duckworth, V. and Ade-Ojo, G. (eds) (2015) *Landscapes of Specific Literacies in Contemporary Society: Exploring a social model of literacy*. London: Routledge.

Duckworth, V. and Smith, R. (2017) 'Further education in England: Transforming lives and communities'. London: University and College Union. Online. www.ucu.org.uk/media/8461/transforming-lives/pdf/ucu_transforminglivesFE_report_jan17.pdf (accessed 11 April 2017).

Freire, P. (2005) *Pedagogy of the Oppressed*. Trans. Ramos, M. London: Continuum.

Giroux, H.A. (1997) *Pedagogy and the Politics of Hope: Theory, culture, and schooling*. Boulder, CO: Westview Press.

Gramsci, A. (1971) *Selections from the Prison Notebooks of Antonio Gramsci*. Ed. and trans. Hoare, Q. and Nowell-Smith, G. London: Lawrence & Wishart.

Macedo, D. (1994) *Literacies of Power: What Americans are not allowed to know*. Boulder, CO: Westview Press.

Machiavelli, N. (1908) *The Prince*. Trans. Marriott, W.K. Originally 1515. Online. www.constitution.org/mac/prince.pdf (accessed 1 April 2017).

Robinson-Pant, A. (2016) *Promoting Health and Literacy for Women's Empowerment*. Hamburg: UNESCO Institute for Lifelong Learning. Online. http://unesdoc.unesco.org/images/0024/002456/245698e.pdf (accessed 1 April 2017).

Shor, I. (1992) *Empowering Education: Critical teaching for social change*. Chicago: University of Chicago Press.

Wiggins, N. (2011) 'Critical pedagogy and popular education: Towards a unity of theory and practice'. *Studies in the Education of Adults*, 43 (1), 34–49.

Part Four

4

Introduction: FE Utopia: Towards a New Republic

Kevin Orr

Challenging the common image of Machiavelli as a kind of calculating Tony Soprano figure, his biographer Erica Benner (2017b) contends that Machiavelli's 'life and words inspire us to become sharper readers of political danger signs, and ruthless warriors for our freedoms'. Machiavelli remains relevant because his close examination of Florentine politics in the early sixteenth century reveals the universal: political power will be variously wielded and interpreted depending on position or interest. Context as well as purpose are everything in understanding power and what it might achieve, and that is as much the case in FE as anywhere else. Machiavelli, according to Benner (2017a: xxi), had a 'steely determination to change the corrupt world he lived in' and also the conviction that any individual 'could do their bit to change things for the better'. The writers of this final part of the book share that latter Machiavellian conviction as they discuss how aspects of FE might be transformed. They also each share with Machiavelli the conviction that nothing should be taken on authority (Benner 2017a: 7).

Craig Hammond describes *The Prince* as 'a political speculum loaded with a range of latencies and tactical potential'. That speculum in hand, Hammond turns towards the latencies and potential contained within tactics inspired by Guy Debord and the Situationists. Hammond describes how in college-based higher-education settings these tactics might inform teachers' pedagogical decisions and especially their design of modules to enable the challenge of received ideas. Hammond specifically addresses the 'problem of navigating the realpolitik of the educational environment' in colleges while 'experimenting with democratic modular practices'. To be successful in that worthwhile and tricky endeavour, however, 'one must be a fox in order to recognize traps, and a lion to frighten off wolves' (Machiavelli, 2004: 74).

Peter Shukie, similarly, urges us to search beyond 'institutional norms and conventions' in order to re-examine our values and even what we understand by learning. Traditional education based in institutions, he argues, tends to privilege knowledge created and valued by the powerful elite, and to denigrate other forms of learning. In response, Shukie advocates forms of distributed teaching and learning, including Community Open Online Courses (COOCs), which have the potential to emancipate students from the strictures of a hierarchical education system. Beware, however, for the 'innovator makes enemies of all those who prospered under the old order' (Machiavelli, 2004: 24).

Rania Hafez describes trainee teachers in FE as 'Trojan horses, primed to be unleashed on the sector with the skills, knowledge and disposition to one day take control of the profession'. The aim of teacher education, Hafez argues, 'should be to create teachers as independent audacious thinkers and actors', which is more likely if those teachers have a grip on the philosophy, history and sociology of education. Hafez is therefore less equivocal than Shukie in her support of the academy, and specifically of its role in teacher education, which she defends against the reductive condescension of recent policy that has sought to marginalize the role of universities.

Machiavelli was in exile when he wrote *The Prince*, and for Rob Peutrell this is reminiscent of those in FE who have similarly been denied their public voice by the powerful. 'Machiavelli would have remarked that corruption is the price the commonwealth pays when the power of the elite is unrestrained by the popular voice.' Peutrell discusses his home city, Nottingham, to illustrate the consequences of recent political decisions affecting FE, and identifies resources upon which to draw in order to reinvigorate democracy in the sector and consequently to reinvigorate the sector itself.

Lou Mycroft and Jane Weatherby are critical of Machiavelli's role in the formation of 'a logical über-human' or a kind of 'David Beckham of his time' 'against whom the rest of us are measured and found to be other'. They propose an antidote to this potent spectre that haunts educational leadership through Spinoza's concept of *potentia*, which offers the possibility of resistance and regeneration. Mycroft and Weatherby have had enough of heroic, charismatic leaders; hope lies in the anti-heroes and their role in social purpose education. Like Shukie, they see opportunities in virtual as well as real spaces in which 'careful and deliberative listening is key to thinking and acting differently'.

James Avis has a warning: we risk complicity with the powerful while we are presenting ourselves as radicals. This reflects what Avis refers to as comfort radicalism, which seeks to provide opportunities for the disadvantaged while posing no threat to the structures that reproduce disadvantage. Indeed, Avis suggests, the wise educational prince will appeal to such radicalism (perhaps expressed in an expansive definition of teacher professionalism) to achieve what management practices based on performativity cannot. Such a realization might, of course, lead to cynicism and stasis. For Avis, however, the 'point is to work on what might be called the good side of the conditions within which we are placed, recognizing the limitations but pushing the possibilities as far as possible'.

Like Avis, each of the contributors to this part comprehends education's complexity, and so they cannot propose easy routes to FE utopia. Rather, they offer alternative visions of education as well as ways of thinking and acting outside current restrictions, for Machiavelli reminds us that we need not play others' games. Benner paraphrases his advice:

> Nothing is stupider than to sink to the level of mindlessly competitive men in hopes of beating them. You might win, but you might end up as mindless as they are. Before long, someone slightly less stupid will beat you.
>
> (Benner, 2017a: 8)

References

Benner, E. (2017a) *Be Like the Fox: Machiavelli's lifelong quest for freedom*. London: Allen Lane.

— (2017b) 'Have we got Machiavelli all wrong?' *The Guardian*, 3 March. Online. www.theguardian.com/books/2017/mar/03/have-we-got-machiavelli-all-wrong (accessed 17 April 2017).

Machiavelli, N. (2004) *The Prince*. Trans. Bull, G. London: Penguin Books.

Callum Davis

'Power resides where men believe it resides. It's a trick, a shadow on the wall. And a very small man can cast a very large shadow.'

Lord Varys (*Game of Thrones*)

Chapter 16

Machiavelli, tactics and utopia?

Craig Hammond

Antonio Gramsci suggests that *The Prince* was not necessarily written for the use of powerful strategists: 'Machiavelli had in mind "those who are not in the know", and ... it was they whom he intended to educate politically' (Gramsci, 1992: 135). For Gramsci, the Machiavellian modern prince is a phenomenon that should be conceived as a collective and revolutionary possibility, not as an individual person. It is an organism, a 'complex element of society in which a collective will, which has already been recognised and has to some extent asserted itself in action, begins to take concrete form' (ibid.: 129). With reference to the Gramscian redefinition in *The Modern Prince*, Louis Althusser notes that Machiavelli's tract is 'a revolutionary *utopian* manifesto' (Althusser, 2000: 23), a revelatory text that provides a potent insight into and liberating exposé of the architectural innards of politics and political manipulation. And yet *The Prince* as a text does not provide a set of instructional blueprints for social, or educational, transformation. Following the Gramscian line of argument, it should be regarded more as a catalyst for insurgents, a political speculum loaded with a range of latencies and tactical potential. As Althusser remarks, *The Prince* offers a scattering of insights and techniques for a transformation-hungry 'nation' (here, we could replace 'nation' with 'learning community'), which can be creatively adapted and incorporated for radical political use. In the context of college-based higher education (CBHE), Machiavellian tactics and strategies can be discovered and promoted through the writing and delivery of alternative degree modules and assessments, which are aimed at uncovering and unleashing democratic and utopian potential (Gramsci, 1992: 176).

While Machiavelli makes numerous references to the warfare-based concepts of tactic and strategy, *The Prince* does not offer a concise definition of these terms. Usefully, however, Michel de Certeau in *The Practice of Everyday Life* (1984) does establish such a definition. For de Certeau, the notion of strategy frames the pervasiveness of organizational and institutional power, encompassing all types of processes, policies, laws and bureaucratic activities. Powerful elites shape and execute strategies to dominate the parameters of regulated space. The notion of the tactic, on the other hand, identifies more radical principles associated with personal action and creative agency. 'Tactic' refers to a range of liberating possibilities, that can challenge and contradict strategy and strategists.

This notion of the de Certeau-infused Machiavellian tactic, bolstered by the Gramscian refraction of the collective, utopian and democratic counter-strategy, has been useful within my own practice as a CBHE practitioner. As an FE lecturer working in CBHE, I write and deliver modules as part of a degree programme that is validated by a large UK university. The college-based validation process for the programme produces rampant surveillance and scrutiny, with the potential to render the dynamism of the subsequent learning environment a stifled space of strategic conformity. Despite the intimidating structures of bureaucratic and organizational regulation, however, spaces of agency remain, where possibilities of academic freedom aligned with subjective tactics of empowerment can still be found and defended. Here, the de Certeau-infused Machiavellian distinction between strategy and tactic provides a flexible and powerful schema that can be effectively applied to the context of CBHE. For example, as part of the development and writing of my degree modules, I have experimented with and incorporated the pedagogical practices of creative autobiography and peer assessment. Creative autobiography, as a pedagogical and learning technique, embraces subjective and experiential characteristics unique to each student; as a method – or indeed a tactic – for reflection and discovery, it is a fluid and exploratory mechanism, which enables the refracted inner-world of student hopes, cultural reference points and memories to be explored and articulated in creative ways. This means that potentially dry and objectively distantiated curricular material can be brought to life in unique ways. To promote and protect the unpredictable diversity that inevitably emerges from each creative autobiographical artefact, I devised and implemented a peer assessment scheme, with the aim of lessening the singular control exercised by the typical expert lecturer in the allocation of an assessment grade, and, as part of the wider creative process, incorporated the democratic engagement of the whole student group. Combined, these pedagogical innovations and practices – as tactics – operate to highlight the often hidden institutional mechanics associated with power and academic control, and the assumptions that belie the institutional sanctioning of meaningful knowledge (for more detailed analyses and explanation, see Hammond, 2017). Creative autobiography and peer assessment operate as micro-political manoeuvres, adaptive tactics that generate conditions for democracy, creativity and empowerment amongst both practitioners and students. These tactics can, moreover, flourish in the gaps and spaces of the organizational context where subversive tacticians can practise and hone the art of academic subterfuge with an agenda to outflank conformist expectations.

Approaching the writing and development of a module in such adaptive and creative ways serves as a reminder that academic agency within a CBHE context still has a vital (and arguably largely untapped) role to play. Each organization and political environment contains within itself empty spaces of possibility, where the actions of an individual or a group can emerge; in my own particular context and institutional environment, this was the programme and module validation process. Supported by the academic and pedagogical arguments advanced by Paulo Freire, bell hooks, Henry Giroux and Peter McLaren, the experimental pedagogical practices were to be sanctioned by both the college and the validating university. In a Machiavellian sense, shards of alternative pedagogic possibility ripped and glimmered through the arcs and seams of strategic and traditionalistic rules. Where strategic power is bound by policy enshrinement and visibility, the invisibility and flexibility associated with the innovative subjective tactic means that alternative academic practices expanded in the openings between institutional rules and expectations.

Again, here we are confronted with the problem of pragmatism. The problem of navigating the realpolitik of the educational environment with a view to experimenting with democratic modular practices requires more concrete tactics and mechanisms. In order to guide practitioners and students towards the open terrain of liberation, empowerment and democracy, I bolstered the Machiavellian sentiments by developing and splicing two Situationist-based tactics as part of my pedagogical practice: the dérive and détournement, as explained below.

Two Situationist-based creative autobiographical tactics

Guy Debord (1931–94), a French Marxist theorist and provocateur, was the leader of a group of intellectuals known as the International Situationists (referred to throughout this chapter as the Situationists). At the 1957 founding meeting of the Situationists, Debord issued his manifesto (with the unwieldy title of *Report on the Construction of Situations and on the Terms of Organization and Action of the International Situationist Tendency*; Debord, 2004), which set out the key Situationist principles as well as its constitutional basis. The Situationists developed a number of tactics (but here we will focus specifically on the dérive and détournement) aimed at challenging the mundane routine of everyday life. For Debord, cultural, academic and political concerns need to be defibrillated from the strategic stultification and soul-crushing power of bureaucracy and consumption; radical action – at the level of subjective agency – is required to confront and tackle the democratic malaise generated by the malignant tendrils of these anti-dynamic forces. The spread of neoliberal markets and consumer activities across colleges and universities, replete with marketing, advertising and branding departments, has rendered radical action based on dérive and détournement more necessary than ever.

Tactic one: The dérive

In his essay 'Theory of the dérive' (1958), Debord defines the Situationist adaptation of the dérive '(literally: "drifting")' as 'a technique of rapid passage through varied ambiances. Dérives involve playful-constructive behavior and awareness of psychogeographical effects, and are thus quite different from the classic notions of journey or stroll' (Debord, 1958: para 1). In one sense, the dérive is associated with the physical act of wandering, a kind of purposeful getting lost in the city. Essentially, and of paramount importance for Debord, it is about actively shifting away from psychic states of uncritical conformity. The Situationist dérive is not, however, confined to a specific set of practical instructions for getting lost, it is more fluid than this. Wark (2015) clarifies that the Situationist dérive should be understood as 'aquatic, conjuring up flows, channels, eddies, currents, and also drifting, sailing or tacking against the wind. It suggests a space and time of liquid movement, sometimes predictable but sometimes turbulent. The word dérive condenses a whole attitude to life' (Wark, 2015: 22).

The fluidity and non-specificity associated with Debord's dérive means that it is an excellent creative-autobiographical vehicle, which can be used in a modular and teaching context to elicit emergent and creative thoughts from individual students. Rather than instructing students to critique theoretical principles and concepts, through the technically distanced modes of academic writing, to then regurgitate them as part of functional essayistic renderings, lecturers can invite students to dérive, explore and write in open and non-legislated ways. As an adaptive conceptual mechanism, the dérive is a potent pedagogical tool, one that educationalists can practise and adapt in different ways, and in so doing challenge themselves to resist conforming to established expectations for module structures and forms of assessment. The dérive can manifest as adventurous ideas and activities that jolt the normally passive participant out of the ruts of banality and familiarity. As an open and flexible approach to thinking and organizing, the dérive can resituate the wider framing of knowledge and reset the connection between the practitioner and the student in many educational settings to allow collaborative relationships to emerge.

Tactic two: Détournement

The tactic of détournement – basically, to detour – identifies reinterpretive cultural practices. To détourne is to seek to liberate 'a word, statement, image or event from its intended usage and to subvert its meaning' (Coverley, 2010: 95). The Situationist essay *Détournement as Negation and Prelude* identifies two related aspects of the practice of détournement: initially, the object being détourned must be stripped of its reified context and ownership, in order to be perceived as a fluid and contributory building block of culture. Secondly, once stripped of its false value, the object should become part of a new ensemble: a new and creative expression. There is no particular size, shape or context that must be associated with the source of a détourned object; as Wark notes, it could be 'a single image, a film sequence of any length, a word, a phrase, a paragraph' (Wark, 2015: 40). What matters is that the fresh and refracted association that a new learning context brings to the artefact generates a new meaning.

As part of my experimental approaches to pedagogy, any cultural or theoretical fragment can be chaotically chosen by each eclectic student; serving as a creative catalyst, the source of an original academic artefact – which could be a theorist, a concept, a theoretical excerpt from a publication – is decomposed and opened up to a fecund territory of new and fresh reinterpretations. Aligning the dérive and détournement with student encounters with theories, philosophies and concepts (such as Roland Barthes's notion of the punctum, or Ernst Bloch's notion of utopia) means that students can be empowered to resist the imposition of expectations associated with established learning strategies. Creative-autobiographical expositions, incorporating the dérive and détournement, directly and subversively engage with the powerful hierarchy of academic knowledge in micro-political ways. The dérive and détournement, as Machiavelli-inspired tactics within a pedagogy of empowerment, ultimately challenge the authority and surveillance of knowledge, characterized by more traditional modular constructions and assessments.

The financial imperative generates strategies of routine and conveyance in colleges as well as an increasingly weakened consumer-student, who becomes initiated into a 'rehearsal for his [sic] ultimate role as a conservative element in the functioning of the commodity system' (Situationist International and member of Strasbourg University,

2006: 408–9). The strategies associated with traditional types of module – such as the expert lecturer imparting knowledge to passive students – serve to preserve and perpetuate a pedagogy of imposition. In response, the malleable Machiavellian proxies of the dérive and the détournement, as pedagogical tactics, supplemented by the additional tactics of creative autobiography and peer assessment, are all the more necessary. Rather than accept and obey the imposition of institutional expectations for acceptable modular structures and assessments, we should open our practice up with a new cartography of dynamic knowledge, 'characterised by a complete disregard for the traditional and habitual practices' (Coverley, 2010: 90). Machiavellian tactics that inform alternative and transformational practice may lead to educational developments that are utopian, in that they are loaded with democratic potential and, as yet, undefined.

References

Althusser, L. (2000) *Machiavelli and Us*. London: Verso.

Coverley, M. (2010) *Psychogeography*. Harpenden: Pocket Essentials.

de Certeau, M. (1984) *The Practice of Everyday Life*. Trans. Rendall, S. Berkeley: University of California Press.

Debord, G. (1958) 'Theory of the dérive'. *Internationale Situationniste*, 2. Online. http://library.nothingness.org/articles/SI/en/display_printable/314 (accessed 25 April 2017).

— (2004) 'Report on the construction of situations and on the terms of organization and action of the international situationist tendency'. In McDonough, T. (ed.) *Guy Debord and the Situationist International: Texts and documents*. Cambridge, MA: MIT Press, 29–50.

Gramsci, A. (1992) *Selections from the Prison Notebooks of Antonio Gramsci*. Ed. and trans. Hoare, Q. and Nowell Smith, G. Originally 1971. New York: International Publishers.

Hammond, C.A. (2017) *Hope, Utopia and Creativity in Higher Education: Pedagogical tactics for alternative futures*. London: Bloomsbury Academic.

McDonough, T. (2004) 'Situationist space'. In McDonough, T. (ed.) *Guy Debord and the Situationist International: Texts and documents*. Cambridge, MA: MIT Press, 241–65.

Situationist International and students of Strasbourg University (2006) 'On the poverty of student life'. In Knabb, K. (ed. and trans.) *Situationist International Anthology* (rev. ed.). Berkeley, CA: Bureau of Public Secrets, 408–29.

Vaneigem, R. (2004) 'Comments against urbanism'. In McDonough, T. (ed.) *Guy Debord and the Situationist International: Texts and documents*. Cambridge, MA: MIT Press, 119–28.

Wark, M. (2015) *The Beach beneath the Street: The everyday life and glorious times of the Situationist International*. London: Verso.

Rob Roach

'You underestimate the power of the Dark Side. If you will not fight, then you will meet your destiny.'

Darth Vader (*Return of the Jedi*)

Chapter 17

Seeking emancipation in a world of online emancipators

Peter Shukie

> [T]here is nothing more difficult to take in hand ... than to take the lead in the introduction of a new order of things.
>
> (Machiavelli, 1908: 24)

This chapter argues for a new order of learning that broadens who can be involved in the creation of learning spaces, while responding to the problems that arise when such a new order of things is introduced. Since the mid-2000s, the emergence of massive open online courses (MOOCs) has promised something of a transformation in adult education (AE). Predominantly focused on higher education (HE), the notion of 'access to the world's best education' (Coursera, 2017) suggests that all that is needed is access to that education. Emancipation comes through a breaking down of campus walls to let the wealth within permeate outwards.

Such a position, however, already situates knowledge within established institutions of learning (to which MOOCs may give access), and it does not disrupt the Enlightenment framework of teacher–student–knowledge. Such thinking reifies the teacher/academic as the creator of knowledge, the students as deficient, and learning as the accumulation of knowledge along designated pathways under teacher guidance. The technology of MOOCs is harnessed to preserve this hierarchical model with no change in the objectives. Existing skills and conventions, styles of writing, course materials, hierarchical roles and locations of knowledge are familiar even if the means of distribution are virtual rather than campus-based.

Community open online courses (COOCs) are an innovation that challenges these Enlightenment models. Rather than the same faces in the same places, learning through COOCs is redistributed: everyone can teach and everyone can learn. The idea of distributed knowledge finds little support in *The Prince*, where wise men 'ought always to follow the paths beaten by great men, and to imitate those who have been supreme' (Machiavelli, 1908, 22). If, however, any path can be tinged with greatness, then the paths to be followed become many, the search for supremacy finding multiple routes. Technology becomes important as the means of sharing with others, not merely through escaping the physical restrictions of institutions, but also through escaping the conventions they are built around. Machiavelli's avowal of the difficulty inherent in creating a new order of things is, nevertheless, noted: 'the innovator has for enemies all those who have done well under the old conditions' (ibid.: 24).

Anderson and Dron (2011) wrote of three generations of distance learning: from behaviourist traditions of teacher domination, through peer-to-peer social connectivism, and finally into the networks of connectivism that the roles of teacher and student loosen. In establishing a pattern of liberation that shifts from teacher-led to collaborative learning, these technology-driven generations indicate the potential for change. As Anderson and Dron highlight, however, the earlier generations have not simply gone away: they all coexist today. Connectivism might challenge the mission of the institution (Feldstein, 2014: 7), but the Enlightenment preference for clearly articulated roles and ownership of knowledge creation continues to dominate. In defining the principles of connectivism, Siemens (2005) generates a dialogue of openness and networked learning that offers new models without teachers. He suggests that learning occurs across machines and people in expanding networks that reflect an era dominated by web-based communication. The technological imperative, the network as liberating space, also influenced the creation of COOCs through the initial connectivist MOOCs (cMOOCs).

The appropriation of these ideas by corporate-institutional hybrid xMOOCs came later. Each of the three approaches, cMOOCs, xMOOCs, COOCs, reflects how a similar idea, the Web as open-accessed network, has very different applications:

1. xMOOCs: institutional traditional pedagogies need updating and, while the same people, the same institutions and the same canon remain, the Web provides emancipatory potential by allowing the walls of the campus to become permeable.
2. cMOOCs: the basis of education needs to be transformed in recognition of global networking possibilities. Teacher, student, institution all become malleable concepts, and knowledge is a fluid idea shaped by multiple nodes in the network, including machines as well as people.
3. COOCs: open and online means can enable communities to be built and to link with each other as forms of resistance to the dominant principle that academics are the primary knowledge creators. That is, openness is not just about access to knowledge, but also about recognizing different

> concepts of expertise, of validity across knowledge, of subject areas, and of types of engagement that are not linked back to institutional knowledge as the core.

From a COOCs perspective the difference between generations of distance learning and between both cMOOCs and xMOOCs comes through purpose. xMOOCs describe a purpose of providing 'universal access to the world's best education, partnering with top universities and organizations to offer courses online' (Coursera, 2017). The aim here is to widen who can access learning with an acceptance that what is accessed is universally vital, relevant and appropriate to all. Connectivist theorists, however, want to disrupt the mission of institutions, they recognize that the Web has led to a situation in which '[a]n entirely new approach is needed' (Siemens, 2005: 3), but with little other justification or explanation. Liberating roles and the location of knowledge outside convention makes emancipation possible, but connectivist theorists provide little rationale for it. In contrast, proponents of COOCs argue that the emancipatory purpose is primary, that academic-facing knowledge and institutional dominance are forms of oppression. Prioritizing what happens in the school, college or university, while denigrating what happens beyond those walls, crushes the opportunity for authentic engagement outside institutions. The COOCs ethos, by contrast, is one based on education as a tool for change, not as the means by which privilege is maintained.

> This coolness arises ... partly from the incredulity of men, who do not readily believe in new things until they have had a long experience of them.
>
> (Machiavelli, 1908: 24–5)

It is not that the institutions must be replaced, but that a blurred space between community and institution needs to be recognized. Authentic engagement cannot begin with a focus on teachers granting students the right to contribute, which leads to nothing more than what Freire describes as 'false charity' (Freire, 2005: 45). False here is the pretence of welcoming a contribution, only to subsume it into the structures of an existing curriculum. Coming to learn is thus infused with an element of surrender, of subjugation to a more knowledgeable other in which the qualities, experiences and expertise of others' lives are reduced to nothing in the glare of a prescribed and narrow curriculum. Despite institutional student-led discourses, in practice there is a deception in which multiple voices are carefully selected to reflect only institutional priorities. Such approaches resonate more with rhetoric ('the customer is always right', or 'our customers are our priority') than they do with emancipatory transformation.

The alternative approach of the COOCs platform is that anyone signing up can teach, create courses, develop networks and promote learning in any subject area. From the first stages of development, the concept, of course, is thrown open to everyone. This is not anarchic; it is an acknowledgement that Enlightenment structures have a purpose based on retaining the status quo. It is necessary to resist assuming that this as a common-sense foundation if anything approaching real emancipation is to occur.

> Thus it happens that whenever those who are hostile have the opportunity to attack they do it like partisans.
>
> (Machiavelli, 1908: 25)

Laurillard (2012) argues that professional educators are needed more than ever and that COOC-type approaches are to be attacked. Laurillard's argument rests on the idea that:

> Technology opportunists who challenge formal education argue that, with wide access to information and ideas on the web, the learner can pick and choose their education – thereby demonstrating their faith in the transmission model of teaching. An academic education is not equivalent to a trip to the library, digital or otherwise. The educationist has to attack this kind of nonsense, but not by rejecting technology. It is a stronger attack when first we must ask what learners need from education and therefore from technology.
>
> (Laurillard, 2012: 4)

This position is the one that perhaps most defines the opposite stance from that of COOCs: Laurillard's later work on MOOCs further establishes open networks primarily as a means of teaching professional educators. Such an approach is based in a contention that only through the reification of a professional class can knowledge find its way to diverse communities. Although Laurillard does counter with discussion of 'informal learning', this is very much of the 'something we can all do' (2016: 41) variety. This view is not uncommon: Grossman (2005) describes the use of 'only' as a prefix to much knowledge outside the centre ground: 'only' informal learning, 'only' community learning. This exemplifies the use of derogatory language that undermines value in learning outside officially sanctioned institutions.

Feldstein (2014: 7) suggests that ideas such as cMOOCs and COOCs are weaker the further from established convention they wander. Similarly, Bourdieu describes the autodidact who does not learn 'in the legitimate order established by the educational system' as existing in a 'miniature culture', their knowledge no more than a 'collection of unstrung pearls' (1984: 328). If the status of knowledge and meaning-making rests only inside of the institutions, the outside becomes automatically impoverished. The collapse of knowledge into neat binaries, of institutional and community learning, only ever raises the status of the first. As a professor commented at a conference presentation I gave at an FE college, COOCs 'is a nice idea for hobbyists and the like, but hardly a place for higher learning'.

If

In the memorable closing scene of *If ...*, Anderson's (1968) film about a public school, Malcolm McDowell's character and his fellow insurgents clamber on the school rooftop and shower grenades and machine-gun fire on the collected establishment figures below. This is an act born of frustration at their continued humiliation and subjugation, and such was the cinematic metaphor playing out in my own head in response to the frustratingly elitist view that learning could not occur in a space open to anyone with an interest in non-institutional education. This is a common sensation when one is faced with an oppressive force, so often an institutional one, which dominates by first ridiculing, then devaluing, and finally attacking any attempt to challenge institutional power.

COOCs as a space for reimagining institutional relationships with community are based on this frustration. Learning outside institutions suggests communities as valid and relevant spaces for different knowledge, not already processed through institutional norms and conventions – a practical application of Freirean praxis, a distributed knowledge that Wiggins describes as 'the idea that the wisdom gained through life experience is in no way inferior (and in some cases superior) to the knowledge gained through formal study' (2011: 46).

Lovett (1988: 4) relates to 'really useful knowledge' that realigns the formation of knowledge away from abstract and alienating institutions, instead placing knowledge creation in the hands of those that are engaged with learning they decide on themselves. This is distinct from 'merely useful knowledge' (ibid.: 27), a technical knowledge handed down to communities from institutions. This merely useful, distilled knowledge frames the community in narrow terms, with impoverished concepts of economic necessity and funding based on function and utility. The approach of COOCs follows what Lovett defines as the purpose of really useful knowledge, that is, 'knowledge calculated to make you free' (ibid.: 22). The contention is that knowledge can come from anywhere and teacher–student roles are in continual flux. It also heeds a warning from Freire that replacing one set of oppressive values with another, the oppressed becoming the oppressors, does not realize any greater social justice. This is not a call for revolution that reduces the institutions to rubble; machine guns and grenades on the school roof are not the answer. It is a call for mutual respect and understanding that knowledge exists in many places.

> This man abolished the old soldiery, organized the new, gave up old alliances, made new ones.
>
> (Machiavelli, 1908: 26)

In this description of Hiero the Syracusan Machiavelli depicts the importance of innovation coming from unexpected places. We could find similar challenges to the old order by looking to pubs, parks and other playgrounds of the intellect. Once we start to shift the notions of expertise as being already the preserve of the institution we are faced with a wild, exhilarating and perhaps threatening range of possibilities. My experience at the Ragged University (discussed in chapter 11) helped forge the first stages of a network of free, non-institutional thinking and practice.

Ragged pubs

Having been invited to attend and present at a Ragged University event I made my way to a new venue. The back room of a Manchester pub created a familiar unfamiliarity, a third space in which the activity of learning became dislocated from its usual spaces, and enriched in the process. My presentation challenged the skills I had previously learned. What was appropriate in such a space: a presentation, a poem, a narrative or a lecture? I merged my interest with Debuffet's concept of Art Brut, or Raw Art, that valued untaught practice, creating a video: bubbling springs representing rhizomatic wanderings, statuesque figures in the park representing classical transcendence. This played as a loop above the wooden stage and provided a silent illuminating backdrop to a part-written, part-spontaneous treatise on the values of free learning. The real difference, the power of this dislocation, came from the space and the participants involved. No measures of attendance – people came because they wanted to, without compulsion or promise of reward beyond an immediate opportunity to engage.

Questions were wide and deep, discussion diverse and sparking beyond anything anticipated. What remained most influential was that in this third space the background of the people did not matter. Interrogation was likely to be incisive and articulate, critical, sceptical or illuminating, regardless of academic foundation. Emancipation came through a liberation from expected roles and established expertise. It was akin to what Deleuze and Guattari (1988) describe as rhizomatic thinking, which sees learning, experience and life as a series of non-hierarchical connections, a networking of people and ideas that defy the certainty and fixity of accumulating accredited knowledge.

The references, experiences and anecdotes were the ingredients that brought richness and depth to the discussion. The approach to learning was a coming together of ideas and approaches not already tied into metaphors of trees of knowledge, or of branches of thought that followed established links verified by disciplines. The diversity, the multiplicity, were instrumental to how knowledge was created. A relocation of space and people did not impoverish or lessen, but enhanced, as we encountered each other's ideas. The experience of being beyond the walls of an institutional space can be exhilarating: instead of being harangued by posters proclaiming 'Innovate', 'Inspire' or 'Achieve', we were inspired to reflection by the sounds of life.

The community in COOCs is not based entirely online, it is a reflection of the conflicts and frustrations, the non-linear randomness of how lives are lived. Community focus allows meaning to be generated through embracing diversity, and not immediately framed by state and institutional requirements. Decisions about what is taught, who teaches and how can be thrown open to all of us, without default positions that continually refer to conventional sources, university mission statements or academic lineage. Community learning of the kind represented by COOCs offers a real, corrupted and responsive mess of living that reflects lives rather than an insulated, immunized and closed institutional rhetoric of education that seeks to maintain its relevance.

Trojan horses

This is not a simple response based on a 'let people teach themselves and all will be fine' approach. It is a recognition that expertise is already distributed, and that change and ownership of this expertise must be reflective of this. It is a call to resist domination through what Holland (2011) calls an assertive nomadology. Nomadology is action that is wandering rather than located, creating new routes rather than being indoctrinated into filling existing spaces. This approach sees resistance as a realignment of actions, not overthrowing oppressive force, but establishing new practices of emancipation. Holland says an affirmative nomadology attempts to 'renew, enrich and invigorate … by displacing the monopoly of the State citizenship with plural nomad citizenship' (Holland, 2011: xi).

The approach of COOCs aligns with this, foregrounding learning as the basis of Holland's citizenship. Both institutional and community learning practices are valid, and the aim is to reduce the imbalance of power that continues to prioritize one and impoverish the other. If we continually find value only in the same measures as in institutional space then there is only failure and disappointment. An example might be in Stewart's description of MOOCs as 'Trojan horse[s]' (2013: 229): unconvincing as vehicles for their intended knowledge purposes, but leading vicariously to increased digital literacy as people navigate these wide, complex spaces. The hidden benefits might still be fixed on institutionally defined digital literacy, but they might also create space for new knowledge, developed through new digital practices working to displace powerful knowledge by infusing it with diverse, emergent, distributed knowledge.

> Hence it is that all armed prophets have conquered, and the unarmed ones have been destroyed.
>
> (Machiavelli, 1908: 25)

Once voices are freed and action is redistributed across society, then what occurs next evades predictive, ideological encampments. Perhaps it makes possible crude, inauthentic populism that casts out expertise as a negative and elitist weapon. It should not do so, because the call here is not based on knowledge being respected but only on its popularity. Rather than meekly accepting web-based learning as a continuation of old hierarchies, approaches such as COOCs and the Ragged University suggest that 'the popular' is something that emerges from all sectors of society. This is not a call to massiveness; instead, it is a call for recognition of the rights of all to create meaningful interpretations of the world. We are all the experts of our lives, and higher learning is possible for all. If we are silenced and subjugated, our only alternative is to assume the laws and theories of others, a distant elite who inhabit a small institutional space with immense power. Emancipation built on the same hierarchies and distributed along controlling principles of privilege and marginalization is no emancipation at all.

What is the purpose of the chapter? We must continually revisit what we mean by learning and see in our own practice where our authentic values lie. This is as likely to be beyond institutional norms and conventions as within them. Only with authenticity of purpose can we escape a moribund travail around tired and conforming practices based on general political and economic trends that support the continued dominance of a narrow and uninspiring elitism. While we may recognize Machiavelli's warning of the vulnerability of the unarmed prophet, we may find better news in his tale of Hiero of Syracuse. Hiero's ascent came from the support of the people that recognized his ability, and despite his lack of noble heritage or entitlement his armoury was the support of the people. By establishing the rights of all to learn, to teach and to be involved in the creation of knowledge we make possible a world in which power can be transferred from the old guard and a world that recognizes with impartiality a new, distributed concept of learning.

References

Anderson, L. (1968) *If ...* Film. Elstree: Memorial Enterprises.

Anderson, T. and Dron, J. (2011) 'Three generations of distance education pedagogy'. *International Review of Research in Open and Distance Learning*, 12 (3), 80–97.

Bourdieu, P. (1984) *Distinction: A social critique of the judgement of taste*. Trans. Nice, R. London: Routledge and Kegan Paul.

Coursera (2017) Coursera homepage. Online. www.coursera.org (accessed 7 August 2017).

Deleuze, G. and Guattari, F. (1988) *A Thousand Plateaus: Capitalism and schizophrenia*. Trans. Massumi, B. London: Athlone Press.

Feldstein, M. (2014) 'MOOCs and technology to advance learning and learning research: The MOOC and the genre movement'. *Ubiquity*, September, 1–9. Online. http://ubiquity.acm.org/article.cfm?id=2591681 (accessed 18 April 2017).

Freire, P. (2005) *Pedagogy of the Oppressed*. Trans. Ramos, M. London: Continuum.

Grossman, J. (2005) 'Workers, their knowledge and the university'. In Crowther, J., Galloway, V., and Martin, I. (eds) *Popular Education: Engaging the academy: International perspectives*. Leicester: NIACE, 77–87.

Holland, E.W. (2011) *Nomad Citizenship: Free-market communism and the slow-motion general strike*. Minneapolis: University of Minnesota Press.

Laurillard, D. (2012) *Teaching as a Design Science: Building pedagogical patterns for learning and technology*. New York: Routledge.

— (2016) 'The educational problem that MOOCs could solve: Professional development for teachers of disadvantaged students'. *Research in Learning Technology*, 24 (1), Article 29369. Online. www.tandfonline.com/doi/pdf/10.3402/rlt.v24.29369?needAccess=true (accessed 18 April 2017).

Lovett, T. (ed.) (1988) *Radical Approaches to Adult Education: A reader*. Beckenham: Croom Helm.

Machiavelli, N. (1908) *The Prince*. Trans. Marriott, W.K. Originally 1515. Online. www.constitution.org/mac/prince.pdf (accessed 21 April 2017).

Siemens, G. (2005) 'Connectivism: A learning theory for the digital age'. *International Journal of Instructional Technology and Distance Learning*, 2 (1), 3–10.

Stewart, B. (2013) 'Massiveness + openness = new literacies of participation?' *Journal of Online Learning and Teaching*, 9 (2), 228–38.

Mason Thew

The most common way people give up their power is by thinking they don't have any.

Alice Walker

Chapter 18

Inside the Trojan horse: Educating teachers for leadership

Rania Hafez

> The universities, in educating the educators of the people, had thus been 'to this nation, as the wooden horse was to the Trojans'.
>
> (Bejan, 2010: 2, citing Hobbes, *Behemoth*: 40)

In this chapter teacher educators are cast as Machiavellians at the gates of Troy, grooming a host of princes, building their students up as vessels of change, and preparing them to be radical leaders for renewal. Educational leadership, I argue, starts in the classroom. Hobbes believed in the absolute authority of a central ruler, so it is unsurprising that he should have accused universities and academics of being Trojan horses. Similarly, teacher educators have been construed as radical agents fomenting discord and rebellion (Daley, 2015); certainly as a teacher educator I think of my trainee teachers as Trojan horses, primed to be unleashed on the sector with the skills, knowledge and disposition to one day take control of the profession. Hobbes was right in that respect: educating the educators of the people, or teacher education, is a revolutionary endeavour, but not in the negative way he implied. The aim of teacher education should be to create teachers as independent audacious thinkers and actors, able to bring about an educational transformation, not only in themselves and their students, but also in society.

Some may misconstrue the Trojan horse metaphor as academics fashioning novice teachers into ticking time bombs. That would be erroneous. Education is not war, nor are duplicitous tactics worthy of educators. In the long run subterfuge and subversion can only harm the profession. Engaging teachers in spurious quixotic battles risks the dual scourge of charging endlessly at shadows while at the same time feeling like the eternal victim. Rather, what I propose has its roots in the classical idea of leadership and the 'philosopher kings' of Plato's *Republic*. The role of the teacher as leader resides in the conceptualization of leadership as emanating from knowledge and wisdom.

Robinson's (2013) research on effective school leadership has established that successful leadership in educational institutions starts with the teachers. Hence, for our novices to grow into future leaders, it is during their initial teacher education that we need to sow the seeds that will come to fruition with their entry into the profession and the subsequent formation of their professional identity. We must give them not only the ideas and principles that will allow them to develop the disposition of leadership, but the awareness and readiness to question, assert and propose. As Hobbes rightly points out, it is the notions and thinking that students imbibe in the academy that are the seeds of future sedition, or, as I prefer to see it, of future liberation.

> Desiring therefore to present myself to your Magnificence with some testimony of my devotion towards you, I have not found among my possessions anything which I hold more dear than, or value so much as, the knowledge of the actions of great men, acquired by long experience in contemporary affairs, and a continual study of antiquity.
>
> (Machiavelli, 1908: Dedication)

In *The Prince*, Machiavelli distils the knowledge and wisdom gained from years of experience in politics and from the meticulous study of the actions of princes and rulers in history, with the purpose of equipping his royal protégé with the skills to subdue opponents and gain power. But vanquishing enemies can hardly be the purpose of leaders in education and it is certainly not the purpose of teacher educators. However, like Machiavelli, we teacher educators must transmit to our novice teachers the wisdom of our experiences. Unlike him we are not doing so to gain favour or to encourage sedition; we do not want our princes to conquer new territories, except those of minds and hearts. Nor should that conquering require deception and cunning. Instead, it requires the vision to see different futures and the skills to work collegiately to achieve them. This requires our princes to be prepared with a foundation of theoretical knowledge that hones their intellect, cultivates their dispositions and equips them for their role as pedagogic leaders.

It is worth remembering that the very word education derives from the Latin *educare*, which is related to *educere*, 'to lead out': to lead out of ignorance into the world of knowledge. Hence, fundamentally, the teacher is the leader, the one who will lead his or her students out from their inexperience into thinking and knowing. A teacher is a leader not in the modern managerial terms that have blighted the FE sector, but in the mould of the ancient educators Socrates, Aristotle and Comenius. This is where teacher educators, the Machiavellis of the sector, come in. For if we want to prepare teachers to lead, it will take more than simply training them in educational techniques. The teacher education curriculum needs to be more than a manual for behaviour management and lesson planning, and educating teachers necessitates more than an automatic transmission of experience. Educators who simply regurgitate insights gained from a few years at the chalkface will not equip their protégés with the means to conquer new intellectual territory. What Durkheim asserts in his *Evolution of Educational Thought* also applies to trainee teachers:

> [I]t is not enough to prescribe to them in precise detail what they will have to do; they must be in a position to assess and appreciate these prescriptions, to see the point of them and the needs which they meet.
>
> (Durkheim 1977: 4)

Education is a complex discipline rooted in philosophy, history and sociology, and a thorough grounding in the knowledge and ideas of these disciplines is vital for teachers so they may start to understand what teaching is and what their role should be. Philosophy in particular allows teachers to address key questions. What is education? What should its values and aims be? How should it be governed? The answers have to be grounded in an appreciation of the history of education, its social construction, and the psychology of learning. As Aristotle once proclaimed:

> [W]hat should be the character of ... public education, and how young persons should be educated, are questions which remain to be considered. As things are, there is disagreement about the subjects. For men are by no means agreed about the things to be taught, whether we look to excellence or the best life. Neither is it clear whether education is more concerned with intellectual or with moral excellence. The existing practice is perplexing; no one knows on what principle we should proceed – should the useful in life, or should excellence, or should the higher knowledge, be the aim of our training? Again, about the means there is no agreement; for different persons, starting with different ideas

> about the nature of excellence, naturally disagree about the practice of it.
>
> (Aristotle, *Politics*, quoted in Curren, 2007: 78)

These are perennial concerns that teachers should continuously strive to address through the principles and practice of their profession, which are rooted in their professional formation (Hafez, 2015). As Michael Young expounds in an essay entitled 'What can higher education offer teacher education?':

> Teachers' pedagogic knowledge contains three elements. The first is conceptual tools for interrogating teachers' specialist knowledge for its pedagogic and curricular relevance for pupils at different stages. ... The second is a knowledge-base for evaluating their practical experience in schools. Finally, the third is access to the educational disciplines – history, sociology and comparative studies in particular – for reflecting on the wider responsibilities of members of a profession. This also equips teachers to engage in debates about educational policy.
>
> (Young, 2011: 26)

Regrettably, however, Hobbesian mistrust of the academy amongst recent education ministers has moved the teacher education curriculum in England away from philosophical questions and away from the educational disciplines that Young identifies. Instead, new teachers are initiated into the profession by observing and imitating current practitioners (Lawes, 2011; Young, 2011). Although trainee teachers can learn much from the experience of veterans, unquestioned imitation is insufficient as a pedagogical foundation for the science and art of teaching. From the erroneous perspective that teaching is a craft to be learnt by imitation, teachers are learning what to do, but they are failing to examine why. Socrates offers a different perspective on knowledge that challenges not only teachers' own assumptions but what they are told by managers, inspectors and policy-makers. The Socratic technique of challenging received wisdom and common sense clears the mind of hubris and makes space for true knowledge to form. Every teacher needs to be a Socrates, questioning the instrumentalism and educational policies that seek to control the minds of practitioners and students alike.

Teachers need the courage to ask who defines subject knowledge, who decides what the aims of education are and, more importantly, who holds the power to answer these questions. The changes in teacher education have gone quite a way in pandering to Hobbesian concerns, and tragically in doing so they may have deprived teachers of the ability they need to be leaders: that of becoming and being autonomous thinkers. Denuding the teacher education curriculum of its critical academic content risks giving the inspectors and principals what they think they need, a conformist and compliant workforce, but depriving the profession of its independent expert professionals. Teachers may be skilled in performing in the classroom, but they may lack the political and theoretical nous to critically examine practice and take a principled stand on education. The losers will be not only the teachers, but also those who seek to lead them, and, ultimately and more importantly, the students.

Principals and senior managers may believe that their authority as leaders lies in a strict hierarchy that sharply demarcates lines of accountability, allocates distinct roles and defines key performance indicators. It is worth remembering that this management terminology did not originate in education, or even in the public sector, but has been borrowed uncritically from industry. It is the language of factories and production lines. It is a terminology that contradicts the very essence of a collegiate profession, that reduces teachers to assembly workers, and students to products. Simply forcing new teachers to comply will erode their confidence and initiative, and lead to a workforce more akin to an army of forced labour than the independent professionals that education needs. If teachers are unable to justify, defend and advocate for their own practice, how can we trust them to develop those very same traits in new generations?

We need to go back to the basics of collegiality if we want to secure a viable, successful future for leadership in education. For too long management-speak has taken over the discourse in FE colleges. It is time to let education speak for itself again. And this can only happen if we let the classroom become once again the centre of power and if we realize that educational leadership is not simply management. The next educational revolution is, then, to put teachers back at the heart of education.

As the Machiavellis of teacher education, our responsibility to our pedagogical princes and princesses lies in our own dedication to the principles, practice and art of educating. It is not our purpose to foment dissatisfaction and restlessness in our novice teachers but to foster critical understanding, a capacity for a visionary outlook and an impatience for excellence. Like Machiavelli, teacher educators can use knowledge and experience to build future teachers who know the territory of education as well as professional journeys through it, battles won and lost, territory gained and ceded. As teacher educators we may be fashioning Trojan horses, but our hope for them is that they conquer ignorance and liberate the intellect.

Florentine princes may have thought themselves leaders but it is their adviser Machiavelli who is remembered. The same goes for education. It is not the principals and the managers that students will remember, but the teachers. As for teacher educators, we must be content with being the catalysts – the horse whisperers and the guides for the future leaders of education.

References

Bejan, T.M. (2010) 'Teaching the Leviathan: Thomas Hobbes on education'. *Oxford Review of Education*, 36 (5), 607–26.

Curren, R. (ed.) (2007) *Philosophy of Education: An anthology*. Oxford: Blackwell.

Daley, M. (2015) 'Why teach? Not afraid to dance'. In Daley, M., Orr, K., and Petrie, J. (eds) *Further Education and the Twelve Dancing Princesses*. Stoke-on-Trent: Trentham Books (13–24).

Durkheim, É. (1977) *The Evolution of Educational Thought: Lectures on the formation and development of secondary education in France*. Trans. Collins, P. London: Routledge.

Hafez, R. (2015) 'Beyond the metaphor: Time to take over the castle'. In Daley, M., Orr, K., and Petrie, J. (eds) *Further Education and the Twelve Dancing Princesses*. Stoke-on-Trent: Trentham Books (157–64).

Lawes, S. (2011) 'Who will defend teacher education?' In Hayes, D. and Marshall, T. (eds) *In Defence of Teacher Education: A response to the Coalition Government's White Paper for Schools (November 2010)*. Derby: Standing Committee for the Education and Training of Teachers, 24–5. Online. www.scett.org.uk/media/3583/in_defence_of__teacher_education_scett_march_2011.pdf (accessed 18 March 2017).

Machiavelli, N. (1908) *The Prince*. Trans. Marriott, W.K. Originally 1515. Online. http://www.gutenberg.org/files/1232/1232-h/1232-h.htm#link2H_4_0006 (accessed 17 July 2017).

Robinson, V. (2013) 'Dimensions of an effective leader'. *Teaching Times*. Online. www.teachingtimes.com/news/dimensions-of-an-effective-leader.htm (accessed 24 November 2016).

Young, M. (2011) 'What can higher education offer teacher education?' In Hayes, D. and Marshall, T. (eds) *In Defence of Teacher Education: A response to the Coalition Government's White Paper for Schools (November 2010)*. Derby: Standing Committee for the Education and Training of Teachers, 26. Online. www.scett.org.uk/media/3583/in_defence_of__teacher_education_scett_march_2011.pdf (accessed 18 March 2017).

Tony O'Connell

'Ask the powerful five questions: what power have you got; where did you get it from; in whose interests do you exercise it; to whom are you accountable; how can we get rid of you? Only Democracy gives us that right. That is why no one with power likes democracy and that is why every generation must struggle to win it and keep it.'

Tony Benn

Chapter 19

Exiled to Sant'Andrea: The excluded voices of FE

Rob Peutrell

Introduction

In 1513, exiled on his farm at Sant'Andrea, Machiavelli writes *The Prince*, a coded appeal to the Medicis to be allowed his public voice again. Machiavelli in exile is a reminder of the exiled voices of teachers and communities in further education (FE). In this chapter, I reflect on our sector's democratic malaise, which I illustrate with examples from my home city, Nottingham. I consider why democracy matters, and I argue that we should not acquiesce to our exclusion but draw on our democratic resources to advocate for change.

My argument is simple: teacher and community voices should be included in policy debate and decision making at all levels in our sector. Excluding them wastes a rich resource of knowledge and experience, and undermines the simple democratic principle that those affected by policy (professionally or through the opportunities it affords or denies them) have a right to shape it. Teacher and community participation are essential for the accountability of decision-makers; the history of fraud in our sector shows the importance of that (see Belgutay, 2016; Cutler, 1999; Linford, 2011). Despite a narrowing interpretation of its educational role, FE still has a responsibility to foster democratic citizenship and should aspire to embody its values and practices. Yet, in our undemocratic sector, this is not how it is; some voices count more than others.

FE's democratic malaise

Since colleges were removed from local authority control in 1993, FE's trajectory has been an undemocratic one. Among the effects of the quasi-market, the centralized funding and the managerialism that together have formed the post-incorporation system have been the erosion of teachers' status and working conditions, the loss of curriculum and student places, and a shift in culture from collegiality to compliance. The language of education has become dominated by the slippery discourses of learning, delivery and employability (Coffield, 2008; Sutter, 2006). Students have become customers, colleges brands and principals chief executives. There is little in common between governing bodies, run in Victorian style, largely by white businessmen, and the communities from which FE students are mostly drawn (Graystone *et al.*, 2015).

This is not to deny that FE needed improving at the time of incorporation; retention, financial waste, inconsistent teaching and inclusion were pressing issues (Hodgson *et al.*, 2015). But rather than including teachers and communities as participants in a process of democratic change, developments were driven by beliefs that have become commonplace across public institutions – in health, welfare and other education sectors. The first was that public institutions lacked the private sector's competitive creativity and efficiency; the second was that policy-making was essentially a technical matter concerned with cost-effective delivery and customer satisfaction. The shift of public provision to businesses or quasi-private bodies immunized the decision making of national and local state and business elites from wider democratic scrutiny and debate. Although the word democracy is still widely invoked in this post-democratic system (Crouch, 2004), the anticipated role of citizens – 'passive, quiescent, even apathetic' (ibid.: 4) – responding to the decisions made by others on our behalf undermines the very notion of professional and public participation in the decisions that affect us.

Just as Machiavelli observed particular states and actors, we can witness these undemocratic processes at work locally. Nottingham has seen 'several decades of imposed "solutions" in which community, user and producer voices have been marginalised' (Nottingham Campaign for Education, 2016). These voices include an early example of a principal setting out 'to change the old order of things for new' (Machiavelli, 1908: 35). In 'Re-engineering a college culture', Nick Lewis (1994) recalled that management's primary task when preparing Broxtowe College for incorporation was to target the forces that resisted cultural change. These forces included long-serving staff, and the FE teachers' union, NATFHE, whose relationship with the local education authority, Lewis contended, gave it 'what amounted to a veto on change' (ibid.: 261). Tellingly, these resistant forces also included the 'strong priority commitment given by lecturers to students, teaching and curriculum matters' (ibid.: 259). In the new order of things, the value of teachers' educational commitments was to be measured by their compliance with the executive's agenda.

More recently, New College Nottingham was the setting for an experiment inspired by the Gazelle group of colleges, formed in 2011, of which the then principal was a founder member. Many aspects of Gazelle (including its membership costs, investments and philosophy) have been controversial (Burke, 2017; Fletcher, 2012). Gazelle's (Cole and Donohue, 2014) pitch was that colleges had to adapt to the new, globally networked, fast-capitalist economy. By embracing 'entrepreneurial learning methods' and the 'transformative nature of technology', colleges would 'deliver graduates ... ready for the new world of work' (ibid.: 5). The approach included training in the six or so learning companies the college set up and funded, including a garage and café run on commercial lines. Although the case for authentic experience in vocational learning is self-evident, teachers expressed doubts over the viability and validity of this entrepreneurial approach. For some, Gazelle's agenda glossed over the job insecurity, poor contracts and precarious forms of self-employment endemic in the economy it championed. Many were at a loss when the college's new tagline, Excellence, Employability and Enterprise, made no reference to education. Their worries about the college's new direction were ignored, despite representations to the board and a vote of no confidence in the principal in 2013. Where was the scrutiny?, teachers asked, as the experiment ended in financial near-collapse and the principal moved on. The subsequent investigation by the Further Education Commissioner (2015: 3) concluded that a 'largely unnecessary budget deficit' was the result of inadequate financial management and the principal's 'expansionist policy' (ibid.: 5) (which included investments in India). It criticized the corporation for being 'too willing to accept' the principal's enthusiasm (ibid.: 6), although no board members resigned as a result.

The FE Commissioner's intervention was instrumental in the decision to merge the two remaining city colleges, which local observers saw as a test run for the national FE area reviews that followed, which were designed to regionalize college provision. Both processes typified the sector's democratic void. No provision was made in the area reviews for teacher or community representatives on its steering groups, alongside those of college corporations, local authorities, local enterprise partnerships (LEPs) and other institutions (Coffield, 2015). Similarly, local campaigners argued that the Nottingham merger consultation was window dressing for a decision already made, and a missed opportunity to engage Nottingham people in thinking about the future of FE in the city (Nottingham Campaign for Education, 2016).

Machiavellian themes run through these local examples: the prince destroying the old and imposing the new, the charismatic seduction of courtiers and hangers-on, fantasy, hubris and contempt for the people.

Machiavelli would have remarked that corruption is the price the commonwealth pays when the power of the elite is unrestrained by the popular voice.

Why democracy matters

Democracy is a powerful idea, if an equivocal one. As a minimum, I take it to include the right and opportunity for all to speak, the responsibility to listen to the views of others, and practices that allow genuine participation in shaping decisions. For Dewey (2012), democracy emerges from the multiple connections and points of interest between the individuals who participate in a community. In Dewey's account, democracy enables our shared capacity for reflection and reconstruction, communicative potentials that are suppressed when democracy is missing. While the demand that teachers reflect on their practice has become a ritual in the FE sector, there is no reciprocal commitment to the democratic conditions that would make genuinely reflective learning cultures possible. Such cultures would allow individuals to raise conflicts and dilemmas in open, productive ways, and organizations to critically rethink their values and practices (Schön, 1983).

It is not that we lack ideas of what democratic education systems might be like. For example, Stevenson (2015) argues for participatory systems at institutional, national and even global levels that empower teachers' professional agency. Through such systems, teachers would be able to shape the conditions of their work and their students' learning, exercising professional judgement in their classrooms, influencing local and national policy, and deciding their own professional learning needs rather than complying willy-nilly with mandated schemes. There are similar arguments about how communities can participate in education decision making. Hatcher and Jones (2015) advocate having community representatives sit alongside those of teachers, heads, governors, students, parents and local authorities on local education forums and committees, the former responsible for long-term strategy, the latter for overseeing schools.

While Hatcher and Jones are concerned with democratizing local education systems fragmented by the academy and by free school programmes, their proposals are equally suited to FE. Thus, we can begin to imagine how democratized colleges could be integrated into democratic local lifelong learning systems. Teacher and community participation would be taken for granted, as would (given our sector's vocational role) employer and trade union representation. Democratization would help bridge the gaps between governance, teachers and the community, and open the issue of what matters in FE to wider public debate.

Of course, a little Machiavellian caution might be advisable here. Machiavelli was not a radical democrat but thought all constitutions were corruptible, the democratic included. If princes could become tyrants and aristocrats could become oligarchs, then democracy could slide into self-interestedness: 'every one living in his own way, a thousand injuries ... inflicted every day' (Machiavelli, 1940: 8). For this reason, Machiavelli proposed a mixed constitution that balanced princely, aristocratic and popular power. Corrupted democracy, he observed, could lead to the restoration of a prince, much as managerialism was justified as a response to some of the poorer practices in our sector, such as mediocre teaching and inadequate inclusion of students with diverse needs. Demanding our democratic voice implies accepting responsibility that our professional judgements are accountable and sound.

Machiavelli proposed only a limited democracy. He nonetheless understood that popular participation was a condition for a commonwealth's vitality and freedom in an uncertain world. The democratic voice might be expressed through elected tribunes in government, or in more direct forms of dissent when popular freedoms were at stake. Either way, democracy was essential if a commonwealth were to mobilize its popular resources while restraining the self-aggrandizing tendencies to which elites were dispositionally prone.

Democratic resources

The democratic potential of FE has been progressively degraded. We could respond in either of two ways: by resigning ourselves to the post-democratic culture, or by reclaiming our democratic entitlements as teachers and citizens and linking our critique of what is wrong to a democratic vision of what our sector could be. If teacher and community voices and agency are central to realizing such a vision, then they are not merely ideals postponed until change is achieved. In attempting this change, we are not without democratic resources to draw on. These include:

- *Reaffirming our shared identity as educators.* In our multi-site colleges, we know our immediate colleagues but often not those in other departments. Teachers have different vocational identities and have followed different routes into teaching. Finding common purpose in our fragmented professional culture (Jephcote and Salisbury, 2009) is challenging. The FE teachers' union, UCU, remains critical to promoting our common professional interests and identity, although the potential of unions for critical thinking about education is often underused. We should additionally recognize the potential of subject specialist bodies and networks to link teachers from different institutions. The National Association for Teaching English and Community Languages to Adults (NATECLA) or Research and Practice in Adult Literacy (RaPAL) come to mind. Where such bodies do not exist, we should create them.

- *Recognizing the democratic potential of social media.* We teachers are increasingly involved in online communities that affect our professional identities and learning (Macià and García, 2016). Even if electronic communities are not a substitute for real-world action, they can cross institutional boundaries to give individuals access to fresh ideas and research, opportunities to share problems and good practice, and assistance in developing self-confidence and autonomy.
- *Exploring coalition-building.* We can learn from collaborations between education unions and communities (Tattersall, 2011), and from campaigns such as Action for ESOL (Peutrell, 2014), which successfully challenged government plans to cut ESOL funding, about the powerful possibilities available to us in our own grass-roots 'stakeholder' alliances of teachers, students and community groups advocating change or defending provision.
- *Recovering our own forgotten democratic traditions.* Against the vacuous idea of always embracing change (see Hall, 2016), we should value our traditional commitments to students, the curriculum and an ethics of care. Hindsight allows us to see both where we have been and what routes we might take. Among the strands within our rich tradition are the participatory ideals of adult, community and critical education (see, for example, Brookfield, 2005; Bryers, 2015; Coare and Johnston, 2003; Fairclough, 2000), and (apropos the contemporary concern with skills preparation) the attempt by rank-and-file teachers to bring a social dimension to the vocational curriculum (Simmons *et al.*, 2014).
- *Building on our knowledge of professional learning.* Years of enquiry into teachers' professional learning has highlighted the importance of autonomy, responsibility, dialogue, criticality and reflection. Managerialism is hostile to these democratic principles, which underlie the many different forms professional learning can take, from action research to communities of enquiry, TeachMeets to mentoring and peer observation.

A final appeal to the people and the princ(e/ipal)

Democracy is not a panacea for our sector. As Machiavelli well knew, it brings its own dilemmas. But although democracy cannot provide a guarantee against self-interest, without it we cannot hope to genuinely mobilize our professional potential or respond to our communities' aspirations and needs.

Across the sector, teachers, managers and principals too have struggled with the uncertainties for which policy-makers are responsible. Although many principals welcomed the independence and status incorporation promised (Hodgson *et al.*, 2015), some are aware of the damage that has been done and are also aware that education is too important for fast-capitalist slogans.

The argument for democracy is about rights and accountability. It is also a recognition of education's complexity. Drawing on our wealth of knowledge and experience to consider (and reconsider) our priorities, needs, practices and values might help bring about an educational system that models democratic ideals. To adapt the political thinker Hannah Arendt, in FE we have nothing in our grasp but perplexities; it is best that we share them with each other.

References

Belgutay, J. (2016) 'Threat of "shocking fraud" in new apprentice system'. *TES*, 13 May. Online. www.tes.com/news/further-education/breaking-news/threat-shocking-fraud-new-apprentice-system (accessed 28 November 2016).

Brookfield, S.D. (2005) *The Power of Critical Theory for Adult Learning and Teaching*. Maidenhead: Open University Press.

Bryers, D (2015) 'Participatory ESOL'. *Language Issues*, 26 (2) Winter, 55–7.

Burke, J. (2017) 'Gazelle Group on its last legs after its director and most members quit'. *FE Week*, 6 January. Online. http://feweek.co.uk/2017/01/06/gazelle-group-on-its-last-legs-after-its-director-and-most-members-quit/ (accessed 31 January 2017).

Coare, P. and Johnston, R. (eds) (2003) *Adult Learning, Citizenship and Community Voices: Exploring community-based practice*. Leicester: National Institute of Adult Continuing Education.

Coffield, F. (2008) *Just Suppose Teaching and Learning Became the First Priority ...* . London: Learning and Skills Network.

— (2015) 'A cause worth fighting for'. Paper presented at Tutor Voices Conference, Northern College, Barnsley, 26 September.

Cole, H. and Donohue, F. (2014) 'Further education reimagined: Preparing for the future workforce'. Mirosoft, Gazelle Group and Intel. Online. www.thegazellegroup.com/docs/Further%20Education%20Reimagined.pdf (accessed 20 September 2016).

Crouch, C. (2004) *Post-Democracy*. Cambridge: Polity.

Cutler, J. (1999) 'Educational notes: Fraud and scandal in further education'. *The Independent*, 11 May. Online. www.independent.co.uk/arts-entertainment/educational-notes-fraud-and-scandal-in-further-education-1093059.html (accessed 18 November 2016).

Dewey, J. (2012) *Democracy and Education*. La Vergne, TN: Simon and Brown.

Fairclough, N. (2000) *Critical Language Awareness*. Harlow: Longman.

Fletcher, M. (2012) 'Gazelle biting off more than they can chew?' *FE Week*, 6 March 6· Online. http://feweek.co.uk/2012/03/16/gazelle-biting-off-more-than-they-can-chew/ (accessed 31 January 2017).

Further Education Commissioner (2015) 'Further Education Commissioner assessment summary: New College Nottingham'. London: Department for Business, Innovation and Skills. Online. www.gov.uk/government/uploads/system/uploads/attachment_data/file/436361/New_College_Nottingham_-_Further_Education_Commissioner_Assessment_Summary.pdf (accessed 13 May 2017).

Graystone, J., Orr, K., and Wye, R. (2015) 'Governance and governors'. In Hodgson, A. (ed.) *The Coming of Age for FE? Reflections on the past and future role of further education colleges in England*. London: Institute of Education Press, 135–54.

Hall, D. (2016) 'It's time to look to the future of FE – not the past'. *TES Magazine*, 1 April. Online. www.tes.com/news/tes-magazine/tes-magazine/its-time-look-future-fe-not-past (accessed 20 September 2016).

Hatcher, R. and Jones, K. (2015) 'For an empowered, democratised and properly resourced local school system'. In Stand Up for Education (NUT) *Reclaiming Schools: The evidence and the arguments*. London: National Union of Teachers, 24–5. Online. www.teachers.org.uk/files/reclaimingschools-essays-9963.pdf (accessed 31 January 2017).

Hodgson, A., Bailey, B., and Lucas, N. (2015) 'What is FE?' In Hodgson. A. (ed.) *The Coming of Age for FE? Reflections on the past and future role of further education colleges in England*. London: Institute of Education Press, 1–23.

Jephcote, M. and Salisbury, J. (2009) 'Further education teachers' accounts of their professional identities'. *Teaching and Teacher Education*, 25 (7), 966–72.

Lewis, N. (1994) 'Re-engineering the culture of a college'. In Gorringe, R. and Toogood, P. (eds) *Changing the Culture of a College* (Combe Lodge Report 24 (3)). Bristol: The Staff College, 253–64.

Linford, N. (2011) 'Colleges must learn from the financial mistakes of the past'. *The Guardian*, 24 May. Online. www.theguardian.com/education/2011/may/24/colleges-subcontracting-scandals (accessed 28 November 2016).

Machiavelli, N. (1908) *The Prince*. Trans. Marriott, W.K. Originally 1515. Online. www.constitution.org/mac/prince.pdf (accessed 1 March 2017).

— (1940) *Discourses on the First Ten Books of Titus Livius*. Trans. Detmold, C.E. New York: The Modern Library. Originally 1517. Online. www.constitution.org/mac/disclivy.pdf (accessed 1 March 2017).

Macià, M. and García, I. (2016) 'Informal online communities and networks as a source of teacher professional development: A review'. *Teaching and Teacher Education*, 55, 291–307.

Nottingham Campaign for Education (2016) 'The people of Nottingham should decide what kind of Further Education they need! Response to the FE merger consultation document: *Delivering Excellence in Further Education in Nottingham*'. Online. https://nottinghamcampaign4ed.files.wordpress.com/2016/04/nottingham-campaign-for-education-response-to-the-nottm-fe-merger-consultation-april-2016.pdf (accessed 13 May 2017).

Peutrell, R. (2015) 'Action for ESOL: Pedagogy, professionalism and politics'. In Daley, M., Orr, K., and Petrie, J. (eds) *Further Education and the Twelve Dancing Princesses*. Stoke-on-Trent: Trentham Books, 139–56.

Schön, D.A. (1983) *The Reflective Practitioner: How professionals think in action*. New York: Basic Books.

Simmons, R., Waugh, C., Hopkins, M., Perry, L., and Stafford, R. (2014) 'Liberal and general studies in further education: Voices from the "chalk face"'. *Teaching in Lifelong Learning: A Journal to Inform and Improve Practice*, 6 (1), 32–42.

Stevenson, H. (2015) 'A real voice for teachers: Teacher professionalism and teacher unions'. In Stand Up for Education (NUT) *Reclaiming Schools: The evidence and the arguments*. London: National Union of Teachers, 29–30. Online. www.teachers.org.uk/files/reclaimingschools-essays-9963.pdf (accessed 31 January 2017).

Sutter, J. (2006) 'The "delivery" metaphor in education – return to sender?' *Reflect: The Magazine of NRDC*, 5, 20–1.

Tattersall, A. (2011) 'The power of union–community coalitions'. *Renewal: A Journal of Social Democracy*, 19 (1), 75–82. Online. www.renewal.org.uk/articles/the-power-of-union-community-coalitions (accessed 10 November 2016).

James Richards

You need power only when you want to do something harmful. Otherwise, love is enough to get everything done.

Charlie Chaplin

Chapter 20

Social purpose leadership: A new hope

Lou Mycroft and Jane Weatherby

> No future is achieved until it is first imagined.
>
> Ashcroft (2014)

There's a strong argument for crediting Machiavelli – and his contemporary Leonardo da Vinci – with fashioning a leadership template that dominates education in the UK to this day. When Machiavelli's prince and Leonardo's Vitruvian man are grafted together a hero is born, a David Beckham of his time, a logical über-human against whom the rest of us are measured and found to be other. In Europe at least, the natural order saw the heroic leader ensconced firmly at the top, there by merit rather than birth, his pursuit of knowledge bringing the desired freedom and happiness of Enlightenment. As feminist, post-colonial and post-human thinkers point out, this adoption of Vitruvian man as the symbol of ultimate human perfection provided philosophical fertilizer for centuries of oppression and colonization, based on othering everyone who by reason of gender, skin colour, economic value or other privilege could not aspire to Vitruvian status.

The stories that survive are those that win the floor. There is another Enlightenment genealogy, one that was obscured for nearly three centuries: Baruch Spinoza, survivor of the Dutch year of disaster in 1672, revived by Gilles Deleuze and others at their renegade university Paris 8 during the late 1960s. In these contemporary, perhaps revolutionary, times, Richard Wilson (2013) claims that our historical way of leading just doesn't work any more. This chapter imagines how a different kind of leadership – one based on the Spinozan notion of *potentia*, rather than *potestas* – could ignite profound change in further and adult education. According to Rosi Braidotti (2015), *potestas* is politics as usual, the leadership style inherited from Machiavelli, ultimately a negative, regressive force, as it works hardest of all to maintain the power differential of the norm. *Potentia*, on the other hand, offers possibilities, producing resistance to the status quo particularly when energies are combined around an affirmative project: an event, an exhibition, a utopian vision. *Potestas* works via strongly rooted hierarchies, *potentia* via organic, rhizomatic networks.

The new millennium has seen the pace of change quicken in education; collateral damage is the morale of a workforce that has largely withdrawn its goodwill. Traditional heroic-model leaders, caught up in managerialist structures, have their energies drained by dragging demotivated staff along behind them. The notion of a heroic, charismatic leader is, of course, highly seductive – someone with a vision who can not only persuade followers out of their *ennui* but successfully win the day. When the future for education – and its jaded workforce – seems so uncertain, it is not hard to understand why the heroic leader clings on in the hope of a return to more abundant times. Yet even twenty years ago Noam Chomsky (1993) was arguing that, rather than looking for heroes, we should be looking for good ideas. More recently, Wilson's work around a new anti-hero metaphor (2013) offers *potentia*, separating leadership from management and depositing it firmly in the lap of the entire workforce. Anti-heroes sit tight in zones of new tension, ready to capitalize on fresh opportunities, ready to offer and act upon good ideas. Anti-heroes think, allowing the new to come into the world (Rushdie, 1988). The thesis is not hard to grasp: heroic leadership has had its day. Why do we persist in applying its simple logic to an increasingly complex world? How can we foster a climate in education in which Wilson's anti-hero approach can take root?

Wilson's concept of the anti-hero finds a welcome in social purpose education, a democratic pedagogy based on transformational principles originally laid down by hooks (2003) and Freire (1972). Social purpose education is based on four cornerstones of practice: teaching your values, reflexive practice, win/win/win, and embedding diversity. It is concerned with developing students' agency so that they can recognize and challenge prevailing power relations, a process Freire names conscientization. We suggest that the collective low self-esteem of the teaching profession in the UK, particularly the fractured workforce of further, adult, community and skills education, needs social purpose leadership in order to conscientize its own agency and bring about change. The model we propose is a leadership of hope and *potentia* working at the margins of what is possible, inspired by differently imagined futures – digital, dialogic and democratic.

Social purpose digital leadership

The digital revolution means access to knowledge on an unprecedented scale and a disturbance to the power structures of old, so that material that was once available only to privileged groups is now open to anyone with access to the internet. It means networks and connecting across traditional demarcation lines of geography, race and class.

Different voices are amplified in different real and virtual spaces (Mycroft and Weatherby, 2014). Digitization allows greater possibilities for people from marginalized groups not only to find information for themselves, unfiltered by the paternalism of others, but also to shape the telling of their own stories. As Arundhati Roy (2004) writes, 'there's really no such thing as the "voiceless". There are only the deliberately silenced, or the preferably unheard' (2004). Digital platforms such as Media Diversified (2016) generate *potentia* working to resist what Toni Morrison called the 'solitary heroes' stereotype of writers of colour, accelerating networks that have long existed but had previously operated at a slower pace. White, male-centred reading lists and book-pricing cartels are exploded by the availability of dissident thinking, supported by open movements such as Creative Commons (Price, 2013) and promoted via social media platforms like Twitter.

Such disruptive energy needs a leadership to suit. The heroic leader finds the *potentia* of digital life terrifying; he needs to tame its chaos in policy. The anti-hero builds digital resilience, willingly leading and participating in Freirean processes of conscientization in order to address complex challenges, to create diverse alliances which share *potentia* and draw courage and strength from thinking differently, together.

The first thing that fascists seize, claims Rosi Braidotti, is the curriculum (2016). The anti-hero anticipates this; she ensures her team has access to the digital capital – resources, resilience, infrastructure, not just kit – which will help them develop cross-subject curricula, fostering critical thinking for both themselves and their students. Led well, digitization is a democratizer. It is about connectedness to each other, being open to new and disruptive information, and the belief that another world is possible.

Social purpose dialogic leadership

Digital has opened up a myriad of new ways to engage in dialogue with others, unfettered by geographical or social boundaries, once the confidence is there to find a language of mutuality. Whereas *potestas* expresses power through a relationship involving domination by one party over others, the concept of *potentia* sees power as being articulated through a relationship with the whole world. Dialogue shaped by *potentia* is shared, open-minded, open-ended and rhizomatic. In this model, listening (or reading) holds equal status to speaking (or writing). Heroic leaders may well see their role as one of giving information, issuing diktats or presenting stirring calls to action; anti-heroes understand that careful and deliberative listening is key to thinking and acting differently.

Dialogic processes such as the Thinking Environment (Kline, 2009), Community Philosophy (SAPERE, 2016) and Non-Violent Communication (Rosenberg, 2003) are *pro-social*: they co-create knowledge and – crucially – new understandings through dialogue. Listening is vital; dialogue needs new thinking too, the courage to go to the very edge of all that is assumed and taken for granted. It is impossible to be part of working this way without contributing, and for many people this is a terrifying prospect. But in the boardroom – as in the classroom and everywhere in between – there are silent voices and unspoken thoughts. The work of anti-heroes is to unlock this creativity.

Potentia is not about finding new ways to do the old: *potestas* does that job. Anti-heroes take every opportunity to transcend existing ways of thinking, seeking out diverse perspectives by engaging on equal terms with those whose experience is located outside traditional hierarchies of power. In this way, dominant discourses can be challenged and overthrown, and new possibilities have the chance to emerge (Freire, 1972).

Social purpose democratic leadership

Education's future relies on a leadership of new ideas, and that means challenging old tropes of what democracy means. Committed as he was to *potestas*, Machiavelli was certainly not anti-democratic. He would have been with Spinoza in recognizing that universal values are in fact the values of the elite. Machiavelli believed in what we might now call creative tension: disruption, dissonance and struggle. None of the dialogic processes described above primarily aim to seek consensus. That consensus is desirable at all costs – more desirable than messy, dangerous change – has come to be taken for granted in a climate in which patterns of compromise hold sway, and in which neoliberal ideology shapes understandings of what is possible.

Anti-heroes provide decision-making spaces that generate new thinking. The same spaces also contain disagreement, tension and misunderstanding. Machiavelli would certainly have recognized this as democracy. He may not have welcomed the smiling faux-democracy on display in many organizations today, where consultation abounds but much of the real *potestas* is hidden from view. For *potentia* work to happen, the tooth and claw of democracy need to be exposed and handled with respect in the decision-making space.

A democratic leadership of hope also means looking beyond the boundaries of the organization and contributing to the greater whole, the *reimagining* of education. In a capitalist economy, the concept of competition has been genetically engineered into the DNA of every public service, but it is still possible to resist. *Potentia* work forms alliances, it scans the horizon for possibilities, it recognizes that the language we use forms the thinking that we do. Connecting with others in *potentia* is the democratic responsibility of the anti-hero.

Conclusion: Why a leadership of hope?

Social purpose leadership is not easy work. It would be far simpler for everyone concerned to collude in axiomatic thinking: that economic growth is desirable, that a five-day week is full-time, that some people know better than others. Not only does the anti-hero have to contend with colleagues desperately holding on to their personal *potestas*, she also has to unsettle those who don't want to think. Culture change takes time, and not everyone has an appetite for it. Endurance is difficult to maintain, when the constant rhetoric of scarcity drives out ease.

In order to explore new ways of thinking about leadership, we have resorted to false dichotomies. In truth, as soon as we have any influence, we are all in *potestas* – politics as usual – all of the time. Any work that is a hundred per cent *potentia* may be brimful of new possibilities, but won't get a foot in the door. A good career, according to Rosi Braidotti (2016), is one which is two-thirds *potestas* and one-third *potentia*: get to a place of influence and then get dangerous. Machiavelli would see the wisdom of this. For the leader of hope, the anti-hero, it seems a reasonable maxim to ensure longevity to make change happen.

In these hardened, market-led times, what place is there for hope? Isn't hope, after all, the last resort of the sentimental, the unrealistic and the romantic, the stuff of greeting cards and social media memes, which tritely encourage us to bear our troubles passively and without complaint? In place of hope, is not *potestas*-led pragmatism a better bet? Why, in the face of current challenges for education, should we turn to hope, when hope is not victory? (Ashcroft, 2014).

The reason is that, for educators grounded in social purpose practice, the concept of hope is fundamental. Freire (1972) and hooks (2003) frame hope as intrinsic to transformative practice. Here, hope is deeply pragmatic and political, because it is hope that allows us to imagine a better, more equal future. In the *potentia* work of the anti-heroic leader, '[hope] can learn to estimate the opposition' (Ashcroft, 2014: 8.53 mins). It can help us see beyond that which is taken for granted, to the margins of possibility, where we can pool our *potentia* energy and work dialogically with others for affirmative change.

References

Ashcroft, B. (2014) 'Revolution, transformation and utopia: The function of literature'. Recording of keynote address given at the 4th Asian Conference on Literature and Librarianship, Osaka, Japan, 4 April. Online. https://iafor.org/revolution-transformation-utopia-function-literature-bill-ashcroft (accessed 11 April 2017).

Braidotti, R. (2015) 'Punk women and Riot Grrls'. *Performance Philosophy*, 1, 239–54. Online. www.performancephilosophy.org/journal/article/view/32/64 (accessed 13 May 2017).

— (2016) 'A posthuman ethics'. Paper presented at Utrecht University, 23 August.

Chomsky, N. (1993) 'Interview with Noam Chomsky by David Cogswell'. Online. www.davidcogswell.com/Political/Chomsky_Interview_93.htm (accessed 11 April 2017).

Freire, P. (1972) *Pedagogy of the Oppressed*. Trans. Ramos, M. London: Penguin.

hooks, b. (2003) *Teaching Community: A pedagogy of hope*. New York: Routledge.

Kline, N. (2009) *More Time To Think: A way of being in the world*. Pool-in-Wharfedale: Fisher King.

Media Diversified (2016) 'About us'. Online. https://mediadiversified.org/about-us/ (accessed 11 April 2017).

Mycroft, L. and Weatherby, J. (2014) 'Social purpose spaces'. Barnsley: Northern College. Online. https://practitionerledactionresearch2014.files.wordpress.com/2014/08/the-northern-college-report_web.pdf (accessed 11 April 2017).

Price, D. (2013) *Open: How we'll work, live and learn in the future*. London: Crux Publishing.

Rosenberg, M.B. (2003) *Nonviolent Communication: A language of life*. Encinitas, CA: PuddleDancer Press.

Roy, A. (2004) 'Arundhati Roy – The 2004 Sydney Peace Prize Lecture'. *University of Sydney News*, 4 November. Online. http://sydney.edu.au/news/84.html?newsstoryid=279 (accessed 11 April 2017).

Rushdie, S. (1988) *The Satanic Verses*. London: Penguin.

SAPERE (Society for the Advancement of Philosophical Enquiry and Reflection in Education) (2016) 'SAPERE: Philosophy for children, colleges, communities'. Online. www.sapere.org.uk (accessed 11 April 2017).

Wilson, R. (2013) *Anti Hero: The hidden revolution in leadership and change*. London: Osca Agency. Online. www.cloresocialleadership.org.uk/userfiles/documents/Research%20reports/2012/Research,%20Richard%20Wilson,%20FINAL.pdf (accessed 11 April 2017).

Curtis Tappenden

When Kleon heard the news from Capua he rose early one morning, being a literatus and unchained, crept to the room of his Master, stabbed him in the throat, mutilated that Master's body even as his own had been mutilated: and so fled from Rome with a stained dagger in his sleeve and a copy of *The Republic* of Plato hidden in his breast.

Lewis Grassic Gibbon (*Spartacus*)

Chapter 21

Beyond cynicism, comfort radicalism and emancipatory practice: FE teachers

James Avis

Machiavelli's *The Prince* has clear affinities with current political and management practices. For Machiavelli, rulers are concerned with two key issues, glory and riches. We need only consider the way senior executives pursue their goals, and the strategies they embrace to achieve them. *The Prince* provides a commentary on these practices and the way brute force, along with softer forms of control, can be mobilized. In the following an analysis of FE practice is rooted in Machiavellian machinations and cynicism. Such an understanding can point towards the contradictory relations in which we are enmeshed and the manner in which we become complicit with those wielding power while presenting ourselves as radical. At the same time this type of understanding can become disabling, as it can lead to a focus on the pursuit of self-interest. The final section offers a corrective that moves beyond cynicism towards a radical politics committed to a socially just society. I draw on two translations of *The Prince* (Machiavelli, 1988, 2015), which, unsurprisingly, differ.

I Concerning the assumption of power

> A wise prince should have no other concern than war and its methods.
>
> (Skinner, 2000: 35; and see Machiavelli 1988: 51–2)

Following the 1992 Further and Higher Education Act, colleges of further education (FE) were incorporated in 1993 and were no longer under local education authority control. This represented a loss of democratic community control mediated by the local council and was replaced by centralized fiscal control. This change brought in its wake a transformation of labour relations, a shift from a patrician style of leadership to a much harsher, masculinized and aggressive managerial culture. These changes occurred alongside the ascendancy of Thatcherism and neoliberalism.

Two points follow. Firstly, the new public management (NPM) had sought to establish the right of managers to manage. This is a right that has to be continuously secured as it encounters resistance of various kinds, but is nevertheless embodied in hegemonic language that has come to be part of our taken-for-granted common sense. This can be seen in the way, without much thought, we mobilize terms such as line manager, appraisal and targets, and repeatedly refer to education as a business. Such terms seep almost unnoticed into our vocabulary.

The second point is that this was a period in which large numbers of teachers left the sector, taking redundancy or early retirement or simply moving on. Perhaps it was enough 'that the family of their former lord [was] extinguished' (Machiavelli, 2015: 19) and that opposition was quelled in the FE sector. College leaders who were uncomfortable with these changes may have preferred to take redundancy or retire rather than remain in post, and so they opened up a space for a new kind of leader more in keeping with the *zeitgeist*. There emerged an aggressive and more masculinized leadership, which aimed to assert a style of control based on a culture of fear and that held a particular understanding of what it meant to run a college along business lines. Incorporation has facilitated the embedding of antagonistic relations into the system, which, from time to time, has led to industrial conflict and strike action, but most of the time is characterized by small acts of individualized resistance. It is important not to eulogize the state of the sector before incorporation; it was complicit in the reproduction of the social relations of class, gender and race, as can be seen from the fact that FE was described as the handmaiden of industry, or indeed as the sector for the education of other people's children. This issue is reflected in the erstwhile call for the vocational to be accorded parity of esteem with the academic.

College leaders are not all of a piece. The excesses following incorporation, when some leaders adopted idiosyncratic practices, have been superseded by bureaucratization, performativity, audit, targets and surveillance. Such practices shuffle through institutions, being used to reward or punish behaviour, and are in turn aligned with Ofsted inspections and college self-assessment. To some extent these practices have softened the excesses of managerialism by systematizing low-trust relations. However, the manner in which managerial power is exercised will be mediated by the balance of force present in the institution. Not all managers are the same and clearly not all are male. Edwards (1979) illustrates the strategies that may be adopted to ensure control, which range from the patriarchal to forms of bureaucratic, hierarchal and technical control. Indeed,

Simmons and Thompson (2007) have examined the feminization of teacher educators in the sector, and a *Journal of Further and Higher Education* special issue (2000) has addressed gender and managerialism. Gleeson and Shain (1999) have discussed different forms of compliance that straddle further education from rank-and-file teachers to senior managers, from unwilling to willing and strategic compliance. In the latter case there is a concern to work on the progressive or good side of the opportunities that arise in any particular situation. Thus, there may be an attempt to push the social justice implications of change as far as possible. Those who engage in unwilling compliance are unlikely to remain long in the sector, while willing compliers buy into the neoliberal and audit culture. While strategic compliance offers some respite from the harshness of neoliberalism, as do less abrasive forms of management, it is important to place this respite within the broader socio-economic context and the economizing of educational relations. Notions of competitiveness and the knowledge economy are hegemonic in the policy discourse that surrounds education in general and further education in particular. A truly felt commitment to social justice and the provision of educational opportunities for disadvantaged groups can be easily set within this doxic discourse. After all, mobilizing these ideas may win resources that would otherwise not be forthcoming. The downside is that notions of competitiveness and the knowledge economy not only operate on a capitalist terrain but also carry with them assumptions about up-skilling and the possibility of social mobility. These assumptions are at best overstated and at worst simply wrong. This is evidenced by an overqualified, under- and unemployed labour force in which large numbers of people face intermittent employment as they churn between periods of unemployment and of low-waged work (Allen and Ainley, 2014; Keep and James, 2012). They are effectively surplus labour that has been eliminated and is no longer required by capital.

The commitment to social justice can become lodged, not only in a particular and dominant understanding of the economy, but also with the manner in which capitalism is understood. Neoliberalism becomes associated with a pathological, if not criminogenic, version of capitalism. This is the irresponsible and toxic capitalism that those on the left, or more precisely the Labour party, castigate (McDonnell, 2015; Miliband, 2012). This version of capitalism is set against a fairer, more just form that reflects sensibilities rooted in social democracy. It believes that the excesses of capitalism can be effectively managed for the good of all, and that neoliberal capitalism is an aberration that celebrates greed and is antithetical to societal needs (Hutton, 2015). There is a reformist politics here, that comes close to accepting that there is no viable alternative to capitalism but offers mitigation of neoliberal excesses. For college leaders such sensibilities readily align with their addressing the needs of not only local industry and employers but also local communities – that is to say the provision of opportunities for disadvantaged communities. Such a stance can reflect a form of comfort radicalism, in that, despite its radical pretensions, it offers no real threat to the maintenance of capitalist relations and downplays the antagonistic relations that surround waged labour. The success of college leaders is predominantly based upon the labour of others, much of which is unpaid, in the sense that, to get work done, weekends and evenings are frequently used. Exploitation is an inevitable feature of waged labour in capitalist societies. Social democratic concerns to address the needs of students resonate with the moral and pedagogic sensibilities of teachers together with their understanding of what it is to be a professional, which can lead to complicity in their own exploitation. Machiavelli (1988: 85) reminds us of 'the end which everyone aims at, that is, glory and riches'.

II Concerning the art of fabrication

Stephen Ball (2003) has discussed the 'terror of performativity' and its relationship with fabrication. I address two rather different interpretations of this concept. The first relates fabrication to new public management (NPM), whereas the second refers to a notion of contrived collegiality and its association with an apparent radicalism.

The NPM, with its audit culture and its preoccupation with performative targets, encourages fabrication. Such managerial practices serve as a technology of control that, along with neoliberalism, assumes that the effectiveness and efficiency of the public sector can be enhanced through quasi-marketized relations. The presumption here is that those who work in the sector need to be managed so as to ensure that their practices align with those of the institution. This is a context in which we all have to be kept up to the mark (after Olssen, 2003: 200), with these practices being set within hierarchical and low-trust relations, echoing the significance of cultures of fear and Machiavelli's (2015: 51) adage that 'it is much safer to be feared than loved'. However, performativity encounters two difficulties. Firstly, the attainment of targets is dependent upon teachers' labour, which may or may not be freely offered, and once the targets are achieved there may be no attempt to go beyond them. Secondly, and more importantly, the data used to evidence success may be fabricated. In oppressive and low-trust work contexts targets may be negotiated on what has already been achieved. Using publication as an example, the target in HE may be to write two journal papers in a particular year. This may already have been achieved, though the articles may not yet be in the public domain – hence the notion of fabrication, a theme explored by Rob Smith (chapter 1 in this volume) in relation to the manipulation of performance metrics in FE. Crass management practices based on performativity do not easily secure the prince's interests, as they can engender resistance because of their aggressive attempts to shape compliant subjectivities and identities. After all, they are working on 'obstinately resistant material' (Johnson, 1979, cited in Avis, 1981: 155). The wise prince will adjust his strategy accordingly and draw on the rhetoric of professionalism, autonomy and empowerment to offer the public sector worker and the FE teacher an illusionary sense of control and even radicalism.

Machiavelli suggests that the prince should appear to be moral and upright, to possess the qualities and virtues that are valued in wider society (see *The Prince*, chapter 18). Two presumptions follow: firstly, that people are naïve and will take the prince's morality at face value, and secondly, that people are treacherous, self-serving and adept at breaking their word. In order to secure their position a prince should be prepared to dissemble and engage in wrongdoing – to do what is necessary to maintain their position of power. This reflects a second type of fabrication, in which skilful leaders may portray themselves as having a commitment to the professional development of teachers as well as to students. They may draw on a radical language that mobilizes notions of social justice, a commitment to serving the disadvantaged and so on. Teachers may be encouraged to exercise their professionalism and be given a degree of autonomy and empowerment in the classroom.

There are several issues that flow from the above. Such a stance can coexist, albeit uneasily, with an audit culture and performativity, which may be presented as a systemic feature of the socio-economic context of the institution. This is a feature that cannot be challenged, shaped as it is by the logic of capitalism, or, to break with the Machiavellian metaphor, by state diktat. While this cannot be changed, teachers should nevertheless be given as much space as is practicable to exercise their professionalism. The trick is that teachers become complicit in their own exploitation and college leaders are able to feel good about themselves and their radicalism. This is a form of comfort radicalism (see Hayes, 2003) that does little to challenge existing power and capitalist relations but which appropriates a suitably radical language. I am reminded of the notion of 'interest convergence' derived from critical race theory, whereby the concerns of black and white appear to converge but offer greater benefit to the latter (Delgado, 1995: 48).

Much the same could be said about the relation between college leaders and teachers.

III Concerning comfort radicalism

Two points follow. Firstly, if the inequities of capitalism are tied to neoliberalism then any critique of the latter can be construed as radical and seen as part of the struggle for the development of a fairer and more just society. However, if neoliberalism is a species of capitalism, one that seeks to claw back the concessions gained by the working class during earlier periods, a rather different politics ensues. The ascendancy of neoliberalism reflects the balance of power between labour and capital. This is an ongoing site of struggle, with earlier concessions being set on a capitalist terrain. In other words, they serve to soften capitalist antagonism but ultimately fail to move beyond these, being lodged within a reformist politics that accepts capitalist relations. In this sense, the critique of neoliberalism can serve as a form of comfort radicalism. We can rail against neoliberalism without fundamentally challenging capitalist relations, yet at the same time feel good about our radicalism. Much the same critique can be made of some types of structural analysis that emphasize the reproduction of class relations and the privileges accorded to the middle class. This type of analysis can skirt around the capitalist relations in which class is embedded and can be diverted into a struggle for positional advantage, veering towards a stance that appears radical but is merely concerned with shuffling positions of advantage.

Capitalism is not all of a piece, with different fractions having divergent interests. A concern with professional autonomy can comfortably coexist with particular fractions of capital. The development of students, their autonomy, creativity and critical engagement with knowledge can serve capitalist interests, contributing to the development of the next generation of managers or maybe even FE teachers. However, if teacher autonomy is located in the safe space of the classroom it can veer towards a form of comfort radicalism, that, while seeking to challenge the status quo, does so only in appearance. Such radicalism is readily appropriable by the prince and may paradoxically be drawn on to buttress his position.

IV Concerning cynicism

Machiavelli offers a particularly jaundiced view of social relations, drawing attention to our baser instincts. His negativity is also disabling to those of us committed to the development of a socially just society. One response would be to argue that Machiavelli was a creature of his time, but that would be too easy. However, *The Prince* draws attention to the contradictory aspects of our practices, lodged as they are in a capitalist and often criminogenic system. Another response to the book calls for reflexivity and critical interrogation of our practices and politics. This can sit within a broader politics, which acknowledges different sites of struggle that are often in tension with one another. For example, pedagogic practices in the classroom may benefit disadvantaged students while simultaneously contributing to the myth of meritocracy. The point is to work on what might be called the good side of the conditions within which we are placed, recognizing the limitations but pushing the possibilities as far as possible. This is a type of revolutionary reformism that takes an existing capitalist tendency and pushes it to its limits, seeking to move beyond capitalist social relations (Srnicek and Williams, 2015: 109). This type of reformism would aim to build alliances with other progressive forces in order to contribute to social change. The trick is to see education as the starting point but to see also that by necessity we need to develop an expansive politics that extends beyond education, moving beyond cynicism towards a revolutionary practice. Perhaps the last word should be given not to Machiavelli but to Stephen Ball (1997: 258):

> Careers and reputations are made as our research flourishes upon the rotting remains of the Keynesian Welfare State. Both those inside the policy discourse and those whose professional identities are established through antagonism towards the discourse benefit from the uncertainties and tragedies of reform. Critical researchers, apparently safely ensconced in the moral high ground, nonetheless make a livelihood trading in the artefacts of misery and broken dreams of practitioners. None of us remains untainted by the incentives and disciplines of the new moral economy.

References

Allen, M. and Ainley, P. (2014) 'A new direction for vocational learning or a great training robbery? Initial research into and analysis of the reinvention of apprenticeships at the start of the 21st century'. Paper presented at HIVE-PED ESRC Research Seminar, University of Greenwich, 28 February.

Avis, J. (1981) 'Social and technical relations: The case of further education'. *British Journal of Sociology of Education*, 2 (2), 145–61.

Ball, S.J. (1997) 'Policy sociology and critical social research: A personal review of recent education policy and policy research'. *British Educational Research Journal*, 23 (3), 257–74.

— (2003) 'The teacher's soul and the terrors of performativity'. *Journal of Education Policy*, 18 (2), 215–28.

Delgado, R. (1995) *The Rodrigo Chronicles: Conversations about America and race*. New York: New York University Press.

Edwards, R. (1979) *Contested Terrain: The transformation of the workplace in the twentieth century*. London: Heinemann.

Gleeson, D. and Shain, F. (1999) 'Managing ambiguity: Between markets and managerialism: A case study of "middle" managers in further education'. *Sociological Review*, 47 (3), 461–90.

Hayes, D. (2003) 'New Labour, new professionalism'. In Satterthwaite, J., Atkinson, E., and Gale, K. (eds) *Discourse, Power, Resistance: Challenging the rhetoric of contemporary education*. Stoke-on-Trent: Trentham Books, 27–42.

Hutton, W. (2015) *How Good We Can Be: Ending the mercenary society and building a great country*. London: Little, Brown.

Johnson, R. (1979) *Popular politics: Education and the state*. Course unit. Milton Keynes: Open University.

Journal of Further and Higher Education (2000) Special issue on gender and management, in FE, 24 (2), 157–260.

Keep, E. and James, S. (2012) 'A Bermuda triangle of policy? "Bad jobs", skills policy and incentives to learn at the bottom end of the labour market'. *Journal of Education Policy*, 27 (2), 211–30.

Machiavelli, N. (1988) *The Prince*. Ed. Skinner, Q. and Price, R. Cambridge: Cambridge University Press.

— (2015) *The Prince*. Trans. Marriott, W.K. Ballingslöv: Wisehouse Classics.

McDonnell, J. (2015) 'Full text: Shadow Chancellor John McDonnell's speech to conference'. *LabourList*, 28 September. Online. http://labourlist.org/2015/09/full-text-shadow-chancellor-john-mcdonnells-speech-to-conference/ (accessed 7 Oct 2015).

Miliband, E. (2012) Speech on responsible capitalism, 19 January. Online. www.labour.org.uk/ed-miliband-on-responsible-capitalism,2012-01-19 (accessed 10 July 2013).

Olssen, M. (2003) 'Structuralism, post-structuralism, neo-liberalism: Assessing Foucault's legacy'. *Journal of Education Policy*, 18 (2), 189–202.

Simmons, R. and Thompson, R. (2007) 'Teacher educators in post-compulsory education: Gender, discourse and power'. *Journal of Vocational Education and Training*, 59 (4), 517–33.

Skinner, Q. (2000) *Machiavelli: A very short introduction*. Oxford: Oxford University Press.

Srnicek, N. and Williams, A. (2015) *Inventing the Future: Postcapitalism and a world without work*. London: Verso.

Conclusion

Ann-Marie Bathmaker

What hope is there for an aspirational, radical and democratic vision for further education (FE) in England, in sympathy with Machiavelli's less prominently celebrated republican and utopian world view? This was the question – the challenge – presented at the start of this book, with Machiavelli's *The Prince* as the starting point and stimulus for contributions. This chapter highlights a number of key themes from the chapters and specifically articulates lessons for practitioners and the sector.

Il Principe, *The Prince*, written in about 1513 by Machiavelli (1909–14), is an example of what have been called 'mirrors for princes'. They were a form of political writing that appeared from the Early Middle Ages to the Renaissance. Best known in the form of texts that directly instructed rulers on how to gain and control power, they could be described as a sort of self-help manual. However, the notion of a mirror for princes hints at the way the authors of these self-help guides needed to balance their advice with flattery of political leaders, in Machiavelli's case Lorenzo di Piero de' Medici, and suggests that the success of the individual leader took precedence over any more common good, except insofar as this enabled a leader or ruler to remain in power.

What is notable about *The Prince* is that Machiavelli took a new and ruthless approach to matters of power. He broke the tie between politics and ethical practices, pointing out that most political situations are unstable and subject to flux, and a common, private version of moral behaviour would not do. He proposed that when circumstances demanded, instead of following a personal ethic, actors should not see themselves as having to be compassionate, humane, trustworthy and honest, but should follow a more instrumental and expedient political ethic (Wolin, 2004). As a result, Machiavelli's name is synonymous with behaviour that is cunning, devious and unscrupulous, and the employment of duplicity in the wielding of power, especially in politics. The *Oxford English Dictionary* (2017) states that the noun 'Machiavellian' refers to 'A person who practises expediency in preference to morality; an intriguer or schemer. Usually derogatory.' The online Merriam-Webster Dictionary (www.merrian-webster.com/dictionary/Machiavellian) defines 'Machiavellian' as 'marked by cunning, duplicity, or bad faith'.

It is this interpretation of Machiavelli that chimes well with popular notions of successful leadership in neoliberal times. To quote one example from a modern-day 'mirror for leaders' (Schiff, 2014), those who are super-successful 'are much, much better at looking out for their self-interests', and in response to the following questions, are likely to answer 'yes':

- Are you more upset by inefficiency than injustice?
- Are you less emotionally affected by social norms and social pressures than most people?
- Are you good at identifying optimal strategies for getting what you want?
- Do you consider your attitude toward business as cool, detached and rational?
- Do you consider yourself opportunistic?

And this approach to power and leadership appears well suited to 'the logic of incorporation', which Lucas and Crowther (2016: 583) argue has characterized FE since the 1992 Further and Higher Education Act, when FE colleges in England were removed from local government control and made independent corporations. The logic of incorporation, which 'set colleges free', involved a business and marketized model of education and training, in which competition replaced notions of public good, and markets replaced social partnership, democratic accountability and concern for community needs. Under these conditions colleges are now positioned as competitors with neighbouring institutions, not as partners within a regional or national sector. Attention has become focused on increased efficiency, in order that colleges can compete in an environment in which economic and financial considerations drive practice.

Lucas and Crowther reach the conclusion that the logic of incorporation has taken on a life of its own that prevents innovation that has any constructive educational or vocational focus. Their bleak prognosis seems hard to deny in the late 2010s, when conditions for FE colleges in England have become increasingly precarious. In 2015, ever-tighter government funding resulted in the sector as a whole posting an annual deficit, which led to area reviews of provision, and a new phase of college mergers to create 'fewer, often larger, more resilient and efficient providers' (BIS, 2015: 3). Optimists may claim that the interest in technical education shown by the Conservative Government elected in 2015 offered some hope for the future. Indeed, the Industrial Strategy Green Paper published in 2017 states that:

> A high-quality technical education system needs high-quality and resilient colleges and other providers to deliver it. The reforms outlined in this chapter will represent a major endorsement of the crucial role that FE colleges play in the economy.
>
> (HM Government, 2017: 41)

Yet colleges are not necessarily the government's institution of choice for the provision of technical and vocational education. To give just one example, not one of the three remaining colleges in the Birmingham area (Birmingham Metropolitan College, South and City College, Solihull College) gained approval to run apprenticeships under the new apprenticeship training arrangements launched in 2017 (Jones, 2017a).

Has the government chosen to ruin the sector, the final option proposed by Machiavelli in *The Prince* (see Rob Smith, chapter 1 in this volume)? The subsequent suspension of the above decision by the Education and Skills Funding Agency while it reviewed its approach (Jones, 2017b) suggests that the government was not entirely sure whether to ruin the sector or not, but the reprieve could well be a stay of execution rather than a presage of a renewed commitment to colleges. It is therefore increasingly hard to have any sympathy with the view that austerity vocationalism is an 'exciting time' in which FE can learn from others, find solutions, and form partnerships – the view of one college principal and chief executive, as reported in *The Guardian* (Swain, 2015) – unless, that is, the use of 'exciting', along with terms such as 'innovation' (see Gary Husband, chapter 10 in this volume), is understood as an appropriation of these words to suit the incentives and disciplines of the new moral economy (see James Avis, chapter 21 in this volume).

Scanning the horizon for possibilities

A number of chapters in this book focus on the increasingly challenging conditions facing FE provision not just in England, but in Ireland, Wales and Scotland, as well as Australia. The account of adult education in Ireland (Fergal Finnegan), battles for the rights of the workforce carried on by UCU Cymru (the University and College Union Wales) (Peter Jones), contradictory policies concerning provision of English for Speakers of Other Languages in Scotland (Steve Brown), and an analysis of the technical and further education sector in Australia (Gavin Moodie), all provide evidence of how FE provision represents a 'wicked' problem for policy-makers that is resistant to ready solutions, even when governments seek to control the sector.

In the English context, Rajiv Khosla offers a highly critical account of the effects of performance management and performativity that are closely associated with the current inspection regime. The ways in which principals (or chief executives as they are now designated) come to align themselves with this world is discussed by Damien Page and presented through a satirical critique of FE 'career-makers' in the chapters by Geoff Brown and Carol Azumah Dennis, who offer their own modern-day versions of 'mirrors for princes'. Their contributions capture the ways in which the moral economy of FE has become steeped in Machiavellian unscrupulousness, with 'strategic myths' used to hide 'wickedity' (Carol Azumah Dennis).

And yet, despite these circumstances, other contributors scan the horizon for the spaces and possibilities that will enable power, agency and professionalism, in particular for those at the grass-roots level of practice. Rob Peutrell emphasizes that 'those affected by policy have a right to shape it'. In this spirit, Rania Hafez discusses how teacher education can help to develop a strong practitioner professionalism. David Powell invites us to set up genuinely democratic, communicative space(s) for dialogue amongst leaders, students and co-workers to debate what constitutes a good education and then to commit to forms of 'communicative action' that change the practices that need to be changed and strengthen those that support these changes. Jim Crawley outlines how acts of connection – practical, democratic, civic and networked – that bring people together to carry out meaningful acts in education can create a bottom-up professionalism, and make a difference to the practices of teaching and learning. The emphasis here is on the possibilities of working in collaboration rather than isolation, moving beyond 'personal professionalism' (Bathmaker, 2006; Bathmaker and Avis, 2013) and 'underground working' (James and Diment, 2003) to engage in realizing change through alliances amongst students, colleagues and leaders.

A number of writers in this book go further than this and argue that we need to build on, but also beyond, what they might term survival radicalism; such building may help to make teaching and learning more meaningful and improve the chances of individual students, but leave underlying conditions unchanged. Craig Hammond roots his chapter in Gramsci's (1992) interpretation of *The Prince* as a revolutionary, utopian manifesto. He recommends two tactics for achieving more radical collective action: firstly, interrogating and reinterpreting cultural practices in order to subvert their meaning; secondly, resisting the compulsion to conform to established expectations, and instead engaging in adventurous ideas and action through collaboration between students and teachers in teaching and learning.

Lou Mycroft and Jane Weatherby turn to the work of bell hooks (2003) and Paulo Freire (1972) for inspiration. They propose that social purpose education and leadership, which develop practitioners' and students' agency to recognize and challenge prevailing power relations, can form the basis for change. Following hooks and Freire, they define hope as an essential feature of transformative practice, because it enables us to look beyond the taken-for-granted, imagine a better, more equal future, and work dialogically with others for change.

Finally, James Avis underlines the limitations of not looking beyond our own practice in seeking to achieve change. In the spirit of an aspirational, radical and democratic vision he argues that we need to undertake a critical interrogation of our practices and politics. We need to build alliances with progressive forces beyond education, in order to push the possibilities for change as far as possible and work towards practices that move beyond unequal capitalist relations.

Maintaining hope and critical scepticism

Throughout this volume we are reminded that FE in its broadest sense plays a crucial role in providing education and training opportunities for disadvantaged young people, vulnerable adults and second-language learners, and second-chance opportunities for those underserved by 'mainstream' educational provision of school and university. Moreover, different examples of practice serve as reminders that FE has a rich and diverse range of purposes, which are not focused just on the generation of human capital in the service of increased economic productivity and global competitiveness. Popular education (Peter Shukie), the Ragged University (Alex Dunedin), refugee education (Steve Brown) and adult and community education (Vicky Duckworth) all have an important place and history as part of a wider and richer conceptualization of the sector.

In a 'post-truth world' of 'post-truth politics' (Hacker, 2017), in which blatant lies have become redefined as acceptable 'alternative facts', it is increasingly hard to hold on to a sense of direction to create a more just and equal education and training system. It would be very easy to fall into a state of 'bodenlose Niedergeschlagenheit', the depths of despair that were experienced by the crew of the Second World War German submarine in the 1980s film *Das Boot*. Yet the chapters in this book encourage us not to give in to despondent cynicism, but to continue to look for the in-between spaces in which alternative practices are possible, and in which we may continue to advocate for change.

References

Bathmaker, A.-M. (2006) 'Alternative futures: Professional identity formation in English further education'. In Satterthwaite, J., Martin, W., and Roberts, L. (eds) *Discourse, Resistance and Identity Formation*. Stoke-on-Trent: Trentham Books, 127–42.

Bathmaker, A.-M. and Avis, J. (2013) 'Inbound, outbound or peripheral: The impact of discourses of "organisational" professionalism on becoming a teacher in English further education'. *Discourse: Studies in the Cultural Politics of Education*, 34 (5), 731–48.

BIS (Department for Business, Innovation and Skills) (2015) Reviewing post-16 education and training institutions (BIS/15/433). Online. http://dera.ioe.ac.uk/23545/ (accessed 16 July 2017).

Freire, P. (1972) *Pedagogy of the Oppressed*. Trans. Ramos, M. London: Penguin.

Gramsci, A. (1992) *Selections from the Prison Notebooks of Antonio Gramsci*. Ed. and trans. Hoare, Q. and Nowell Smith, G. New York: International Publishers.

Hacker, P. (2017) 'Reason, the Enlightenment, and post-truth politics: Rediscovering the dream of the Enlightenment'. *IAI News*, 2 March. Online. https://iainews.iai.tv/articles/reason-the-enlightenment-and-post-truth-politics-auid-785 (accessed 1 March 2017).

HM Government (2017) *Building Our Industrial Strategy: Green paper*. London: Department for Business, Energy and Industrial Strategy. Online. https://beisgovuk.citizenspace.com/strategy/industrial-strategy/supporting_documents/buildingourindustrialstrategygreenpaper.pdf (accessed 1 March 2017).

hooks, b. (2003) *Teaching Community: A pedagogy of hope*. New York: Routledge.

James, D. and Diment, K. (2003) 'Going underground? Learning and assessment in an ambiguous space'. *Journal of Vocational Education and Training*, 55 (4), 407–22.

Jones, T. (2017a) 'Birmingham colleges snubbed in new apprenticeship push'. *Birmingham Post*, 21 March. www.birminghampost.co.uk/news/regional-affairs/birmingham-colleges-snubbed-new-apprenticeship-12770197 (accessed 14 June 2017).

— (2017b) 'Reprieve for Birmingham colleges after apprenticeship push'. *Birmingham Post*, 13 April. Online. www.birminghampost.co.uk/news/regional-affairs/reprieve-birmingham-colleges-after-apprenticeship-12886564 (accessed 14 June 2017).

Lucas, N. and Crowther, N. (2016) 'The logic of the incorporation of further education colleges in England 1993–2015: Towards an understanding of marketisation, change and instability'. *Journal of Education Policy*, 31 (5), 583–97.

Machiavelli, Niccolo (1909–14) *The Prince*. Trans. Thomson, N.H. (Harvard Classics, 36, 1). New York: P.F. Collier & Son. New York: Bartleby.com, 2001. Online. www.bartleby.com/36/1/.

Oxford English Dictionary (2017) Oxford: Oxford University Press.

Schiff, L. (2014) 'Are you Machiavellian? Here's how (and why) to find out'. Online. www.linkedin.com/pulse/20140501124102-3943659-are-you-machiavellian-here-s-how-and-why-to-find-out (accessed 16 July 2017).

Swain, H. (2015) 'The future of further education is turbulent, but full of opportunity'. *The Guardian*, 31 March. Online. www.theguardian.com/education/2015/mar/31/future-further-education-turbulent-opportunity (accessed 1 March 2017).

Wolin, S.S. (2004) *Politics and Vision: Continuity and innovation in Western political thought*. Princeton: Princeton University Press.

Coda

Student voice: At the heart of policy but silent in practice?

Shakira Martin

In his critique of student participation Coffield concludes that institutional failings 'provide a perfect preparation for students who will soon be confronted with the feeble version of democracy prevalent in British society' (2016: 90). This coda features a discussion about the role of student voice in FE between Shakira Martin, President of the National Union of Students (NUS), and the editors. At the time of the discussion Shakira was the NUS Vice-President for FE.

Editors: Does Coffield's analysis reflect your experience of FE?

Shakira: Yes, student participation needs to be much stronger, and we need to consider what would make it more effective and then prepare students for democratic citizenship. Over the past two years as the NUS Vice-President for FE I have met many principals from up and down the country, several of them on a one-to-one basis, and have talked about putting student voice at the heart of their colleges. I've stressed the importance of developing a strong students' union, and genuinely engaging with student governors. My experience is that principals appear committed to having processes, policies and structures that promote student voice, but that the joint pressures of reduced funding and policy shifts from the government mean that student representation is rarely a high priority on their lengthy lists of things they must do.

Editors: Have you found principals to be open to what Hall (2017) describes as the democratic and transformational potential of student voice going beyond policy and strategy?

Shakira: Student engagement has to be about transformation and democracy. I have shared the barriers and challenges I've faced with many principals who tell me how inspirational I am, but I find this frustrating; and my response is, I wasn't always like this, there is a Shakira in each of your colleges who needs support to overcome adversity too. Involvement in my students' union played a huge role in giving me something positive to focus on, and allowed me to draw on my own personal experiences to help inspire, empower and motivate other students to create their own opportunities. This isn't about sitting on committees and governing bodies as virtual observers without having valued and meaningful input. Principals need to do more to move from policy-based to genuine student agency.

Editors: Machiavelli's advice to the prince is to be 'a constant inquirer, and afterwards a patient listener' (1908: 115). Should this apply to principals?

Shakira: Of course principals must inquire, as Geoffrey Elliott argues in his preface. They must also listen to the student voice, but more is required. This is my advice to principals:

1. Colleges should engage with students on learning and teaching and other issues core to FE, and student representatives should be supported in facilitating student feedback (NUS, 2015).
2. Invest in your students and students' union. Highlight the benefit of getting involved in extra-curricular activities for all students. Encourage students to take ownership of their education by building a solid engagement structure to ensure student views reach the heart of the college senior management.
3. Provide training for course and student executive representatives, and student governors, to ensure that they understand their roles.
4. Ensure there are well-trained staff that are able to support and develop the students' union through promoting elections and organizing student conferences, incorporating citizenship education of all 16–19 years programmes.
5. Empower student governors by insisting that they are asked about their concerns and invited to formally present the views of their peers, and ensure you can provide evidence that they have genuine impact on policy that isn't restricted to students' union matters.
6. Principals should collectively lobby the government through organizations like the Association of Colleges (AoC), but also the staff trade unions and the NUS, about the importance of student representation, which should be at the heart of all FE provision, and for the funding to do this effectively.
7. Education is more than just learning in the classroom; it must encompass developing personal growth including the ability to engage in democratic debate. For student voice to be taken seriously in every institution across the UK, we need to collectively send a clear message to government about the importance of investing in the development of strong students' unions. Because of the power they have, a commitment to this message must start with the principal.

References

Coffield, F. (2016) 'Teachers as powerful, democratic professionals'. In Higgins, S. and Coffield, F. (eds) *John Dewey's Democracy and Education: A British tribute*. London: Institute of Education Press (76–98).

Hall, V. (2017) 'A tale of two narratives: Student voice – what lies before us?' *Oxford Review of Education*, 43 (2), 180–93.

Machiavelli, N. (1908) *The Prince*. Trans. Marriott, W.K. Originally 1515. Online. www.constitution.org/mac/prince.pdf (accessed 19 April 2017).

NUS (National Union of Students) (2015) 'NUS charter on teaching and learning'. London: National Union of Students. Online. www.nusconnect.org.uk/resources/nus-charter-on-teaching-and-learning (accessed 20 April 2017).

Index